40 Days Through DANIEL

RON RHODES

HARVEST HOUSE PUBLISHERS
EUGENE, OREGON

Cover by Dugan Design Group

Cover photo © JannHuizenga / Shutterstock

40 DAYS THROUGH DANIEL
Copyright © 2016 Ron Rhodes
Published by Harvest House Publishers
Eugene, Oregon 97402
www.harvesthousepublishers.com

Library of Congress Cataloging-in-Publication Data
Rhodes, Ron.
40 days through Daniel / Ron Rhodes.
    pages cm
Includes bibliographical references.
ISBN 978-0-7369-6445-6 (pbk.)
ISBN 978-0-7369-6446-3 (eBook)
1. Bible. Daniel—Devotional use. I. Title. II. Title: Forty days through Daniel.
BS1555.54.R46 2016
224'.506—dc23

                                                    2015017105

Printed in the United States of America

        16 17 18 19 20 21 22 23 24 / LB-JH / 10 9 8 7 6 5 4 3 2

To my beloved wife, Kerri

Acknowledgments

After I became a Christian, I read one prophecy book after another. I could not get enough.

At the time, I seemed to gravitate toward prophecy books written by professors at Dallas Theological Seminary—John F. Walvoord, J. Dwight Pentecost, Charles Ryrie, and others. I found their books to be intelligently and persuasively written. Their words about the prophetic future, based on the Bible, resonated with me.

Little did I know then that in the not-too-distant future, I would actually enroll at Dallas Theological Seminary and take courses under these men, obtaining master of theology and doctor of theology degrees. As I now write about the prophetic book of Daniel, I want to acknowledge my personal indebtedness to these godly teachers of the Word. Their work continues to bear fruit in my life.

I also want to offer continued praise and thanksgiving to God for the wonderful family He has blessed me with—my wife, Kerri, and my two grown children, David and Kylie. With every year that passes, I grow in affection and appreciation for these three.

Thank You, Lord! I am grateful.

Contents

Introduction

Thank you for joining me in this exciting journey through the book of Daniel. You are in for a spiritually uplifting time! My hope and prayer is that as you read *40 Days Through Daniel*, you will experience several significant blessings:

- an awareness that God is a personal being who personally interacts with His people
- a conviction that God blesses righteous living
- an understanding of the need for God's people to maintain faith in Him regardless of the outward circumstances
- an understanding of God's sovereignty and control over the events of human history, including not only kings and nations but also the specifics of each of our individual lives
- an awareness that God will one day providentially cause good to triumph over evil
- an awareness that God is now providentially guiding human history toward its prophetic culmination
- an exalted view of the true majesty and glory of Jesus Christ, the divine Messiah
- an increased conviction of the trustworthiness of the Bible in general and the prophecies in the Bible in particular

As we begin our journey together, I want to address a few things that will lay a foundation for better understanding the book of Daniel. In this introduction, I will briefly look at the big picture. Then, in the chapters that follow, I will zero in on the details.

The Prophet Daniel

Daniel was born into a royal family (Daniel 1:3,6) and was apparently physically attractive (1:4). He became one of the major prophets of the Old Testament. His name means "God is my judge." He was uncompromising in his faithfulness to God. His contemporaries acknowledged both his righteousness and his wisdom (see Ezekiel 14:14,20; 28:3).

Daniel was taken captive as a youth to Babylon by King Nebuchadnezzar in 605 BC. He was likely 15 or 16 years old when this happened. As providence had it, he spent the rest of his life there—perhaps 85 years or more. He was assigned to be a governmental official in charge of assisting with the imported Jews.

There were actually three deportations involved in Babylon's victory over Judah. The first took place in 605 BC and included Daniel and his friends. The second took place in 597 BC and included Ezekiel. The third took place in 586, when the Babylonians destroyed Jerusalem and the temple.

Daniel wrote the biblical book that bears his name (see Daniel 8:15,27; 9:2; 10:2,7; 12:4-5). His book was titled Daniel not only because he was one of the chief characters in the book but also because it was customary in Bible times to affix the author's name to the book he wrote. In the New Testament, Jesus Himself identified Daniel as a prophet of God (Matthew 24:15; Mark 13:14).

Captivity and Exile

In the book of Deuteronomy, God through Moses promised great blessings if the nation lived in obedience to the Sinai covenant. God also warned that if the nation disobeyed His commands, it would experience the punishments listed in the covenant—including exile from the land (Deuteronomy 28:15-68).

Old Testament history is replete with illustrations of Israel's unfaithfulness to the covenant. The two most significant periods of exile for the Jewish people began with the fall of Israel to the Assyrians in 722 BC and the collapse of Judah to the Babylonians in 605 BC. Just as God promised, disobedience brought exile to God's people.

As a backdrop, it is interesting to observe that the first chapter of Isaiah takes the form of a lawsuit against Judah. Judah was indicted by the Lord (through Isaiah) because of Judah's "breach of contract" in breaking the Sinai covenant, which had been given to the nation at the time of the Exodus from Egypt. In this courtroom scene, the Lord called on heaven and earth to act as witnesses as He leveled accusations against the nation (Isaiah 1:2). The whole universe was to bear witness that God's judgments are just.

The Lord indicted Judah for rebelling against Him. It is noteworthy that the Hebrew word translated "rebelled" in Isaiah 1:2 often referred to a subordinate state's violation of a treaty with a sovereign nation. In Isaiah 1, the word points to Judah's blatant violation of God's covenant. Therefore, Judah went into captivity.

The Babylonian captivity was God's means of chastening Judah. This punishment, of course, was intended as a corrective. Both the Old and New Testaments demonstrate that just as an earthly father disciplines his children, so God the Father disciplines His children. His goal is to purify, train, and educate them (Hebrews 12:1-5; see also Job 5:17; 33:19; Psalm 118:18; Proverbs 3:11-12). The prophet Daniel indicates that God yet has a future for His people.

Daniel's Book

The book of Daniel is categorized as apocalyptic literature. It was written in about 537 BC and contains history as well as prophecy of the end times.

Scholars tell us that apocalyptic literature is a special kind of writing that arose among the Jews and Christians to reveal certain mysteries about heaven and earth, especially regarding the world to come. This type of literature is often characterized by visions—and there are plenty in the book of Daniel. Certain themes are common to apocalyptic literature:

- a growing sense of hopelessness as wicked powers grow in strength
- the promise that the sovereign God will intervene

- visions with a heavenly perspective that helps the faithful endure present suffering
- God's intervention in overcoming and destroying evil
- the call to believers to live righteously
- the call to persevere under trial
- God's final deliverance and restoration, with the promise to dwell with His people

We see all of these in the book of Daniel.

An Outline of the Book of Daniel

Daniel's Personal History (1)

Daniel was deported with other young men and placed in a training program in Nebuchadnezzar's court in Babylon. Their names were changed, as were their diets. Daniel, however, refused to eat food dedicated to idols, and the Lord rewarded him for his faithfulness.

God's Prophetic Plan for the Gentiles (2–7)

Daniel was able to interpret Nebuchadnezzar's disturbing dream of a great statue (2). By God's power, Daniel revealed that the dream indicated that God would raise up and then bring down four Gentile empires—the fourth being a revived Roman Empire over which the antichrist would rule. The times of the Gentiles would finally end at the second coming of Jesus Christ.

Nebuchadnezzar set up a golden image and decreed that all bow to it (3:1-7). Shadrach, Meshach, and Abednego (Daniel's three Hebrew friends) refused and were subsequently tossed into a fiery furnace as punishment. (Daniel was engaged in official business at the time, but had he been there, he too would have refused!) God delivered the three Hebrew youths, after which they were all promoted (3:8-30).

The self-inflated, prideful Nebuchadnezzar then had a dream indicating that God was going to bring him down and humiliate him for a time, causing him to dwell with animals. Nebuchadnezzar was eventually restored and afterward offered praises to God (4).

We then read of Belshazzar, the next Babylonian king mentioned in Scripture. He arrogantly defied God. Soon enough, he saw handwriting on the wall signifying that his kingdom had been numbered, weighed, and divided. That very night, the kingdom of the Babylonians fell to Darius and the Medes (5).

While Darius was king, he banned prayer to any god other than himself. Daniel ignored the decree and was thrown into a den of lions overnight. But God delivered Daniel, and Daniel was further exalted (6).

Daniel then had a vision of four strange beasts, representing four kingdoms that play an important role in biblical prophecy. These were Babylon, Medo-Persia, Greece under Alexander the Great, and a revived Roman Empire, which is yet future (7). It is over this latter empire that the antichrist will rule during the future tribulation period.

God's Prophetic Plan for Israel (8–12)

God yet has a plan for Israel. Daniel spoke of 70 weeks of years that constitute a prophetic timetable for Israel (9). Israel's timetable was divided into 70 groups of 7 years, totaling 490 years. The first 69 groups of 7 years, or 483 years, counted the years from the issuing of a decree to restore and rebuild Jerusalem until Jesus the Messiah came (Daniel 9:25). After that, God's prophetic clock stopped. Daniel said there would be a gap between these years and the final 7 years of Israel's prophetic timetable.

The final "week" of 7 years will begin for Israel when the antichrist confirms a covenant for 7 years (Daniel 9:27). The signing of this peace pact will signal the beginning of the tribulation period. Daniel became frightened at this momentous vision. He prayed to the Lord for strength, and an angel eventually arrived in answer to the prayer. The angel promised to show Daniel further things to come in the prophetic future (10).

Daniel revealed that the antichrist will emerge in the end times and will "go out with great fury to destroy and devote many to destruction" (11:44). The tribulation period "shall be a time of trouble, such as never has been since there was a nation till that time" (12:1). Daniel was instructed to "shut up the words and seal the book, until the time of the end. Many shall run to and fro, and knowledge shall increase" (12:4).

How to Use this Book

As you begin each chapter, consider using this prayer:

> *Lord, I ask You to open my eyes and enhance my understanding so I can grasp what You want me to learn today* [Psalm 119:18]. *I also ask You to enable me, by Your Spirit, to apply the truths I learn to my daily life and to be guided moment by moment by Your Word* [Psalm 119:105; 2 Timothy 3:15-17]. *I thank You in Jesus's name. Amen.*

Following this short prayer, you can read the assigned section of the book of Daniel using your favorite Bible. With your Bible still in hand, you can then work your way through the insights, where I provide some fascinating contextual background information. I suggest you go verse by verse through your Bible again, but this time, after reading each verse, also read the appropriate notes in the book.

After the insights on each verse in the passage, I provide four brief summaries:

Major Themes. These topical summaries will help you learn how to think theologically as you study the Bible.

Digging Deeper with Cross-References. These will help you discover relevant insights from other books of the Bible.

Life Lessons. This is where you learn to apply what you have read to your everyday life. You will discover that the book of Daniel is rich in transforming truths!

Questions for Reflection and Discussion. Use these for your personal journaling or for lively group interactions.

> *Lord, by the power of Your Spirit, please enable my readers to understand and apply truth from the book of Daniel. Please excite them with Your Word and instill in them a sense of awe for You—our wondrous and majestic God. I thank You in Jesus's name. Amen.*

Daniel's Historical Circumstances

Daniel 1:1-7

Scripture Reading and Insights

Begin by reading Daniel 1:1-7 in your favorite Bible. Read with the anticipation that the Holy Spirit has something important to teach you today (see Psalm 119:105).

In today's lesson, we will focus our attention on the historical circumstances of Daniel and his friends. With your Bible still accessible, consider the following insights on the biblical text, verse by verse.

Daniel 1:1-2

Third year (1:1): This would have been 605 BC.

Jehoiakim (1:1): See Major Themes.

Judah (1:1): Judah was one of the 12 sons of Jacob. (His mother was Leah.) The tribes of Judah and Benjamin formed the southern kingdom, also known as Judah (see Genesis 29:35; 37:26; 44:14; 49:8-10; Numbers 1:27; Judges 1:8; 2 Samuel 2:4; 1 Kings 12:20,23).

Nebuchadnezzar (1:1): See Major Themes.

Babylon (1:1): Babylon was situated on the banks of the Euphrates River, a little more than 50 miles south of modern Baghdad. Because of its ideal location, Babylon was an important commercial and trade center in the ancient world. The nation was also brimming with paganism.

Jerusalem (1:1): This city rests in the Judean hills at about 2640 feet above sea level. King David of Israel captured the city in the tenth century BC and built his palace there. His son Solomon eventually became king and built a magnificent temple, making Jerusalem the center of Israel's religious life. Jerusalem would later become famous worldwide because it was the scene of Jesus's arrest, trial, crucifixion, and resurrection.

The Lord gave Jehoiakim king of Judah into his hand (1:2): The Lord used the Babylonians as His whipping rod to chastise the people of Judah for their unrepentant sins (see Jeremiah 25:9; 27:6).

Vessels of the house of God (1:2): The house of God was the Jewish temple built by Solomon in Jerusalem. The temple was rectangular, running east and west, and was about 87 feet long, 30 feet wide, and 43 feet high. The walls of the temple were made of cedar, and carved into the wood were cherubim (angels), flowers, and palm trees. The walls were overlaid with gold. The floor was made of cypress.

Solomon's temple had a Holy Place and a Most Holy Place. The Holy Place (the main outer room) housed the golden incense altar, the table of showbread, and five pairs of lampstands, as well as utensils used for sacrifice. Double doors led into the Most Holy Place, where the ark of the covenant was placed. The ark rested between two wooden cherubim, each standing ten feet tall. God manifested Himself in the Most Holy Place in a cloud of glory (1 Kings 8:10-11). This temple—the heart and center of Jewish worship for the kingdom of Judah—was destroyed by Nebuchadnezzar and the Babylonians.

The "vessels" were sacred objects in the temple. The Babylonians seized these sacred objects as spoils, believing this represented the victory of Babylon's gods over the God of Israel. Little did the Babylonians know that it was actually the one true God of Judah who handed His own people over to the Babylonians for chastisement (see Deuteronomy 28:64; Jeremiah 25:8-14).

In any event, the sacred objects of the temple would have included "the golden altar, the golden table for the bread of the Presence, the lampstands of pure gold...the lamps, and the tongs, of gold; the cups, snuffers, basins, dishes for incense, and fire pans, of pure gold; and the sockets of gold, for the doors of the innermost part of the house" (1 Kings 7:48-51).

Shinar (1:2): Another term for Babylon.

House of his god...treasury of his god (1:2): Like other pagan nations of the Ancient Near East, the Babylonians believed in many false gods and goddesses. These gods were thought to control the entire world of nature, so being successful in life required placating the gods. The Babylonians also believed that their military victories indicated that their gods were more powerful than any other nation's gods. However, in the Babylonian religious system, the gods' behavior was considered unpredictable at best.

Each city in Babylon had a patron god with an accompanying temple. Several small shrines were also scattered about each city, and people often met there to worship various other deities. The chief of the Babylonian gods was Anu, considered the king of heaven, and the patron god of Babylon was Marduk. "His god" (1:2) is likely a reference to Marduk.

Daniel 1:3-5

Chief eunuch (1:3): This term does not necessarily refer to a man who was castrated. The Hebrew term *saris* can simply refer to a government official (see 2 Kings 8:6).

Bring some of the people of Israel (1:3): In one section of the Mosaic Law, recorded in Leviticus 26:33,39, God threatened His people with exile if they chose to be unfaithful to the terms of the covenant established at Mount Sinai (see also Deuteronomy 4:27; 28:64). As it happened, the people of Judah disobeyed the Lord for an extended time. The resulting exile did not occur all at once. Initially only "some of the people of Israel" were brought to Babylon, including Daniel and his friends. This would have been in 605 BC. The exile came to full fruition in 597 BC when Babylon destroyed both Jerusalem and its temple, and at that time countless Jews were exiled to Babylon.

Youths (1:4): Young teenagers—probably between 14 and 17 years old.

Teach them (1:4): The Babylonian literature they were required to study probably included writings on agriculture, architecture, astrology, astronomy, law, mathematics, and the difficult Akkadian language.

(One recalls that Moses was likewise trained in Egyptian literature—Acts 7:22.) Nebuchadnezzar wanted these young men to be encultur-ated and assimilated into Babylonian society (see Major Themes). As we will see throughout the rest of the book, however, Babylon influ-enced Daniel and his friends very little. Instead, they greatly influenced Babylon by remaining faithful to the one true God.

Food...wine (1:5): That the king allowed the youths the food and wine he partook of was likely designed to foster dependence, gratitude, and loyalty to the king.

Educated (1:5): The youths were educated for three years, not quite as long as it would take a person to get a college degree today.

Daniel 1:6-7

Daniel (1:6): In the ancient world, a name was not a mere label, as it is today. A name was equivalent to whomever or whatever bore it. A person's name could indicate his or her character, personality, or alle-giance. Knowing a person's name therefore amounted to knowing a great deal about him or her.

We see this illustrated in the names of major Bible characters. The name Abraham, for instance, means "father of a multitude," which was fitting because Abraham was the father of the Jewish nation. The name David means "beloved," and of course, David was a king specially loved by God. The name Solomon comes from a word meaning "peace"—and Solomon's reign was characterized by peace. In each case, we learn something about the individual from his name.

The same is true regarding the names given to the four Hebrew youths mentioned in Daniel 1:6: Daniel, Hananiah, Mishael, and Aza-riah. Daniel's name, for example, means "God has judged," or per-haps "God is my Judge." Note that the ending of Daniel's name, *el*, is a Hebrew term for God. Daniel's parents were apparently God-fearing people.

Hananiah (1:6): This name means "Yahweh has been gracious." Note that the *iah* ending (or *yah*) is an abbreviation for God's name Yahweh.

Mishael (1:6): This name means "Who is what God is?" Again we see the *el* ending, a Hebrew name for God.

Azariah (1:6): Azariah's name means "Yahweh has helped." Again, the *iah* ending (or *yah*) is an abbreviation for God's name Yahweh.

Tribe of Judah (1:6): The Israelites were divided into 12 tribes, descended from the 12 sons of Jacob: Reuben, Gad, Manasseh, Asher, Naphtali, Zebulon, Issachar, Ephraim, Benjamin, Judah, Simeon, and Dan. The tribe of Judah is particularly significant, for Genesis 49:10 prophesied that the Messiah would come from the tribe of Judah and reign as King. Judah is therefore a royal tribe.

Belteshazzar (1:7): Daniel and his friends all had Hebrew names that honored the one true God of Israel. The Babylonians believed their gods were superior to the God of Israel. The young men's names were therefore changed to honor Babylonian deities instead of the God of Israel. Daniel was renamed Belteshazzar, meaning "Bel, protect his life," or "Bel, protect the king's life." (Bel was a Babylonian deity.)

Shadrach (1:7): Hananiah's name was changed to Shadrach, apparently meaning "Command of Aku." (Aku was another Babylonian deity.)

Meshach (1:7): Mishael's name was changed to Meshach, meaning "Who is Aku?"

Abednego (1:7): Azariah's name was changed to Abednego, meaning "Servant of Nebo." (Nebo, also known as Nabu, was yet another Babylonian deity.)

Major Themes

1. *King Nebuchadnezzar of Babylon.* Nebuchadnezzar's name means "Nabu has protected my inheritance." Nebuchadnezzar was the most powerful of the Babylonian kings. He is famous for taking multitudes of Jews into captivity from 605 to 597 BC, among whom were Daniel and his companions (Jeremiah 27:19; 40:1; Daniel 1:1-7). After Daniel's companions were thrown into the fiery furnace and miraculously delivered (Daniel 3), the

king became afflicted with a strange mental disease as a punishment for his pride and vanity. He was eventually restored.

2. *King Jehoiakim of Judah.* Jehoiakim was the second son of Josiah and became the eighteenth king of Judah (2 Kings 23:33-34; 2 Chronicles 36:6-7). He was born about 633 BC. He was a vicious, cruel, selfish, rebellious, and irreligious man who encouraged idolatry (see Jeremiah 19). He flaunted his impiety when he destroyed a prophetic scroll written by the prophet Jeremiah. He died a violent death (2 Kings 24:3-4; Jeremiah 22:18-19; 36:30).

3. *The enculturation of exiles.* Daniel and his Jewish friends were enculturated in Babylon. They were trained in Babylonian language and literature and instructed to eat Babylonian food (though Daniel was able to make other arrangements). They were given Babylonian names that honored Babylonian gods. The idea was to make them suitable for service in the king's palace.

Digging Deeper with Cross-References

Exile as the consequence of disobedience—Genesis 15:13-14; Exodus 1:11-14; Deuteronomy 28:36; Judges 2:14; 2 Kings 17:6-7; Isaiah 39:6; Amos 5:27

Sacred objects of the temple—Exodus 25:29; 37:16; 40:9; 1 Kings 7:51; 2 Kings 14:14; 24:13; 25:14; 2 Chronicles 36:18; Ezra 1:7; 5:14; Jeremiah 28:3

Life Lessons

1. *A failure to repent brings God's discipline.* A failure to repent of sin always brings God's discipline in the life of a believer. Recall that this is what happened to David following his sin with Bathsheba (Psalms 32:3-5; 51). It can happen to us today too (Hebrews 12:5-11). Never forget, "If we would

examine ourselves, we would not be judged by God in this way" (1 Corinthians 11:31 NLT).

2. *God is sovereign over human affairs.* Daniel 1:2 reveals that God sovereignly allowed Judah's captivity. Scripture reveals that God is absolutely sovereign—He rules the universe, controls all things, and is Lord over all. He may utilize various means to accomplish His ends, but He is always in control. You might want to meditate a few minutes on Psalms 50:1; 66:7; Proverbs 16:9; 19:21; 21:30; Isaiah 14:24; 40:15,17; 46:10.

Questions for Reflection and Discussion

1. What does the reality of God's sovereignty mean to you personally? Does this doctrine comfort you, frighten you, or maybe a little of both?

2. If you were forced to live in a part of the world brimming with paganism, do you think you'd still be able to effectively serve God with a good attitude?

3. Has God ever moved you outside of your comfort zone? If so, how did you adapt?

Daniel's Faithfulness

Daniel 1:8-16

Scripture Reading and Insights

Begin by reading Daniel 1:8-16 in your favorite Bible. As you read, remember that the Word of God is alive and working in you (Hebrews 4:12).

In the previous lesson, we studied the historical circumstances of Daniel and his friends, newly exiled in Babylon. In today's lesson, we zero in on Daniel's faithfulness to God while living in a pagan society. With your Bible still accessible, consider the following insights on the biblical text, verse by verse.

Daniel 1:8

Daniel resolved (1:8): The word "resolved" carries the idea, "Daniel purposed in his heart," or "Daniel determined in his heart," or "Daniel set upon his heart." He was a man of strong convictions, and he consistently acted on them.

King's food...wine (1:8): Why didn't Daniel and his friends want to eat the king's food? Here are four possible explanations.

- The food was prepared by Gentiles, so it was "unclean" according to the requirements of the Mosaic Law. Also, the fare probably included foods that were forbidden by the Mosaic Law (see Leviticus 11:1-23; Deuteronomy 14:1-21).

- Pagan nations often devoted food to pagan deities before eating it. If Daniel and his friends had eaten what they were served, they would have defiled themselves by rendering honor to the false gods (see Exodus 34:15).

- Daniel and his friends might have been rejecting the luxurious lifestyle—including the extravagant food—offered to those in the king's court. Perhaps they reasoned that such materialism might defile them or lure them away from complete commitment to God.

- Jewish people drank wine diluted by water (see Major Themes). The Babylonians did not dilute their wine, and "strong drink" was unacceptable to the Jews (see Proverbs 20:1). Moreover, Babylonians poured their wine on pagan altars in the worship of their deities. Daniel and his friends would have wanted no part of this.

Ultimately, Daniel resolved that even though he lived in a land that did not honor God's Law, he himself would nevertheless do everything possible to continue obeying the Lord's commands. Walking in faithfulness to God was harder in Babylon than in Judah, but God rewarded Daniel's faithfulness.

Therefore he asked (1:8): James 2:17 tells us, "Faith by itself, if it does not have works, is dead." Daniel didn't just make a resolution in his heart ("faith") but also acted on that resolution ("works"). He took immediate steps to make other arrangements for food.

Daniel 1:9-10

God gave Daniel favor and compassion (1:9): God has the power to turn the hearts of unbelieving leaders so that they are favorable to God's people (see Exodus 11:3). He also honors those who first honor Him (1 Samuel 2:30; 2 Chronicles 16:9). Proverbs 16:7 tells us, "When a man's ways please the LORD, he makes even his enemies to be at peace with him." (See Life Lessons.)

I fear my lord the king (1:10): The chief eunuch was charged with overseeing the physical and mental development of Daniel and his friends. If the king was not pleased with this development, that would reflect badly on the chief eunuch and he could be punished or even lose his life.

Worse condition (1:10): Evidenced by looking worse.

Endanger my head (1:10): Disappointing the king could result in execution.

Daniel 1:11-14

Daniel said (1:11): Notice that Daniel did not rebel. He did not use harsh language, raise his voice, or get into a heated argument. Instead he used good judgment by courteously offering a reasonable alternative to the steward. He came up with a creative solution that avoided offense and enabled him and his friends to remain faithful to God in the process.

Steward (1:11): Daniel surmised from the chief eunuch's words that his request for a special diet had been denied. Daniel thus approached the steward who had been placed in charge of the four youths. Daniel requested a ten-day period in which they would be fed only vegetables and water. He implied that he and his friends would have a better appearance in ten days than those eating the king's food. The steward had no authority on his own, so he likely okayed this with the chief eunuch before proceeding. The God who brings favor in the eyes of others was clearly at work behind the scenes here.

Vegetables (1:12): The Old Testament word translated "vegetables" means "things grown from seeds." The word could refer either to fresh vegetables or even to wheat or barley grain. Vegetables—things grown from seeds—were a safe choice, for the Mosaic Law did not categorize any vegetables as unclean. Therefore, no matter what vegetables were brought to Daniel and his friends, they would not be defiled.

Some Bible expositors have suggested the possibility that in addition to avoiding defilement, Daniel avoided meat and other foods in order to engage in a kind of fast as an expression of their mourning, having been exiled. One must note, however, that their attitudes before the Babylonians were always upbeat and positive.

So he listened (1:14): Daniel's suggestion was okayed and put into practice.

Daniel 1:15-16

Better in appearance and fatter in flesh (1:15): To be better in appearance and fatter in flesh was taken as evidence that they were healthier than those who ate the king's diet. This was precisely the opposite of what Ashpenaz, the chief eunuch, had feared.

Some scholars have been careful to point out that this verse cannot be taken as a biblical endorsement of vegetarianism. After all, it was ultimately God who made them healthy and gave them the outer appearance of health. The youths had honored God, and now God honored them by keeping them healthy. Though vegetables are definitely healthy, God ultimately blessed them because they obeyed His will, not simply because they ate vegetables instead of other foods.

Scripture stands against legalists who for religious reasons "require abstinence from foods that God created to be received with thanksgiving by those who believe and know the truth. For everything created by God is good, and nothing is to be rejected if it is received with thanksgiving, for it is made holy by the word of God and prayer" (1 Timothy 4:3-5). Acceptable foods certainly include meat (Genesis 9:3).

In Old Testament times the Jews believed—based on divine revelation—that health came from pleasing God, while sickness and disease came from displeasing Him. God Himself affirmed in Exodus 15:26, "If you will diligently listen to the voice of the LORD your God, and do that which is right in his eyes, and give ear to his commandments and keep all his statutes, I will put none of the diseases on you that I put on the Egyptians, for I am the LORD, your healer." God commanded, "You shall serve the LORD your God, and he will bless your bread and your water, and I will take sickness away from among you" (Exodus 23:25). Scripture promises that if you "fear the LORD, and turn away from evil...it will be healing to your flesh and refreshment to your bones" (Proverbs 3:7-8).

So the steward took away (1:16): As a result of the ten-day experiment, a permanent diet of vegetables and water was allowed for Daniel and his friends.

Major Themes

1. *Avoiding defilement.* The ancient Jews believed that a number of things could render a person unclean. For example, a woman was rendered ceremonially unclean during menstruation and following childbirth (Leviticus 12:2-5; Ezekiel 16:4). Touching a dead animal rendered one unclean (Leviticus 11:24-40), as did touching any dead body (Numbers 19:11). A person with a skin infection was considered unclean (Leviticus 13:3). Sexual discharges rendered one unclean (Leviticus 15:2). The Samaritans of New Testament times were considered unclean because they were of mixed ancestry (Israelite and Assyrian— see John 4:9). Likewise, eating certain prohibited foods rendered one unclean or defiled (Leviticus 11:46-47; Ezekiel 4:13-14; Hosea 9:3-4). This is what Daniel was seeking to avoid (Daniel 1:8).

2. *Drinking wine.* In day-to-day meals in biblical times, wine was often mixed with water as a means of purifying it. A popular beverage of ancient times was twenty parts water mixed with one part wine. This was essentially wine-flavored water. In other cases, one part wine might be mixed with one part water (or no water at all), and this was considered strong wine. Drinking wine in moderation is permissible for Christians (John 2:9; 1 Timothy 3:3,8; but also see Romans 14:21; 1 Corinthians 6:12; 10:31). Drunkenness is prohibited (Ephesians 5:18).

3. *A good conscience.* Daniel and his friends were concerned not only about moral purity but also about ceremonial purity. They wanted to avoid *any* kind of defilement. They may have been forced to move to Babylon, but it was

important to them to maintain a good conscience in all things. This is a thread that runs all through Daniel. We are reminded of the apostle Paul's instruction in 1 Timothy 1:19 for young Timothy to keep a strong faith as well as a good conscience (see also 1 Peter 3:16). Daniel is a good example of the kind of man Paul wanted Timothy to be.

Digging Deeper with Cross-References

Unclean foods the Israelites were to avoid—Leviticus 11:46-47; Ezekiel 4:13-14; Hosea 9:3-4; 1 Corinthians 8

Health promised for obedience—Exodus 15:26; 23:25; Deuteronomy 7:15; 2 Kings 20:5; Psalms 30:2; 91:5-6; 103:3; Proverbs 3:7-8; 4:20-22; James 5:14-15; 3 John 2

Life Lessons

1. *Be faithful to God.* Daniel and his companions were faithful to God. You and I are likewise called to be faithful to God (meditate on Proverbs 3:3; Matthew 25:23; Romans 12:12; and Revelation 2:10). Scripture reveals that as we walk in dependence on the Holy Spirit, faithfulness is part of the fruit of the Spirit that will be produced in our lives (Galatians 5:16,22). It makes good sense to therefore depend on the Holy Spirit every day of our lives!

2. *God gives favor.* Scripture often displays God giving His people favor in the eyes of others. For example, when Joseph was in prison, God gave him favor in the eyes of the prison warden (Genesis 39:21). God likewise gave Daniel favor in the eyes of the chief eunuch (Daniel 1:9). God can cause people to look upon us favorably as well (see Exodus 3:21; 11:3; 12:36). Why not incorporate this into your prayers? "Lord, please grant me favor in the eyes of..."

3. *Be a person of integrity.* Daniel was clearly a man of integrity.

The Bible speaks a great deal about what it means to be a man of integrity.

- "Better is a poor man who walks in his integrity than a rich man who is crooked in his ways" (Proverbs 28:6).

- "Better is a poor person who walks in his integrity than one who is crooked in speech and is a fool" (Proverbs 19:1).

- "The integrity of the upright guides them" (Proverbs 11:3).

- "The righteous who walks in his integrity—blessed are his children after him!" (Proverbs 20:7).

Daniel was certainly right in line with Paul's words in 2 Corinthians 8:21: "We aim at what is honorable not only in the Lord's sight but also in the sight of man." In other words, we aim at integrity both before the Lord and before human beings. Here are some helpful verses worthy of meditation: Psalms 25:21; 26:1; Micah 6:8; Acts 24:16; Titus 2:1-14; Hebrews 13:18; James 1:22-25.

Questions for Reflection and Discussion

1. Does Daniel's resolution in verse 8 motivate you to follow his lead and make your own resolution?

2. What do you learn about God's sovereignty in verse 9 in regard to authority figures in your life? (Contemplate how Proverbs 21:1 might relate to this.)

3. What impresses you most about how Daniel handled himself in his circumstances?

Daniel Rises in Favor Before the King

Daniel 1:17-21

Scripture Reading and Insights

Begin by reading Daniel 1:17-21 in your favorite Bible. As you read, remember that those who obey the Word of God are truly blessed (Psalm 119:2; Luke 11:28; Revelation 1:3).

In yesterday's lesson, we considered Daniel's faithfulness to God while living in a pagan society. Today we'll see Daniel's providential rise in favor with the king. With your Bible still accessible, consider the following insights on the biblical text, verse by verse.

Daniel 1:17

God gave them learning and skill (1:17): As a result of God's special gifting, the four Hebrew youths were equipped with reasoning skills that enabled them to think clearly and logically. They gained a heightened discernment that enabled them to interpret events and circumstances in their true light.

Wisdom (1:17): The Hebrew word for wisdom is *hokmah*. This word was commonly used for the skill of craftsmen, sailors, singers, administrators, and counselors. *Hokmah* pointed to the experience and efficiency of these various workers in using their skills. Similarly, a person who possesses *hokmah* in his spiritual life and relationship to God is both knowledgeable and experienced in following God's way. Biblical wisdom involves skill in the art of godly living. This broad wisdom makes for skilled living and empowers people to be successful at home, at work, in human relationships, in finances, in eternal issues, and much more. Daniel and his friends received *hokmah* from God.

We might note in passing that God has not stopped giving His people wisdom when they need it. In James 1:5 we are promised, "If any of you lacks wisdom, let him ask God, who gives generously to all without reproach, and it will be given him." Also, God often uses people with excellent educational backgrounds. This was certainly true of Moses (Acts 7:22), Daniel and his friends, and the apostle Paul (Acts 22:3).

Understanding in all visions and dreams (1:17): Daniel had a gift that set him apart from all others in Babylon. He was given a special ability to understand visions and dreams. Others in Babylon may have known as much about literature as Daniel did, but no one else had his special, God-given ability to interpret dreams. How could they? The false gods of Babylon (who were not really gods at all) could not help the magicians or enchanters understand dreams. Only the one true God knows the meaning of dreams, and as we will see, God conveyed those meanings to Daniel (see Daniel 2:2-11; 4:6-7).

Of course, when God gives His people learning and skill, He doesn't intend for those gifts to lay stagnant in their lives. Rather, He gives His people these qualities so they can be used. We will see throughout the rest of the book of Daniel that these four youths put to excellent use the gifts of learning and skill God gave them.

Daniel 1:18-19

At the end of the time (1:18): This refers back to verse 5—"They were to be educated for three years, and at the end of that time they were to stand before the king." Now the time had come.

Brought them in (1:18): Ashpenaz, the chief eunuch, now displayed his students of three years before Nebuchadnezzar for their final examination. Though Ashpenaz was no doubt confident in his abilities as a trainer, he nevertheless likely experienced some anxiety, knowing that a failure to please Nebuchadnezzar could lead to punishment or even death.

The king spoke with them (1:19): The king gave an oral examination to all those present, likely covering topics that were most important to him and his agenda.

Among all of them (1:19): Recall from verses 5 and 6 that these four youths were among a larger group of youths that the king commanded to be trained. Apparently the entire group of youths now stood before the king.

None was found like (1:19): Daniel and his three friends were the cream of the crop among all those trained. As a result of the special abilities God gave them, they were clearly superior to all others. At this time they would have been about 20 years old—about the age of a modern college student.

Therefore they stood before the king (1:19): One is reminded of Proverbs 22:29: "Do you see a man skillful in his work? He will stand before kings."

Daniel 1:20-21

In every matter of wisdom and understanding (1:20): The final examination was comprehensive. It covered a wide spectrum of topics and issues. The four youths didn't excel in only a few of these topics but rather in "every matter" that was brought up.

Ten times better (1:20): This phrase signifies completeness or fullness. The four youths were completely superior to the others around them. They outshone everyone else. They stood heads and shoulders above the others.

This again brings to mind Joseph, whom God also gave special abilities. Pharaoh "sent and called for all the magicians of Egypt and all its wise men. Pharaoh told them his dreams, but there was none who could interpret them to Pharaoh" (Genesis 41:8). With God's help, Joseph succeeded where all others had failed. "Then Pharaoh said to Joseph, 'Since God has shown you all this, there is none so discerning and wise as you are'" (Genesis 41:39).

Magicians and enchanters (1:20): These individuals typically used divination, astrological charts, and soothsaying to ascertain their answers. They were occultists, and as occultists they were actually energized by demonic spirits, though they claimed to be spokesmen for Babylon's pagan gods.

One must not miss the religious significance of what is going on here. The contest between the four youths and the magicians and enchanters is very much a contest between the one true God and the many false gods of Babylon. The four youths stood out because the one true God was the source of their wisdom and skills. All others dimmed in their presence because they derived their power from false gods, which were in fact nonexistent. The false gods were no competition with the one true God of Israel.

We witness a similar contest between the true God and false gods in Moses's ongoing confrontation with Pharaoh over the Jews' slavery. Moses expressed God's absolute incomparability in two ways. The most common was negation—"There is no one like the LORD our God" (Exodus 8:10). The other way was by rhetorical questions, such as "Who is like you, O LORD, among the gods?" (Exodus 15:11). The implied answer is, "No one in all the universe." This was particularly significant in view of Moses's experience in Egypt, which was brimming with false gods.

God used ten plagues to openly demonstrate His superiority over the gods of Egypt. For example, the first plague, which turned the Nile's water into blood (Exodus 7:14-25), was a judgment against one of Egypt's most prominent gods. The Nile itself was worshipped as a god, and as its water was virtually the lifeblood of Egypt, this blow was devastating. The Exodus account reveals that Nilus, the Egyptian river god, was impotent in the face of the true God of Scripture.

The ninth plague brought darkness to the whole land (Exodus 10:21-29). This was a judgment against the Egyptian sun god, Re. The sun god was regarded as the creator, father, and king of the gods. He was considered the most distinguished god in the pantheon and was praised as stronger, mightier, and more divine than the other gods. But Re was nowhere to be found when the true God of Scripture darkened the land.

Babylon was now learning the same lesson the Egyptians had learned much earlier. But in the present case, the true God's victory over Babylon's false gods was evident in the four youths' superiority over all the magicians and enchanters of Babylon.

Until the first year of King Cyrus (1:21): Daniel's ministry in the royal court of Babylon continued until the overthrow of the Babylonian Empire by Cyrus in 539 BC. Daniel was one of the first captives exiled to Babylon, but he lived to see the first exiles return to Jerusalem in 538 BC under Cyrus's decree.

Major Themes

1. *Dreams in Bible times.* In Old Testament times, God often communicated with believers as well as unbelievers through dreams. Here are a few examples:

Abimelech (Genesis 20:3-7)	Pharaoh's butler and baker (Genesis 40:5)
Jacob (Genesis 28:12; 31:10)	Pharaoh himself (Genesis 41:1-8)
Laban (Genesis 31:24)	a Midianite (Judges 7:13-14)
Joseph (Genesis 37:9-11)	Nebuchadnezzar (Daniel 2:1)

   Such revelatory dreams continued in New Testament times, such as Joseph's dream about Mary's pregnancy by the Holy Spirit (Matthew 1:20; see also 2:12-13,19). Today, we have the Bible as God's primary means of revelation (2 Timothy 3:15-17). Interestingly, however, Acts 2:17 tells us, "In the last days it shall be, God declares, that I will pour out my Spirit on all flesh, and your sons and your daughters shall prophesy, and your young men shall see visions, and your old men shall dream dreams."

2. *Magicians and enchanters.* The king of Babylon often consulted with occultists (magicians and enchanters) for wisdom. It was thought that such individuals had supernatural insights. God, of course, condemns all forms

of occultism, including magic (Exodus 22:18; Leviticus
19:31; Deuteronomy 18:9-13; Ezekiel 13:18; Acts 19:19-20;
Galatians 5:20; Revelation 9:21; 21:8). The magicians were
influenced by demons, while Daniel was influenced by
God. No wonder Daniel could provide answers when the
magicians could not (Daniel 1:20).

Digging Deeper with Cross-References

The interpretation of dreams—Genesis 40:8,12,18; 41:12,25;
    Daniel 1:17; 2:4,28,36,45; 4:20,24

God's people exalted—Genesis 41:41; Exodus 7:1; 11:3; Joshua
    3:7; 4:14; 1 Samuel 2:8; Job 5:11; Psalms 27:6; 37:34; 113:7;
    145:14; 148:14; Isaiah 40:31; Habakkuk 3:19; Matthew
    23:12; 25:21; Luke 13:30; 14:11; Romans 8:18; 1 Corinthi-
    ans 6:2; 1 Peter 5:6

Life Lessons

1. *God gives special abilities.* Daniel 1:17 tells us that God gave
   Daniel and his friends some special abilities that enabled
   them to serve well. Actually, Scripture often reveals God
   giving special abilities to people. Christians today are
   equipped with the gifts of the Holy Spirit, which are to
   be used in serving the body of Christ (see Romans 12:6;
   1 Corinthians 12:4; Ephesians 4:11). The gifts God gives
   one believer are often different from the gifts He gives
   another. But we all serve the same body.

2. *Adapting to new circumstances.* Sometimes God allows us
   to experience circumstances that are outside our comfort
   zone. When that happens, it is best to adapt to our new
   circumstances and find ways to serve God. Daniel and his
   friends excelled in their assigned tasks in Babylon (Daniel
   1:20). Likewise, after Joseph was betrayed by his brothers,
   he served God faithfully in every new circumstance that

befell him (for example, see Genesis 39:4-6,21-23). When the apostle Paul was thrown in jail, he didn't wallow in self-pity, but was used by God in writing some of the New Testament books (Ephesians, Philippians, Colossians, and Philemon). The lesson we learn is simple: Be ready and willing to serve God in every situation!

Questions for Reflection and Discussion

1. Can you think of another person in Scripture who received great learning and wisdom from God? (See 1 Kings 3:12,28.) What does God's gift of such learning say about His sovereignty? What does it say about His grace?

2. Do you think Daniel and his friends were living examples of the truth found in Proverbs 4:23? How so?

3. Do you know what your spiritual gifts are? (Not sure? The best way to find out is to get involved in ministry at your local church. Spiritual gifts typically surface in the context of ministry.)

Nebuchadnezzar's Dreams

Daniel 2:1-6

Scripture Reading and Insights

Begin by reading Daniel 2:1-6 in your favorite Bible. As you read, keep in mind that just as we eat food for physical nourishment, so we need the Word of God for spiritual nourishment (1 Corinthians 3:2; Hebrews 5:12; 1 Peter 2:2). Seek to feed upon God's Word today.

Yesterday we focused attention on Daniel's rise in favor with the king. Now let's shift our attention to Nebuchadnezzar's dreams. With your Bible still accessible, consider the following insights on the biblical text, verse by verse.

Daniel 2:1

The second year of the reign of Nebuchadnezzar (2:1): In Babylonian reckoning, Nebuchadnezzar's accession year would have been the first year of the four youths' training (605–604 BC). Nebuchadnezzar's first full year of reigning would have been the second year of the youths' training (604–603 BC). His second full year of reigning would have been their third year of training (603–602 BC). So Nebuchadnezzar must have had the dreams immediately following the youths' third year of training, toward the end of his second full year of reigning (602 BC).

Nebuchadnezzar had dreams (2:1): The plural reference to dreams apparently means that Nebuchadnezzar was experiencing a recurring dream night after night. This must be the case since Daniel recalled and interpreted only one dream, not several different dreams (Daniel 2:24-26).

His spirit was troubled (2:1): Nebuchadnezzar's troubled heart is an indication that he considered the dream and its meaning significant. He couldn't rest until he found out what it meant.

His sleep left him (2:1): Sleep often eludes people with troubled hearts.

Daniel 2:2-3

The king commanded (2:2): The appearance of the various occultists before the king was not a mere invitation. They were given a direct order to appear before Nebuchadnezzar.

The magicians, the enchanters, the sorcerers, and the Chaldeans (2:2): The Babylonians believed that dreams were messages from the gods. The various occultists in Babylon were expected to be able to interpret them. If one group of occultists couldn't accomplish the task, perhaps another group could. In the present case, they were all summoned to appear before Nebuchadnezzar because the king wanted answers!

The Chaldeans mentioned in this verse were priests who served as astrologers or soothsayers.

Summoned to tell the king his dreams (2:2): Here is where the problem begins for these occultists. If the king told them his dream, they could take a stab at interpreting it. But here Nebuchadnezzar instructs them to actually tell him his dream before giving him the interpretation. This would prove to be an impossible task for these occultists because God was the One who gave this dream to Nebuchadnezzar. Only a man of God would be able to reveal it and interpret it. The false gods of Babylon would prove impotent in this task.

I had a dream (2:3): Nebuchadnezzar's statement, "I had a dream" (singular), qualifies the statement in verse 1, "Nebuchadnezzar had dreams." As noted previously, the king must have had a single dream that recurred over a number of nights. The recurrence of the dream demonstrated its importance.

My spirit is troubled to know the dream (2:3): Nebuchadnezzar may have been troubled that the dream somehow indicated that he would fall from power as a king. He wondered, *What does this dream say about me and my future?*

Daniel 2:4

Aramaic (2:4): Daniel's narrative switches from Hebrew to Aramaic in this verse, and continues through chapter 7, where the narrative then switches back to Hebrew. Aramaic was a common language among the Babylonians, Assyrians, and Persians. The language was often used in diplomacy, commerce, and trade. Aramaic was truly an international language in that part of the world.

One might wonder why the Chaldeans chose to speak in Aramaic. The answer is that the various occultists who appeared before the king came from different provinces and used various dialects, but they all understood Aramaic.

In addition, Daniel 1:1–2:4a and 8:1–12:13 were written in Hebrew likely because the scriptural text deals with Hebrew issues. By contrast, Daniel 2:4b–7:28 was written in Aramaic apparently because the scriptural text deals with issues of interest to the Gentile nations.

O king, live forever! (2:4): The Chaldeans were quite eager to please King Nebuchadnezzar. They accordingly addressed the king with an expression of common courtesy in that part of the world. We see this courtesy elsewhere in Scripture. For example, recall that "Bathsheba bowed with her face to the ground and paid homage to the king and said, 'May my lord King David live forever'" (1 Kings 1:31; see also Nehemiah 2:3; Daniel 3:9; 5:10; 6:21).

Tell your servants the dream (2:4): Notice that no one said, "Tell me the dream." No one wanted to try to interpret the dream alone. Rather, they were confident that with their combined efforts they'd be able to come up with something that would satisfy the king.

Daniel 2:5-6

The word from me is firm (2:5): Negotiation was not an option. Things would be done the king's way, or people would lose their lives. The king was resolved to ensure that the interpretation of his dream would be without deception.

Some have asked whether the king may have forgotten his dream. After all, people today have dreams that are disturbing, but upon awakening, they sometimes forget their dreams. Moreover, some have tried to argue that the clause "the word from me is firm" could be translated "the thing is gone from me," implying that the king forgot the dream.

The latter translation seems foreign to the context in the present case. After all, if the king had forgotten the dream, the occultists could simply make up a dream and reveal it to him. The king wouldn't know any better, and the occultists' lives would be spared. Contrary to such an idea, the context seems to indicate that the king is putting the occultists to a test that goes something like this: "I know what I've dreamed night after night, and if you can't tell me the details of this recurring dream, you're all dead men." So Nebuchadnezzar withheld the facts of the dream before those present not because he forgot them, but because he wanted to test his "wise men."

Let's not forget that in the Bible, when God gave someone a dream, no one ever forgot the details of it. (See "Notable dreams" in Digging Deeper with Cross-References.) Daniel 2:1 indicates that Nebuchadnezzar awoke because the dream was so troubling, and he wasn't able to go back to sleep precisely because he remembered it.

If you do not make known to me (2:5): In the past, the king had likely had other dreams and received satisfactory interpretations from his occultic advisors. Apparently, however, this dream was so important to the king that he imposed extremely stringent requirements on his occultic advisors. The king seemed to reason that if he was going to trust their interpretation of the future based on his dream, they ought also be able to reveal the past—that is, they ought to be able to tell the king his dream. If they botched up the past, they would be likely to botch up the future.

Some Bible expositors have pointed out that Nebuchadnezzar was a young king, while these advisors were quite old, having served Nebuchadnezzar's father. Nebuchadnezzar may have thought that these aged men might be trying to pull the wool over his eyes, thinking he was a naive young man. He therefore may have doubted their loyalty to him.

Nebuchadnezzar's test may have been engineered to sift out the bad with a view to bringing in people he could really trust.

Torn limb from limb...houses...laid in ruins (2:5): The consequences for failure would be severe: Death and destruction of personal property. These words were probably more severe than these aged men had ever heard from Nebuchadnezzar's father.

Gifts and rewards and great honor (2:6): On the other hand, the reward for success would be great. The stakes were very high.

Therefore show me the dream and its interpretation (2:6): The occultists had their backs against the wall, and they knew it. This was an either-or crisis. Either they get it right and get rewarded, or they get it wrong and die. There was no middle option.

Major Themes

1. *Sorcerers.* Sorcery in ancient times sometimes involved conjuring spells (Deuteronomy 18:11). Other times it might involve interpreting omens (Genesis 30:27; 44:5). Still other times it might involve practicing soothsaying by, for example, examining the liver of a dead animal that had been used for sacrifice. If there were any abnormalities in the liver, they would try to interpret those abnormalities as a possible indication of some aspect of the will of the gods. The Bible condemns all forms of sorcery (Exodus 22:18; Leviticus 19:26,31; 20:27).

2. *Astrologers.* Astrology can be traced back to the religious practices of ancient Mesopotamia, Assyria, Babylon, and Egypt. It is a form of divination—an attempt to seek paranormal counsel or knowledge by occultic means. It was believed that the study of the arrangement and movement of the stars could enable one to foretell events and determine whether they will be good or bad (see Daniel 2:10,27; 4:7; 5:7). As well, in Babylon the stars were viewed as being connected to the pagan gods

(Daniel 5:11). Astrology is strictly off-limits for Christians (Deuteronomy 18:9-12; Isaiah 47:13-15).

Digging Deeper with Cross-References

Notable dreams—Genesis 28:12; 37:5,9; 40:5,16; 41:1; Judges 7:13; 1 Kings 3:5,15; Matthew 1:20; 2:12-13,19,22; 27:19

Magicians—Genesis 41:8; Exodus 7:11,22; 8:7,19; Daniel 1:20; 2:2,10,27; 4:7; 5:7

Life Lessons

1. *Sleeplessness versus sound sleep.* We read about sleeplessness not only in the book of Daniel (2:1; 6:18-19), but elsewhere in Scripture as well (Esther 6:1; Job 7:4-5; 30:17; Psalm 77:4; Ecclesiastes 2:23). Scripture also speaks of those who enjoy good sleep (Psalms 3:5; 4:8; 127:2; Proverbs 3:21-24; 6:20-22). Do you want to sleep soundly? Scripture urges us to always trust God, obey God, and fill our minds with God's Word.

2. *Dealing with threats.* In Daniel 2:5 the various occultists were threatened with death if they didn't tell the king what he wanted to hear. God's people, too, are often threatened. For example, in Acts 4:17-21 the Jewish Sanhedrin threatened the apostles to keep silent about Jesus. The apostles responded by praying, "And now, Lord, look upon their threats and grant to your servants to continue to speak your word with all boldness" (verse 29). We can adopt this prayer as our own as we encounter threats in our increasingly anti-Christian culture.

Questions for Reflection and Discussion

1. Can you think of any popular modern occultists who claim to have answers to the mysteries of life? Why might they be so popular?

2. What do the polar opposite consequences in Daniel 2:5-6 reveal about the king's character?

3. We will soon see Daniel clearly explaining that the power to interpret dreams is from God. What source empowered the magicians, the enchanters, and the sorcerers? What does Scripture elsewhere reveal about this source? (See John 8:44; 2 Corinthians 4:4; 11:14; 1 Peter 5:8.)

Nebuchadnezzar Demands an Interpretation

Daniel 2:7-16

Scripture Reading and Insights

Begin by reading Daniel 2:7-16 in your favorite Bible. As you read, remember that storing God's Word in your heart can help you to avoid sinning (Psalm 119:9,11).

Yesterday we focused on Nebuchadnezzar's recurring dream and his demand for an interpretation. Today we will see him prepare to carry out his threats against his "wise men." With your Bible still accessible, consider the following insights on the biblical text, verse by verse.

Daniel 2:7

Let the king tell his servants the dream (2:7): The occultists knew their backs were against the wall. They therefore implored the king again to reveal the dream to them so they could offer him an interpretation.

As is so often the case in the Bible, the occultists were unable to deliver. The same thing had happened twice in the Egyptian Pharaoh's court—once with Joseph (Genesis 41:1-8) and again with Moses (Exodus 8:16-19). The contest between the one true God and the powers of darkness (who energized these occultists) turns out to be no real contest at all.

Daniel 2:8-9

You are trying to gain time (2:8): The king took the second plea from the occultists as an attempt to stall for time. Perhaps they thought that if they could stall long enough, the king would simply acquiesce and not pursue the matter any further. They hoped their stall tactics would provide sufficient time for the king to cool down and forget about the incident.

The word from me is firm (2:8): The king would not bend. His mind was made up. He seemed intent on exposing their hypocrisy. The occultists claimed to be wise men, but how wise were they really? The king suspected they were bogus—all talk and no substance. Their stall tactics were leading them toward an early grave.

As we have seen, these men had worked for Nebuchadnezzar's father. They may have thought the new king was inexperienced, immature, and naive. Perhaps they thought that given enough time, he might grow up and act more kingly, like his father. If so, this was a gross miscalculation on their part, for they were all close to losing their lives.

There is but one sentence for you (2:9): The king reiterates the penalty for failure in order to emphasize the gravity of the occultists' situation. They would either reveal the dream or forfeit their lives (see verse 5).

Tell me the dream (2:9): The king was convinced he could trust the occultists' interpretation of the dream only if they first revealed the dream to him. If they couldn't do that, the king must conclude they conspired against him and "agreed to speak lying and corrupt words...till the times change."

The truth is that only a person with supernatural insight could meet the king's demands. The failure of the so-called "wise men" sets the stage for Daniel's impressive intervention.

Daniel 2:10-11

There is not a man on earth (2:10): In an attempt to save their lives, the occultists pleaded with the king—he was making an impossible and unreasonable request that no one was capable of fulfilling. Of course, they were correct. No man, not even Daniel, has the intrinsic ability to tell another human being his or her dreams.

No great and powerful king (2:10): No other potentate had ever asked wise men to do what Nebuchadnezzar was now asking.

No one can show it to the king except the gods (2:11): Notice the contrast we see in verses 10 and 11 between the earthly and the non-earthly. No one on earth could meet the king's demand (verse 10), only the gods, "whose dwelling is not with flesh" (verse 11). In other words, these gods do not dwell on earth with mere mortals. The truth, of course, is that these gods don't live anywhere, for they don't even exist (see 1 Corinthians 8:4-6).

Another thing is worth noting here. When the occultists said that no one but the gods could reveal the dream to the king, they admitted that their previous interpretations of dreams were bogus, since only the gods can give such information. We might paraphrase the point this way: "Even though we've given many interpretations of dreams in the past, the truth is (*ahem*) that only the gods can do it."

Only the one true God in heaven could answer the king's request. God would soon do this through his beloved servant Daniel (Daniel 4). We are again reminded of the Egyptian magicians in Joseph's time who were unable to interpret Pharaoh's dream. With God's help, Joseph did so. Pharaoh said to Joseph, "Since God has shown you all this, there is none so discerning and wise as you are" (Genesis 41:39). Daniel and Joseph were seemingly cut from the same cloth!

Daniel 2:12-13

The king was angry (2:12): The king became angry for several reasons. The occultic "wise men" were in fact not wise because they could not tell the king his dream. They claimed to be in contact with the divine, but obviously they were not. Instead of immediately granting the king's request, they stalled for time, hoping the incident would be forgotten. The king concluded these men were deceivers who considered him gullible enough to fall for their lies.

To make matters worse, the wise men implied that the king's request was inappropriate and in fact impossible. The king was to be viewed as divine, and the wise men were to be his servants, so they were out of line saying such a thing to a god.

The decree went out (2:13): The king had had enough and ordered the execution of all the wise men in his kingdom. Biblical scholars have noted several examples of ancient potentates executing an entire class of servants or workers (compare with 1 Samuel 22:13-19).

The wise men were about to be killed (2:13): Daniel and his friends were in the class of "wise men" in Babylon even though they were completely unlike any of the occultists. Therefore the king's instruction to kill all the wise men in the kingdom included them.

Daniel 2:14-16

Daniel replied (2:14): Confronted by the captain of the king's guard about the death sentence imposed on all wise men, Daniel again showed his wisdom, prudence, and discretion (see Proverbs 15:1).

Why...so urgent? (2:15): Instead of responding in a reactionary way, Daniel simply inquired why the king made this urgent decree. Arioch then informed Daniel of all that had transpired.

Requested the king to appoint him a time (2:16): Notice three things about this verse. First, notice that Daniel had direct access to the king. This indicates that Daniel was held in high regard. No ordinary person would be granted an urgent appointment with the king.

Second, notice how bold Daniel was. The wise men had previously stalled and delayed in answering the king. Now Daniel asked the king to "appoint him a time"—which, in fact, would also involve a delay. Perhaps the king granted Daniel's request because Daniel had proved himself trustworthy in the past.

Third, notice Daniel's faith. He made an appointment to reveal and interpret the dream for the king even though God had not yet revealed the dream to Daniel. He knew that God would come through for him.

Major Themes

1. *The error of believing in many gods.* The Chaldeans told the king no one could tell the king his dream "except the gods" (Daniel 2:11). Daniel consistently pointed to the one true God in contrast to the many false gods of Babylon.

Scripture consistently testifies that only one true God exists. God himself positively affirmed through Isaiah the prophet, "I am the first and I am the last; besides me there is no god" (Isaiah 44:6; see also 37:20; 43:10; 45:14,21-22). He asserted, "I am the LORD, and there is no other, besides me there is no God" (Isaiah 45:5). He later affirmed, "I am God, and there is no other; I am God, and there is none like me" (46:9; see also Deuteronomy 6:4; 32:39; 2 Samuel 7:22). The New Testament also emphasizes the oneness of God (John 5:44; 17:3; Romans 3:29-30; 16:27; Galatians 3:20; Ephesians 4:6; 1 Thessalonians 1:9; 1 Timothy 1:17; 2:5; 1 John 5:20; Jude 25). Belief in one God is known as monotheism. Belief in many gods is called polytheism.

2. *Royal decrees.* Daniel 2:13 informs us, "The decree went out, and the wise men were about to be killed." The decree came from Nebuchadnezzar. A decree is essentially an order, declaration, or edict from a person in high authority that had the force of law. Royal decrees were common in biblical times (for example, see Esther 1:19-22; Acts 17:7). Most often, such decrees were first spoken aloud by a person in high authority and then committed to writing. To disobey the decree amounted to disobeying the one who issued the decree. In Daniel 2, Arioch, the captain of the king's guard, knew that if he didn't obey the decree, he would likely lose his life.

Digging Deeper with Cross-References

The limits of human understanding—Genesis 41:8; Job 8:9; Proverbs 20:24; 27:1; 30:3; Ecclesiastes 3:22; 8:7; 9:12; Daniel 2:10,27; 4:7,18; 5:8,15; 12:8; Matthew 11:25; 1 Corinthians 13:9; James 1:5

The use of time—Ephesians 5:16; Colossians 4:5

The true God outshines the powers of darkness—Exodus 7–11;
1 Kings 18; Jeremiah 28; Acts 13:1-12

Life Lessons

1. *The Christian and prudence.* God desires that His followers
   be prudent, like Daniel (Daniel 2:14). The prudent person
   always looks ahead to see what is coming (Proverbs 14:8)
   and foresees danger (Proverbs 22:3; 27:12). The prudent
   person always carefully considers his steps (Proverbs
   14:15). He is consistently cautious (Proverbs 14:16). He
   consistently saves money for the future (Proverbs 6:6-11)
   and guards his mouth and his tongue (Psalm 39:1;
   Proverbs 21:23). Moreover, he is aware that consulting
   many counselors is one key to success (Proverbs 15:22).
   One great way to increase prudence is to focus studied
   attention on the book of Proverbs (see Proverbs 1:1-6).

2. *Beware of the deception of occultists.* John 8:44 tells us
   that Satan is the father of lies. It therefore makes sense
   that magicians, enchanters, and sorcerers—all of whom
   are energized by Satan—would be deceptive as well.
   Satan deceives in many ways. He has his own church—
   the "synagogue of Satan" (Revelation 2:9). He has his
   own ministers of darkness who bring false sermons
   (2 Corinthians 11:4-5). He has formulated his own system
   of theology, called "teachings of demons" (1 Timothy
   4:1; see also Revelation 2:24). His ministers proclaim his
   gospel—"a gospel contrary to the one we preached to
   you" (Galatians 1:7-8). He has his own throne (Revelation
   13:2) and his own worshippers (Revelation 13:4). He
   inspires false Christs (Matthew 24:4-5) and employs false
   teachers who bring in "destructive heresies" (2 Peter 2:1).
   He sends out false prophets (Matthew 24:11) and sponsors
   false apostles who imitate the true (2 Corinthians 11:13).
   Christian beware!

Questions for Reflection and Discussion

1. Daniel made an appointment to tell the king the interpretation of the dream (Daniel 2:16) *before* the interpretation had been revealed to him by God (verse 19). What does this show us about Daniel's faith?

2. In today's world, where the tyranny of the urgent rules and distractions confront us at every corner, do you find it difficult to keep God at the forefront of your thinking the way Daniel did? If so, do you want to make any changes today?

3. What are some ways that modern occultists, such as psychics, engage in deception?

God Reveals the Meaning of the Dream to Daniel

Daniel 2:17-23

Scripture Reading and Insights

Begin by reading Daniel 2:17-23 in your favorite Bible. As you read, remember that the Word of God teaches us, trains us, and corrects us (2 Timothy 3:15-17).

In yesterday's reading, Nebuchadnezzar demanded an interpretation of his dream. In today's lesson, God reveals the dream and its meaning to Daniel. With your Bible still accessible, consider the following insights on the biblical text, verse by verse.

Daniel 2:17-18

Daniel went to his house (2:17): Daniel was deliberately calm in this crisis. Though his life and his companions' lives were at stake, he remained tranquil and steady as he trusted in God.

Told them to seek mercy from the God of heaven (2:18): Upon arriving home, Daniel immediately asked his friends to pray to God for mercy. Notice that in this context of intercessory prayer to God, Daniel's associates were addressed not by their Babylonian names but by their Hebrew names—Hananiah, Mishael, and Azariah. They were praying not to the false gods of Babylon but to the God of the Hebrews—the true God.

Daniel knew that their only hope rested with God and His mercy. If God did not intervene, they were all dead men. Daniel knew that in himself he was just as ignorant of the dream and its meaning as the occultists were. From Daniel's perspective, God *had* to intervene. Notice that in their prayer, Daniel and his friends were trusting God to give them a definite answer within definite time parameters. They were stepping out on a limb, and if God did not intervene, they were history.

We again note the contrast between earth and heaven. Earlier in Daniel 2, the occultists informed the king that no man on *earth* could reveal the dream (verse 10). They were right about that. Now, we find Daniel appealing to the God of *heaven* for answers. The ascription "God of heaven" is used four times in this chapter (verses 18-19,37,44). "Lord of heaven" is used in 5:23, and we read, "There is a God in heaven" in 2:28.

Throughout this entire ordeal, we see no sense of panic in Daniel or his associates. They prayed to God, they trusted in God, and they were at peace. One is reminded of the apostle Paul's teaching on prayer in Philippians 4:6-7: "Do not be anxious about anything, but in everything by prayer and supplication with thanksgiving let your requests be made known to God. And the peace of God, which surpasses all understanding, will guard your hearts and your minds in Christ Jesus" (see also Isaiah 26:3).

Concerning this mystery (2:18): Daniel and his friends asked God to enable them to unravel the mystery. In the Bible, a mystery is a truth that cannot be discerned simply by human investigation, but requires special revelation from God. They desperately needed special revelation from God regarding Nebuchadnezzar's dream and its meaning.

Daniel 2:19

The mystery was revealed (2:19): God answered their prayers. He showed them the mercy they requested.

Vision of the night (2:19): The very night Daniel and his friends prayed, God communicated Nebuchadnezzar's dream to Daniel in a vision (compare with Numbers 12:6; 2 Kings 6:8-12; Job 33:15-16). What was hidden from Babylon's occultists was now revealed to Daniel. The former had been impotent to accomplish their task, but God showed Himself strong on Daniel's behalf, thereby rescuing him and his associates from execution.

Daniel 2:20-23

Blessed be the name of God forever and ever (2:20): Notice that Daniel did not immediately rush off to Arioch to tell him the good news. Daniel's highest priority was God. The first thing he did after receiving the vision was to give thanks and praise to God for His mighty deliverance. God, not Daniel, was to get all the credit in this episode. Daniel was truly grateful to God!

This opening statement is significant. God's name represents all that He is (see Major Themes). To bless someone is to pronounce goodness or favor upon them.

Examples of God blessing people abound in Scripture (for example, Genesis 1:22,28; 12:2; 22:17; 24:35; 32:29; Exodus 20:24; Job 42:12; Psalm 45:2). Examples of people blessing people are well illustrated in several famous biblical personalities, including Isaac (Genesis 27:26-40), Jacob (Genesis 49:1-27), Moses (Deuteronomy 33), Joshua (Joshua 22:6-7), and Jesus (Luke 24:50). Scripture indicates that human beings bless God when they recognize and thank Him for His wonderful acts of mercy and grace in their lives (see Psalms 63:4; 104:1; 145:1-2). This is what Daniel was doing in our present context.

Daniel's blessing of God brings to mind Psalm 103:1-2: "Bless the LORD, O my soul, and all that is within me, bless his holy name! Bless the LORD, O my soul, and forget not all his benefits." Daniel was definitely a Psalm 103 kind of person.

To whom belong wisdom and might (2:20): Daniel recognized that God was both wise and mighty, for only a wise and mighty God could have intervened in his life through a vision to rescue Daniel and his friends from certain death.

He changes times and seasons; he removes kings and sets up kings (2:21): In verses 21-22, Daniel provides illustrations of God's wisdom and might. For example, God is so mighty that he can control history (changing times and seasons) and determine the destiny of nations (removing kings and setting up kings). This means Nebuchadnezzar was king of Babylon for only one reason—God sovereignly determined to use him for His providential purposes.

He gives wisdom to the wise (2:21): As a God of wisdom, God is the source of wisdom to those who follow Him (see Proverbs 1:2-5). Daniel and his friends acted wisely in Babylon because God gave them wisdom. Daniel 1:17 says of the four youths, "God gave them learning and skill in all literature and wisdom, and Daniel had understanding in all visions and dreams."

He reveals deep and hidden things (2:22): This includes Nebuchadnezzar's dream.

He knows what is in the darkness (2:22): God is both all-knowing (omniscient) and everywhere-present (omnipresent). This means that nothing escapes His notice, even in the darkest places in the universe. Even a person's dreams cannot escape His notice. Nebuchadnezzar's dream was "darkness" to him, but God's light revealed the meaning of it to Daniel.

The light dwells with him (2:22): In context, this carries the idea that even though people may be in the dark about things (just as Daniel had no knowledge of Nebuchadnezzar's dream), all things are clear to God. Psalm 36:9 says of God, "In your light do we see light." Job 12:22 tells us, "He uncovers the deeps out of darkness and brings deep darkness to light." Psalm 139:12 says of God, "Even the darkness is not dark to you; the night is bright as the day, for darkness is as light with you." In Jeremiah 23:24 God Himself affirms, "Can a man hide himself in secret places so that I cannot see him? declares the LORD. Do I not fill heaven and earth? declares the LORD."

God of my fathers (2:23): This is the God of Abraham, Isaac, Jacob, and the other patriarchs (see, for example, Genesis 31:42). He is the one true God of the universe.

I give thanks and praise (2:23): Through the vision God gave Daniel, Daniel and his friends obtained the knowledge that would save their lives. Daniel's appropriate response was thanksgiving and praise to God. Like Daniel, we should always have praise for God on our lips (see Psalm 34:1). We should praise God in the depths of our hearts (Psalm 103:1-5,20-22) and continually "offer up a sacrifice of praise to

God" (Hebrews 13:15). One means of praising God is through spiritual songs (Psalm 69:30).

You have...made known to me what we asked of you (2:23): Daniel and his friends made a specific request of God in prayer. God gave a specific answer. They asked for wisdom, and God gave it (see James 1:5). The Babylonian wise men were unaware of it at the time, but the true wise men—the four Hebrew youths—would bring about even their deliverance.

Through it all, Daniel and his friends discovered the truth of Psalm 50:15, where God said, "Call upon me in the day of trouble; I will deliver you, and you shall glorify me."

Major Themes

1. *The name of God.* Daniel praised God by saying, "Blessed be the name of God forever and ever." In the ancient world, a name was not a mere label as it is today. A name was considered as equivalent to whoever or whatever bore it. The sum total of a person's being and his internal and external pattern of behavior was gathered up into his name. Indeed, knowing a person's name amounted to knowing his essence (see 1 Samuel 25:25). So when Daniel praised God's name, he was praising everything about God.

2. *God is omnipotent.* Daniel affirmed that God controls the course of world events (Daniel 2:21). Scripture more broadly reveals that God is omnipotent, or all-powerful (Genesis 18:14; Jeremiah 32:17,27; Matthew 19:26; Mark 10:27; Luke 1:37). He is abundant in strength (Psalm 147:5) and has incomparably great power (2 Chronicles 20:6; Ephesians 1:19-21). No one can hold back His hand (Daniel 4:35), and no one can thwart Him (Isaiah 14:27). Therefore He is able to control the course of world events, as Daniel said. The next time life throws you a punch, trust in the all-powerful God of the Bible.

Digging Deeper with Cross-References

> *Seeking God's mercy*—Psalms 6:2; 9:13; 25:7,16; 27:7; 30:10;
> 31:9; 33:22; 40:11; 41:10; 51:1; 57:1; 85:7; 86:3; 119:58,77;
> 123:3
>
> *God as light*—John 1:9; 8:12; 12:45-46; Matthew 4:16; Ephe-
> sians 5:14; James 1:17; 1 Peter 2:9; 1 John 1:5; Revelation
> 21:23

Life Lessons

1. *Mercy.* This term points to compassion and kindness
   shown to another. In the New Testament, God shows
   mercy on the basis of the work of Christ at the cross
   (Ephesians 2:4-5). Theologically, grace and mercy are
   closely related. The word "grace" means "unmerited favor."
   The word "mercy," as related to our salvation, carries the
   idea of withholding deserved punishment. Because of
   what Jesus did for us at the cross, we not only receive God's
   unmerited favor (grace) with a wondrous salvation, we also
   escape the judgment we deserve for our sins (mercy). What
   a wonder is our Jesus! (See 1 Peter 2:10; 2 John 3; Jude 21.)

2. *Intercessory prayer.* Intercession is a common feature of
   the prayers of God's people in the Bible. Jesus urged His
   followers, "Pray for those who persecute you" (Matthew
   5:44). He informed Peter, "I have prayed for you that your
   faith may not fail" (Luke 22:32). Speaking of those who
   crucified Him, Jesus prayed, "Father, forgive them, for
   they know not what they do" (Luke 23:34). Sometime
   later, the apostle Paul spoke of the importance of "making
   supplication for all the saints" (Ephesians 6:18). He said,
   "I urge that supplications, prayers, intercessions, and
   thanksgivings be made for all people" (1 Timothy 2:1).
   Paul urged the Corinthian believers, "Help us by prayer"
   (2 Corinthians 1:11). James speaks of intercessory prayer for

the sick: "Is anyone among you sick? Let him call for the elders of the church, and let them pray over him" (James 5:14; see also Acts 7:60; Philippians 1:19). Praying for others ought to be our regular practice.

Questions for Reflection and Discussion

1. What do you learn about the attributes of God in Daniel 2:20-23? Why does Daniel see these attributes as praiseworthy?

2. Whom can you intercede for in prayer this week?

3. Do you sufficiently engage in thanksgiving and praise to God? We could probably all do better. Why not make Hebrews 13:15 one of your theme verses?

Daniel Informs Nebuchadnezzar That God Has Revealed the Meaning

Daniel 2:24-30

Scripture Reading and Insights

Begin by reading Daniel 2:24-30 in your favorite Bible. As you read, never forget that you can trust everything recorded in the Word of God (Matthew 5:18; John 10:35).

In the previous lesson, God revealed the meaning of Nebuchadnezzar's dream to Daniel. In today's lesson, Daniel reports to Nebuchadnezzar that God told him about the dream and its meaning. With your Bible still accessible, consider the following insights on the biblical text, verse by verse.

Daniel 2:24-25

Daniel went in to Arioch (2:24): Daniel immediately went to see Arioch because the stakes were so high in quickly meeting the king's demands. One should not miss the fact that Daniel not only had easy access to Arioch but also enjoyed some level of influence with him. This indicates the high respect that Arioch and others in the royal service had for Daniel. Daniel had a good reputation.

Do not destroy the wise men of Babylon (2:24): Daniel sought to prevent any further executions of Babylon's wise men. Here again we find Daniel manifesting a godly attitude, focusing on the safety of others. Much later in history, the apostle Paul would describe this attitude in Philippians 2:4: "Let each of you look not only to his own interests, but also to the interests of others." Recall that Jesus himself taught, "You shall love your neighbor as yourself" (Matthew 22:39). Daniel loved and cared for the other wise men even though they were occultists.

Bring me in before the king (2:24): Daniel requested that Arioch take him immediately to see the king, for he now knew the dream and its interpretation. Notice that Daniel had no hesitation in sharing this news with Arioch. He was not unsure of himself. He did not say, "I think I know the dream and its interpretation." He did not say, "I have a good idea what the dream is and its interpretation." Daniel was absolutely sure that God had accurately revealed the dream and its meaning to him. He was completely confident in God.

Arioch brought in Daniel before the king in haste (2:25): Just as Daniel had quickly gone see Arioch, so now Arioch quickly takes Daniel to see the king. Perhaps Arioch thought that if he brought good news to the king, the king might reciprocate by looking upon him more favorably. Perhaps the king might even reward him. Time was of the essence. The sooner he got to the king, the better he would look.

I have found among the exiles from Judah (2:25): Notice how Arioch distorted what really happened. Daniel had come to Arioch, but Arioch boasts that he went out and found Daniel, as if he were busily trying to solve the king's dilemma. Daniel, a man of integrity, did not seek to correct Arioch on this.

Notice that Arioch introduced Daniel as one from "among the exiles from Judah." It is interesting to observe how often God has used a Jewish person to bring deliverance to others. Recall that when a number of kings joined in a coalition to overthrow Sodom and Gomorrah, Lot and many others were taken captive. Abraham, the father of the Jewish race, delivered them from bondage (Genesis 14). God used Joseph to deliver many Egyptians (and others) from the great famine that came upon the land (Genesis 37–50). God used a resistant Jonah to bring a message of repentance to Nineveh, after which they all repented, and God withheld His punishment of the nation (Jonah 1–3). And who can forget the wondrous salvation that has come through the divine Messiah, Himself a Jewish man (Matthew 1:1; John 3:16).

Daniel 2:26

Are you able to make known to me the dream...and its interpretation? (2:26): The king—perhaps a bit cynical after the failure of all the other wise men in Babylon—got right to the point with Daniel. Notice again that the interpretation of the dream would not be enough to satisfy the king. Daniel must first reveal the dream itself and then give the interpretation. Daniel was subjected to the same test of truth that the other wise men experienced.

Recall that the other wise men informed the king, "The thing that the king asks is difficult, and no one can show it to the king except the gods, whose dwelling is not with flesh" (Daniel 2:11). Thus Daniel's claim to know the dream and its message must have seemed extraordinary to Nebuchadnezzar. However, his knowledge of the dream was not from "the gods" but rather from the one true God.

Daniel 2:27

No wise men (2:27): Daniel's main point in Daniel 2:27-28 is that no one could possibly satisfy the king's request on his own. Daniel's reference to "wise men" referred not only to the occultists who failed to reveal the dream but also to himself. Daniel freely admitted that left to his own abilities, he could not tell the king his dream or its meaning. The good news, however, is that the God in heaven does have this ability, and Daniel received revelation from God through a vision.

Daniel 2:28-30

God in heaven (2:28): The phrase "God in heaven" distinguishes Daniel's God from the multiple local deities of Babylon. Daniel was careful to emphasize that he knew the dream and its meaning only because the God of heaven revealed it to him (compare with Genesis 41:16). Unlike Arioch, Daniel had no interest in promoting himself, but rather sought to honor and glorify God.

Who reveals mysteries (2:28): This God in heaven is One who reveals mysteries. In the present case, the mystery involved Nebuchadnezzar's dream and its meaning. In the Bible, a mystery is a truth that cannot be discerned simply by human investigation, but requires special revelation from God. The God of heaven gave special revelation to Daniel about Nebuchadnezzar's dream.

He has made known to King Nebuchadnezzar (2:28): The moment had now arrived. Daniel was about to pass on to Nebuchadnezzar what God Himself had passed on to him.

He who reveals mysteries made known (2:29): Daniel informed Nebuchadnezzar that God was revealing the prophetic future to Nebuchadnezzar.

The Old Testament use of the term "last days" (and similar terms) typically refers to the time leading up to the second coming of the Messiah to set up His millennial kingdom on earth. More specifically, the Old Testament usage of such terms as "latter days," "last days," "latter years," "end of time," and "end of the age" all refer to Israel's time of tribulation, which leads to the second coming of the Messiah.

We will investigate the specifics of this prophetic dream in the next chapter. We will see that Nebuchadnezzar's dream spanned Gentile history and dominion, including the kingdom of his day and the kingdoms that followed, up to the days preceding the coming of Israel's Messiah in the prophetic future. The dream focuses heavily on what Jesus called "the times of the Gentiles" (Luke 21:24). The future sequence of Gentile kingdoms would one day climax with the appearance of God's eternal kingdom.

As for me (2:30): Daniel again took the path of humility. He took no credit for the dream or its interpretation, nor did he claim to be superior to the other wise men in Babylon. The mystery was revealed to him by the God of heaven. Despite Daniel's personal humility on the matter, one must recall that Nebuchadnezzar himself had earlier found Daniel and his friends to be "ten times better than all the magicians and enchanters that were in all his kingdom" (Daniel 1:20).

Take a moment to ponder some of the rich spiritual truths about God we have uncovered in today's biblical text:

- He is the only true God and is infinitely greater than all.
- He is sovereign over all kings and nations and is guiding human history.

- He is omniscient and knows the distant future.
- He answers prayer, gives revelation to human beings, and providentially protects His people.

Our God is an awesome God!

Major Themes

1. *God is omniscient.* Daniel knew that God is omniscient, so he boldly informed the king, "There is a God in heaven who reveals mysteries, and he has made known to King Nebuchadnezzar what will be in the latter days" (Daniel 2:28). Scripture reveals that God knows all things, both actual and possible (Matthew 11:21-23). He knows all things past (Isaiah 41:22), present (Hebrews 4:13), and future (Isaiah 46:10). And because He knows all things, His knowledge can neither increase nor decrease. Psalm 147:5 affirms that God's understanding is beyond measure. God's knowledge is infinite (Psalms 33:13-15; 139:11-12; Proverbs 15:3; Isaiah 40:14; 46:10). Thus God could easily reveal to Daniel the king's dream and its meaning.

2. *God alone knows the future.* Closely related to God's omniscience is the biblical teaching that the one true God can foretell the future: "Fear not, nor be afraid; have I not told you from of old and declared it?" (Isaiah 44:8). "Who told this long ago? Who declared it of old? Was it not I, the LORD?" (45:21). "I declared them to you from of old, before they came to pass I announced them to you" (48:5). You and I may not know what the future holds for us or for anyone else. But we do know the One who knows the future—our all-knowing God.

Digging Deeper with Cross-References

> *God's foreknowledge*—Exodus 3:19; Deuteronomy 31:16; Isaiah 42:9; 44:7; 46:9-10; 48:3; Matthew 21:2; 24:36; Acts 2:23; 3:18; Romans 8:29; 1 Peter 1:2
>
> *Looking out for the interests of others*—Daniel 2:24; Romans 12:10; Ephesians 4:2; 5:21; Philippians 2:3-4; 1 Peter 5:5

Life Lessons

1. *God reveals the prophetic future to human beings.* Someone has rightly said that God *moved* and the prophet *mouthed* prophetic truths. God *revealed* and man *recorded* His words about the future (see 2 Timothy 3:16; 2 Peter 1:21; see also Jeremiah 1:9; Zechariah 7:12; Acts 1:16; 4:24-25). If there's one thing we learn from this, it is that we ought to place our trust not in human psychics, who make many mistakes and who are involved in occultism, but rather in the one true God, who knows the future.

2. *Following Daniel's example of humility.* Daniel was a humble man who pointed away from his own abilities and pointed to God instead (Daniel 2:27-28). The Scriptures tell us that those who would please God must walk in humility. Not only that, but God exalts the humble: "Humble yourselves before the Lord, and he will exalt you" (James 4:10; see also Luke 1:52). Daniel humbled himself all throughout the book of Daniel, and God subsequently exalted him. Scripture exhorts us to clothe ourselves with humility (1 Peter 5:5).

Questions for Reflection and Discussion

1. Can you think of another Old Testament personality who was challenged to interpret a dream for a high government

official? (Hint: The answer is in the book of Genesis.) Try
to think of at least five ways these two are alike.

2. What leadership qualities do you see in Daniel in today's
   Scripture reading?

3. Do a little self-inventory. Ask yourself, *Am I more interested
   in building others up or in building myself up in the eyes of
   others?* What have you learned in this lesson that might
   help you seek the kind of humility Daniel displayed?

Daniel Reveals the Meaning of the Dream to Nebuchadnezzar

Daniel 2:31-49

Scripture Reading and Insights

Begin by reading Daniel 2:31-49 in your favorite Bible. As you read, trust God to open your eyes so you can discover wondrous things from His Word (Psalm 119:18).

In yesterday's lesson, Daniel reported to Nebuchadnezzar that God had provided the meaning of the dream to him. Now Daniel reveals the dream and its meaning to the king. With your Bible still accessible, consider the following insights on the biblical text, verse by verse.

Daniel 2:31-35

A great image (2:31): As a backdrop, apocalyptic literature is a special kind of writing that arose among the Jews and Christians in Bible times to reveal certain mysteries about the end times and the world to come. This type of literature is often characterized by visions, exhortations to make ethical and moral decisions or changes as a result of such visions, and a pervasive use of symbols and imagery. Daniel is an apocalyptic book, so we are not surprised to find kingdoms described as a statue made of gold, silver, bronze, iron, and clay (Daniel 2:32-35).

Its appearance was frightening (2:31): The size and appearance of the image must have been staggering, especially considering the metals from which it was constructed. With a head of gold on top and fragile feet at the bottom, this image seemed likely to topple.

Head...chest and arms...middle and thighs...legs...feet (2:32-33): The various metals and clay make this an interesting image. The head was made of gold, the chest and arms of silver, the stomach area and thighs of bronze, the legs of iron, and the feet a mix of iron and clay. Nebuchadnezzar probably considered this mix to be the most confusing element of the dream. Simply eyeballing the image gave no clue about its meaning. That would require revelation from God.

A stone was cut out (2:34): With a head of gold and fragile feet, the top-heavy image seemed prone to topple, but Nebuchadnezzar's dream revealed that a stone would aid the process by striking the image.

All together were broken in pieces, and became like the chaff (2:35): First the feet and then the rest of the body shattered, and the remaining particles blew away in the wind like chaff. ("Chaff" refers to worthless husks that separate from grain during the process of threshing.) Not a trace of the image could thereafter be found.

The stone that struck the image (2:35): The stone then became a great mountain that filled the whole earth. Nebuchadnezzar must have been baffled by this dream—no wonder it unnerved him.

Daniel 2:36-45

The dream...its interpretation (2:36): Daniel had informed Nebuchadnezzar of his dream. Part two of the process would now begin— the interpretation of the image. We will see that as Daniel explains the image, he is actually referring to the Gentile nations that would rule over Palestine and the people of Israel.

You, O king, the king of kings...you are the head of gold (2:37-38): Daniel first revealed that Nebuchadnezzar—the "king of kings" whom God put into power, not only over human beings but over the animal kingdom as well—is the head of gold. The reference to animals brings to mind Genesis 1:26, where God affirmed after creating human beings, "Let them have dominion over the fish of the sea and over the birds of the heavens and over the livestock and over all the earth and over every creeping thing that creeps on the earth."

Another kingdom (2:39): Nebuchadnezzar was a finite being. He would not live forever, so another kingdom would arise after his. This next kingdom relates to the "chest and arms of silver" we read about in verse 32. The two arms of silver represent the rise of the Medes and Persians, who would conquer Babylon in 539 BC. Though the Medo-Persian empire was strong and would last more than 200 years, it was nevertheless inferior to the kingdom of Babylon, just as silver is inferior to gold.

A third kingdom (2:39): Yet another kingdom would arise after the Medo-Persian empire. It relates to the "middle and thighs of bronze" mentioned in verse 32. The word "middle" refers to the stomach area of the image. This refers to the Greek Empire, which conquered the Medo-Persian Empire between 334 and 330 BC under the leadership of Alexander the Great.

A fourth kingdom (2:40): A fourth kingdom would arise after the Greek Empire. It relates to the "legs of iron" mentioned in verse 32. This refers to the Roman Empire, which conquered the Greeks in 63 BC. Just as iron is the strongest among metals, so this empire would be stronger than all the previous empires. So strong was Rome that it was able to conquer many peoples and subdue any rebellion.

Feet and toes, partly of potter's clay and partly of iron (2:41): Scholars have debated this verse and those that follow, some ascribing the verses to the Roman Empire of old, and others ascribing the verses to the revived Roman Empire in the end times, over which the antichrist will rule. There are several reasons that make the latter view preferable.

First, the ten toes in Daniel 2:41 and the ten horns in Daniel 7 seem to represent the same ten kings. These revelations belong together. These kings will exercise rule in the revived Roman Empire in the end times.

Second, prophecy scholars have noted that the ten toes of Nebuchadnezzar's image have not yet corresponded to anything in history and therefore must relate to the prophetic future. As prophecy scholar John F. Walvoord put it, "According to Daniel's prophecy, the kingdoms represented by the ten toes existed side by side and were destroyed by one sudden catastrophic blow. Nothing like this has yet occurred in history."[1] But this *will* occur in history as the final revived

Roman Empire is shattered at the second coming of Jesus Christ in glory.

Third, Old Testament prophecies commonly gloss over long periods of time. For example, some Old Testament prophecies lump together predictions concerning the first and second comings of Christ without mentioning the extended time between the two. Consequently the legs of Nebuchadnezzar's image can easily refer to the Roman Empire of old, and the toes can refer to the revived Roman Empire in the end times.

Thus we can say that this latter-days Roman Empire will not attain true unity or cohesiveness, but will be like a mixture of iron and clay. It will be strong as iron but will be characterized by divisions.

The God of heaven will set up a kingdom (2:44): Daniel now speaks of the overthrow of all earthly kingdoms, including the revived Roman Empire of the end times. Nebuchadnezzar had witnessed a rock smashing into the image (verse 34). The term "rock" is often used in reference to the divine Messiah, Jesus Christ (see Psalm 118:22; Isaiah 8:14; 28:16; 1 Peter 2:6-8). Christ will not only overthrow earthly kingdoms, but will—following the second coming—set up His own millennial kingdom that will last 1000 years on earth (Revelation 11:15; 19:11-20; 20:4). Following the millennial kingdom, Christ will continue His reign forever and ever.

The dream is certain (2:45): The interpretation of the dream is certain, for the source of the interpretation is God Himself, the Revealer of mysteries (see verses 19,23,28,30).

Daniel 2:46-47

Nebuchadnezzar fell upon his face (2:46): Nebuchadnezzar was "blown away" by Daniel's account of God's interpretation of the dream. He fell down and paid homage to Daniel and commanded that an offering and incense be offered up to him—actions traditionally reserved for the worship of Babylon's deities.

Your God is God of gods and Lord of kings (2:47): Daniel already knew that his God was superior to the gods of Babylon (which actually didn't exist). Now Nebuchadnezzar was forced to admit the superiority of Daniel's God.

Daniel 2:48-49

High honors...great gifts...ruler...chief prefect (2:48): Daniel was rewarded with incredible material wealth as well as greatly increased authority in Babylon.

Daniel made a request (2:49): Daniel did not forget his friends. Through his influence, he was able to secure promotions for them as well. They became administrators under Daniel's authority. Of course, Nebuchadnezzar's promotion of Daniel and his friends was the providential work of the sovereign God.

Major Themes

1. *The supremacy of the one true God.* From the very beginning of the Old Testament, the one true God (Yahweh) is portrayed as incomparable to false, pagan gods. Moses said, "There is no one like the LORD our God" (Exodus 8:10). Rhetorical questions emphasized this same truth: "Who is like you, O LORD, among the gods?" (Exodus 15:11). The implied answer is, no one in all the universe. God is supreme and incomparable. Nebuchadnezzar came to realize this, and the book of Daniel continually emphasizes it.

2. *Nebuchadnezzar paid Daniel homage.* Following Daniel's revelation of the dream and its meaning, the king greatly honored both Daniel and Daniel's God. We should not miss the fact that if Daniel had taken all the credit for himself, the king would have honored only Daniel. But because Daniel gave glory to God in this episode, the king said, "Truly, your God is God of gods and Lord of kings" (Daniel 2:47). Pay special attention to the word "kings," which includes Nebuchadnezzar himself. Because of Daniel's witness, Nebuchadnezzar acknowledged that the true God

was supreme even over him. That's quite an admission for a pagan king who claimed to be divine.

Digging Deeper with Cross-References

God's eternal kingdom—2 Samuel 7:16; Psalms 145:13; 146:10; Isaiah 9:7; Micah 4:7; Luke 1:32-33; Hebrews 12:28; 2 Peter 1:11; Revelation 11:15

The exaltation of the true God—Exodus 15:2; 1 Chronicles 29:11; Nehemiah 9:5; Job 22:12; Psalms 21:13; 46:10; 57:11; 92:8; 97:9; 108:5; Isaiah 2:11; 6:1; 25:1; Ezekiel 38:23

Life Lessons

1. *The humble are exalted.* This theme is repeated over and over again in Daniel. God providentially exalted Daniel in Babylon because he was consistently humble. As 1 Peter 5:6 puts it, "Humble yourselves, therefore, under the mighty hand of God so that at the proper time he may exalt you" (see also James 4:10). Proverbs reminds us, "Humility comes before honor" (15:33), "The reward for humility and fear of the LORD is riches and honor and life" (22:4), and "One's pride will bring him low, but he who is lowly in spirit will obtain honor" (29:23).

2. *True believers.* Daniel and his Jewish colleagues were the "real deal." They not only talked the talk but also walked the walk (see James 2:14-26). Some have said that many today are secret-agent Christians who have never blown their cover. In other words, it's hard to recognize that some people are Christians by their words or actions, for they don't seem very "Christian." But Daniel and his friends lived out their faith for all to see, regardless of the consequences. What a great example they set for each of us!

Questions for Reflection and Discussion

1. Daniel explained, "The God of heaven will set up a kingdom that shall never be destroyed...it shall stand forever" (Daniel 2:44). What do you learn in this passage about the prominence of God's kingdom over the finite kingdoms of the earth? Does that give you a sense of security?

2. What attributes of God do you see highlighted in today's lesson?

3. If somebody accused you of being a Christian, would there be enough evidence to convict you?

DAY 9

Nebuchadnezzar Makes a Golden Image to be Worshipped

Daniel 3:1-7

Scripture Reading and Insights

Begin by reading Daniel 3:1-7 in your favorite Bible. As you read, ask God to help you understand His Word (Psalm 119:73).

In yesterday's reading, Daniel revealed the dream and its meaning to Nebuchadnezzar. In today's lesson, Nebuchadnezzar constructs a golden image to be worshipped by all the people in his kingdom. With your Bible still accessible, consider the following insights on the biblical text, verse by verse.

Daniel 3:1

Image of gold (3:1): Having been identified as the head of gold on the image in his dream (Daniel 2:38), Nebuchadnezzar in his megalomania erected a full golden image of himself—gold from head to toe—to put an exclamation point on his greatness. Some Bible expositors suggest that Nebuchadnezzar may have also been trying to bring greater unity to his kingdom by affirming his authority as king and by centralizing worship. As we will see shortly, there were many varying ranks of government officials in Babylon, but this image portrays Nebuchadnezzar as the one who is over all. No one else in the kingdom would have such an image.

The image was ninety feet high but only nine feet wide. If the image were in the form of a human being, this ten-to-one ratio would make

69

him appear to be very skinny. (The ratio of a normal human being is more like five to one.) It may be that the image pictured a more normal-looking human figure elevated on some type of massive base that made him appear high and exalted.

The construction of this golden image shows Nebuchadnezzar's true colors. Recall from Daniel 2:47 that following Daniel's revelation of the meaning of Nebuchadnezzar's dream, Nebuchadnezzar had exulted to Daniel, "Truly, your God is God of gods and Lord of kings." Apparently his high thoughts of Daniel's God were short-lived, for he now had only high thoughts of himself.

In any event, because of its height and the gold appearance, the image was no doubt an imposing symbol of Nebuchadnezzar's majesty and authority. Because it was to be worshipped, it is properly categorized as an idol. (See Major Themes.)

Plain of Dura (3:1): "Dura" comes from an Akkadian word meaning "walled," "walled area," or "walled enclosure." Therefore, the plain of Dura may have been a plain surrounded either by walls or perhaps by mountains or hills. Archaeologists have uncovered a site that may be where the golden image stood, but there is no certainty on this as of yet.

Daniel 3:2-3

Satraps (3:2): These were chief representatives of the king over specific regions. Note that the seven positions listed in verse 2 are apparently in descending rank.

Prefects (3:2): These were military chiefs or commanders of armies.

Governors (3:2): These were civil administrators, lieutenants, or viceroys.

Counselors (3:2): These were legal experts or lawyers. They may have assisted the king in the formation of new laws. Or they may have been counselors to those in various levels of governmental authority.

Treasurers (3:2): These were in charge of Babylon's treasure houses and administered the funds of the kingdom.

Justices (3:2): These were government arbiters and administrators of the law.

Magistrates (3:2): These were judges who passed judgment in keeping with the law.

And all the officials (3:2): These were all other types of civil leaders in Babylon.

The dedication of the image (3:2): All seven classes of government officials would be required to bow in worship of the image to show their full and unqualified allegiance to Nebuchadnezzar. Note that Daniel would not have been present with this group because he remained in the capital city "at the king's court" (Daniel 2:49). Daniel's three friends—Shadrach, Meshach, and Abednego—were called to Dura to show their loyalty. As we will see, they refused to bow down, just as Daniel would have refused had he been there.

They stood before the image (3:3): In obedience to Nebuchadnezzar, the seven classes of government officials all showed up to the dedication and demonstrated their respect by standing before the image. They were required to bow down and worship the image, so it had both religious and political significance. Bowing to the image acknowledged not only acceptance of Nebuchadnezzar's divine status but also submission to his political power and authority. This would unify the kingdom religiously and politically.

Daniel 3:4-5

The herald proclaimed (3:4): Heralds publicly announced the king's decrees on various matters. In the present case, the herald indicated to all seven classes of government officials that by their act of bowing before the image, they would recognize Nebuchadnezzar's political and religious power and authority. Bowing would be an open act of submission.

When you hear (3:5): Music was used for a variety of purposes in biblical times (see Major Themes). In the present case, music was a cue to bow down and worship the golden image.

Horn (3:5): There were various kinds of horns in biblical days. The *geren* was a form of trumpet, made from the horn of an animal (see Leviticus 25:9; Joshua 6:4). A trumpet made from a ram's horn was called a *shofar* and was used for special occasions during the Jewish year, particularly on the Hebrew New Year's Day and the Day of Atonement. The horn used in Babylon was no doubt something similar.

Pipe (3:5): The pipe was a wind instrument. An example of this type of instrument was the *halil*, which was basically a hollow pipe made of cane or wood that utilized a reed to make a musical sound.

Lyre (3:5): The lyre was a stringed instrument with a wooden frame (see Genesis 4:21; 2 Samuel 6:5; 1 Kings 10:12). David, the shepherd king of Israel, was apparently able to play both the lyre and the harp and often used such musical instruments to soothe the nerves of King Saul (1 Samuel 16:16,23).

Trigon (3:5): This was a small harp with smaller strings and high tones.

Harp (3:5): Similar to the lyre, the harp was a musical instrument made from a wooden frame that had strings on it. Again, David was a gifted harpist, with the ability to play several different kinds of harps (see 1 Samuel 16:18-23). David was also a proficient poet, as evidenced in the psalms he wrote, many of which were accompanied by music. He was known as the "sweet psalmist of Israel" (2 Samuel 23:1).

Bagpipe (3:5): Unlike the modern bagpipe, Babylon's bagpipe was apparently some type of percussion instrument.

Fall down and worship (3:5): The sound of the music would be the cue to worship the idolatrous image. (See Major Themes.)

Daniel 3:6-7

Whoever does not fall down and worship...a burning fiery furnace (3:6): The penalty for refusing to bow down and worship the image was incineration in what was apparently an industrial-sized oven used for smelting metals and baking bricks. This is a punishment Nebuchadnezzar had elsewhere used of two Judean false prophets, Zedekiah and Ahab (Jeremiah 29:22). The Code of Hammurabi (sections 25, 110, and 157) indicates that this may have been a common Babylonian means of execution.

As soon as all the peoples heard (3:7): An awesome and formidable image stood before the people. The king had given the command. Now the music started. On cue, all the government officials showed their submission by bowing before the image in worship. Nebuchadnezzar thereby achieved what he wanted—an open display of leaders vowing political and religious submission.

Major Themes

1. *The making of idols.* Daniel had told Nebuchadnezzar that the head of gold in his dream represented him (Daniel 2:38). It must have gone to his head! Now the king had a 90-foot-high gold image of himself constructed—not just a head, but apparently the entire body—to reflect his greatness, glory, and self-proclaimed deity. This image was likely not made of solid gold but rather featured a gold overlay, similar to other objects discovered in the ruins of Babylon (see Isaiah 40:19). An image that large made of solid gold would have been entirely too difficult to handle because of its incredible weight. Regardless of how glorious it appeared, Daniel's friends refused to bow down and worship it. The New Testament consistently urges Christians to avoid all forms of idolatry (1 Corinthians 5:11; 2 Corinthians 6:16; Galatians 5:19-21; Colossians 3:5; 1 John 5:21). (More on this in the next lesson.)

2. *Musical instruments in biblical times.* Music was used for a variety of purposes in Bible times. Music was played for the homecoming party of the prodigal son (Luke 15:25). It was also used at banquets and feasts (Isaiah 5:12; 24:8-9) as well as for laments (Matthew 9:23). Music was performed at the coronation of kings (2 Chronicles 23:11-13) as well as temple ceremonies (1 Chronicles 16:4-6; 2 Chronicles 29:25). Music was often performed during pilgrimages (2 Samuel 6:5). Sometimes music was used to enable a prophet to enter into a trance so he could receive divine oracles (see 2 Kings 3:15). Music was also used to celebrate military victories (Exodus 15:1; 2 Chronicles 20:27-28). In

the present case, music was used as a signal to bow down and worship a pagan idol (Daniel 3:10).

Digging Deeper with Cross-References

Execution by burning—Genesis 38:24-25; Leviticus 20:14; 21:9; Daniel 3:6,21

Idolatrous images of gold—Exodus 20:23; 32:2-4; Deuteronomy 7:25; 1 Kings 12:28; Psalms 115:4-8; 135:15; Isaiah 2:20; 30:22

Life Lessons

1. *Worship is reserved for the one true God.* Worship involves reverencing God, adoring Him, praising Him, venerating Him, and paying homage to Him, not only externally (with words, songs, and rituals) but also in our hearts (Isaiah 29:13; see also 1 Samuel 15:22-23). The Hebrew word for worship, *shaha*, means "to bow down" or "to prostrate oneself" (see Genesis 22:5; 42:6). Likewise, the New Testament word for worship, *proskuneo*, means "to prostrate oneself" (see Matthew 2:2,8,11). In Old English, "worship" was rendered "worthship," pointing to the worthiness of the object that was worshipped. Such worship is the proper response of a creature to the divine Creator (Psalm 95:6). Worship can be congregational (1 Corinthians 11–14) or individual (see Romans 12:1). Worship does not stop on earth, but continues in heaven when believers enter into glory (see Revelation 4–5). Some have said that true worship is the missing jewel in the modern church. Let's resolve to recover that jewel!

2. *False objects of faith.* It has been well said that everybody has faith in something. Even members of cults and false religions can have a strong faith, but their faith is misdirected to a false object of faith. The people

commanded to bow down and worship Nebuchadnezzar's golden image had no hesitation in doing so, not only because they were accustomed to worshipping pagan gods but also because of the death penalty for refusing. Daniel's friends—Shadrach, Meshach, and Abednego—were present at this ceremony. They had faith in the one true God, and their faith was unwavering in the face of persecution and even the threat of death (compare with Psalm 118:8; Proverbs 3:5; Jeremiah 17:7; 2 Corinthians 5:7; 1 Peter 1:7). In the next chapter, we will see that their faith in God and their faithfulness to God landed them in a fiery furnace (Daniel 3:20-21).

Questions for Reflection and Discussion

1. Daniel and his friends did not obey the command to worship the golden image. Do you think peaceful civil disobedience is ever justified? If so, under what circumstances? (See Acts 5:29.)

2. Can you say without hesitation that God is your foremost object of faith? Are you sometimes tempted to trust other things in place of Him?

3. Why might music have been used in this worship ceremony? In what ways can music affect people?

Shadrach, Meshach, and Abednego Are Accused

Daniel 3:8-12

Scripture Reading and Insights

Begin by reading Daniel 3:8-12 in your favorite Bible. As you read, remember that reading Scripture can strengthen your faith in God (Romans 10:17).

Yesterday we saw Nebuchadnezzar construct a golden image to be worshipped. Now let's watch as Shadrach, Meshach, and Abednego get in life-threatening trouble for refusing to worship the image. With your Bible still accessible, consider the following insights on the biblical text, verse by verse.

Daniel 3:8

Chaldeans (3:8): The word "Chaldeans" can be used in different senses in Scripture. It can function simply as a general ethnic term for the Babylonian people. In the present case, however, the term is used more narrowly in reference to priests who functioned as astrologers, soothsayers, and wise men in Nebuchadnezzar's government.

Maliciously accused the Jews (3:8): The phrase "maliciously accused" translates a rather vulgar expression that means, "devour the pieces of flesh torn off a person's body." It came to connote doing injury to another person through malicious slander. The Chaldeans were making a serious accusation against Shadrach, Meshach, and Abednego in order to destroy them.

The motivation of the Chaldeans for maliciously accusing the Jews was probably threefold. First is the issue of racism, for many Babylonians hated the Jews. We see this same type of hatred elsewhere in Scripture. Esther 3:5-6 tells us, "When Haman [a Persian] saw that Mordecai [a Jew] did not bow down or pay homage to him, Haman was filled with fury. But he disdained to lay hands on Mordecai alone. So, as they had made known to him the people of Mordecai, Haman sought to destroy all the Jews, the people of Mordecai, throughout the whole kingdom of Ahasuerus." The psalmist laments to God of attempted genocide against the Jews: "For behold, your enemies make an uproar; those who hate you have raised their heads. They lay crafty plans against your people; they consult together against your treasured ones. They say, 'Come, let us wipe them out as a nation; let the name of Israel be remembered no more!'" (Psalm 83:2-4). Many Babylonians would have been happy to completely do away with the Jews.

Second, aside from hatred of the Jews, there was also the issue of jealousy. When one nation took the people of another nation into captivity, the captives were generally assigned positions of servitude in the conquering nation. They were not typically elevated to positions of authority, but Daniel and his friends had become governing officials in the kingdom. Nebuchadnezzar himself had previously spoken of them with high praise: "In every matter of wisdom and understanding about which the king inquired of them, he found them ten times better than all the magicians and enchanters that were in all his kingdom" (Daniel 1:20). The Chaldeans no doubt bitterly resented this praise and their high appointments. We recall from Daniel 2:49 that Daniel himself "made a request of the king, and he appointed Shadrach, Meshach, and Abednego over the affairs of the province of Babylon. But Daniel remained at the king's court." The Chaldeans referred to the king's appointment of these Jews during their accusation of them: "There are certain Jews *whom you have appointed* over the affairs of the province of Babylon: Shadrach, Meshach, and Abednego" (Daniel 3:12). One can almost see the jealousy dripping from their lips.

Third, their accusation was ultimately self-serving. The Chaldeans had bowed before the golden image, whereas Shadrach, Meshach, and Abednego had not. Perhaps they were trying to make themselves look good at the expense of Shadrach, Meshach, and Abednego. Perhaps they were seeking personal favor from the king.

Notice that Daniel was not among the accused. Daniel would not have been present with this group because he remained in the capital city "at the king's court" (Daniel 2:49). Besides, these Chaldeans may have considered it risky to say anything negative about Daniel, who was a higher official and was highly regarded. Let us be clear, however, that Daniel would have refused to bow before the image with as much fervor as Shadrach, Meshach, and Abednego had he been there.

Daniel 3:9-11

O king, live forever (3:9): Before launching their verbal attack against Shadrach, Meshach, and Abednego, the Chaldeans said, "O king, live forever." This was apparently a common show of respect when beginning a conversation with the king. Later in the book of Daniel, when the high officials and satraps appeared before another king with the intention of entrapping Daniel, they began their conversation, "O King Darius, live forever" (Daniel 6:6). Daniel ended up in the lions' den as a result of their entrapment. But the next morning, the king rushed down to the den to see if Daniel was okay. Daniel answered, "O king, live forever! My God sent his angel and shut the lions' mouths" (6:21-22).

You, O king, have made a decree (3:10): The unscrupulous Chaldeans reminded the king of his decree that the penalty for not bowing before the golden image was death by incineration.

Every man who hears (3:10): The cue for bowing before the image was to be the sound of musical instruments playing. As the music played, however, Shadrach, Meshach, and Abednego didn't budge. They continued to stand upright.

Whoever does not (3:11): The word "whoever" communicates the idea that there were to be no exceptions. Any person who failed to bow before the image was to experience capital punishment by burning.

Cast into a burning fiery furnace (3:11): A form of capital punishment that was not only effective but also terribly painful.

Daniel 3:12

Certain Jews...Shadrach, Meshach, and Abednego (3:12): Notice the subtle insinuation that the king made a mistake in assigning foreigners high positions of leadership. One can almost see the finger pointing: "There are certain Jews whom *you* have appointed over the affairs of the province of Babylon."

Pay no attention to you; they do not serve your gods or worship the golden image (3:12): Shadrach, Meshach, and Abednego were acting under clear instructions from God's Law.

> You shall have no other gods before me. You shall not make for yourself a carved image, or any likeness of anything that is in heaven above, or that is in the earth beneath, or that is in the water under the earth. You shall not bow down to them or serve them, for I the LORD your God am a jealous God (Exodus 20:3-5).

Shadrach, Meshach, and Abednego had to choose between King Nebuchadnezzar and the one true God, who is the King of kings. They chose wisely!

The three Hebrew youths likely recalled some of God's promises. Here's one example.

> Fear not, for I have redeemed you; I have called you by name, you are mine. When you pass through the waters, I will be with you; and through the rivers, they shall not overwhelm you; when you walk through fire you shall not be burned, and the flame shall not consume you (Isaiah 43:1-2).

Based on their faith in the God of promises, Shadrach, Meshach, and Abednego stood tall when all other leaders bowed low.

This brings up a controversial question. Are God's people ever justified in disobeying civil authorities? Many Christians have con-cluded that they must obey the government *unless* the government explicitly commands them to go against one or more of God's com-mands found in Scripture. In such a case, believers must obey God rather than the government.

The New Testament illustrates this principle. After being com-manded by the Sanhedrin (the Jewish government) not to preach any further, "Peter and the apostles answered, 'We must obey God rather than men'" (Acts 5:29). God commanded Peter and the others to preach; the Jewish government commanded them not to preach. So they chose to obey God rather than human government.

Shadrach, Meshach, and Abednego likewise chose to obey God instead of men. Sometime later, Daniel righteously disobeyed when the government commanded him to go against God's revealed will (Daniel 6).

Of course, believers must guard against abusing this principle, for Scripture elsewhere instructs them to obey government (Romans 13:1). So for example, believers would certainly *not* be justified in disobeying the government in cases where they simply disagreed with its policies.

Major Themes

1. *Nebuchadnezzar's golden image.* The large image con-structed by Nebuchadnezzar was not unique to him. Archaeologists have discovered other large statues from the Babylonian, Persian, and Greek Empires. Herodotus, a Greek historian who lived in the fifth century BC, speaks of an 18-foot golden image of a man in a Babylonian temple. Diodorus Siculus, a Greek historian who wrote *Bibliotheca Historica* (*Universal History*) between 60 and 30 BC, mentions a 40-foot image of Zeus atop a Bel temple. Nebuchadnezzar's golden image was 90 feet tall, thus pointing to the highly exalted view he had of himself.

2. *Death by burning.* History reveals that Assyria, Babylon, Persia, and Greece all used burning as a method of capital

punishment. In a sixth-century BC Mesopotamian record, a king instructs that a corrupt priest be burned in an oven. Nebuchadnezzar burned two Judean false prophets to death, Zedekiah and Ahab (Jeremiah 29:22). Burning as a form of execution is sanctioned in the Hammurabi Code. The oven was likely not originally constructed for capital punishment but rather to cast and smelt metal and to bake bricks and pottery.

Digging Deeper with Cross-References

The decrees of kings—Ezra 5:13; 7:21; Esther 1:20; 2:1; 4:8; 8:14; Daniel 2:13; 3:4,10,22,29; 6:9,26; Jonah 3:7; Luke 2:1

Troublemakers—Proverbs 6:16-19; 16:28-30; Matthew 5:44; Romans 12:18; 16:17; Titus 3:10

Life Lessons

1. *Obey God no matter what.* Daniel and his friends were committed to obeying God no matter what. Daniel and his friends remind us that obeying God may often entail sacrifice, but it also has many benefits. For example, obedience brings great blessing (Luke 11:28), long life (1 Kings 3:14; John 8:51), happiness (Psalms 112:1; 119:56), peace (Proverbs 1:33), and a state of well-being (Jeremiah 7:23; see also Exodus 19:5; Leviticus 26:3-4; Deuteronomy 4:40; 12:28; 28:1; Joshua 1:8; 1 Chronicles 22:13; Isaiah 1:19). Never get discouraged in your obedience to God.

2. *Enduring despite pressure.* Daniel and his friends patiently endured whatever they faced in Babylon—including persecution for refusing to worship an idol. You and I are also called to patiently endure whatever comes our way. Hebrews 12:1-2 exhorts believers, "Let us also lay aside every weight, and sin which clings so closely, and let us run with endurance the race that is set before us, looking

to Jesus, the founder and perfecter of our faith." Jesus described Christian commitment this way: "If anyone would come after me, let him deny himself and take up his cross and follow me. For whoever would save his life will lose it, but whoever loses his life for my sake will find it" (Matthew 16:24-25). Let's not forget, "Blessed is the man who remains steadfast under trial, for when he has stood the test he will receive the crown of life, which God has promised to those who love him" (James 1:12).

Questions for Reflection and Discussion

1. Have you ever been maliciously accused by someone who sought to get you in trouble? Were you able to forgive that person?

2. Do you think you'd have the courage to obey God in a circumstance that might lead to your death?

3. Can you think of any modern-day examples of Christians standing strong in their faith and losing their lives for it?

Shadrach, Meshach, and Abednego Remain Faithful to God

Daniel 3:13-18

Scripture Reading and Insights

Begin by reading Daniel 3:13-18 in your favorite Bible. As you read, allow the Word of God to bring revival to your soul (Psalm 119:25,93,107).

In yesterday's reading, the Chaldeans accused Shadrach, Meshach, and Abednego of not bowing before Nebuchadnezzar's golden image. Today we'll see the three Hebrews remain unbendingly faithful to God in the face of accusation. With your Bible still accessible, consider the following insights on the biblical text, verse by verse.

Daniel 3:13

Nebuchadnezzar in furious rage (3:13): It would have been one thing for Shadrach, Meshach, and Abednego to privately refuse bowing before the golden image. But the three youths publicly refused to bow before the image and worship it. To Nebuchadnezzar, this represented a public defiance of his religious and political authority. He was therefore enraged. He immediately ordered that these three be brought before him.

Nebuchadnezzar had previously held these three youths in high esteem (Daniel 1:20), but that did not exempt them from submitting to his decree regarding the golden image. They now had to answer for their defiance.

We note in passing the growing evidence that Nebuchadnezzar may have had an anger problem. Recall that when the wise men could not tell the king his dream, "the king was angry and very furious" (Daniel 2:12). Now, when he hears that Shadrach, Meshach, and Abednego refused to bow down to the golden image, he is "in furious rage" (3:13). Later, when the three youths definitively state to the king that they will not worship the image, he is "filled with fury" (3:19). He seemed to *react* far more often than he *responded*.

Notice again that Daniel is not part of this group. This is only because Daniel was not at the dedication ceremony. Had he been there, he too would have refused to worship the golden image, and he too would have found himself being dragged before Nebuchadnezzar.

Daniel 3:14-15

Is it true, O Shadrach, Meshach, and Abednego (3:14): It appears that once Shadrach, Meshach, and Abednego arrived before Nebuchadnezzar, he had gained a bit more control of his emotions. Instead of passing immediate judgment on the three, he instead asked them if the Chaldeans' accusation was true. If it turned out that the accusation was false, he would drop the matter.

If you are ready...well and good (3:15): Nebuchadnezzar gave the three lads a second chance—perhaps due to his former high esteem of them. He informed them that if they would bow before the image upon hearing the music, then all would be forgiven. They would escape punishment, and life would go back to normal.

If you do not worship (3:15): If the three lads refused to bow before the image, they would be cast into a fiery furnace. That is the consequence for defying the king's authority.

Who is the god who will deliver you out of my hands? (3:15): Nebuchadnezzar's question no doubt stimulated the three lads' faithfulness to the one true God. This reminds us of Pharaoh's defiant statement to Moses: "Who is the LORD, that I should obey his voice and let Israel go?" (Exodus 5:2).

Nebuchadnezzar apparently considered himself to be higher than all other gods, for no other god could turn back his hand. No other god could circumvent his authority. Nebuchadnezzar was here claiming for himself what is ultimately true only of the one true God. Indeed, God affirms, "My counsel shall stand, and I will accomplish all my purpose...I have spoken, and I will bring it to pass; I have purposed, and I will do it" (Isaiah 46:10-11). He asserts, "For the LORD of hosts has purposed, and who will annul it? His hand is stretched out, and who will turn it back?" (14:27).

Nebuchadnezzar would soon learn that he will lose any contest with Yahweh. Nebuchadnezzar asked, "Who is the god who will deliver you out of my hands?" Yahweh would soon indicate, "That would be Me" (see 3:25-29).

Daniel 3:16-18

O king, we have no need to answer (3:16): The three youths may initially appear to be disrespecting the king with an in-your-face attitude. This is not the case, however. Their point was that their commitment to Yahweh was so firm and so rock solid that they would not consider doing anything to offend Him. They knew Him to be the true and living God, so they had "no need to answer" because they could take no other course of action. They would remain forever faithful to God.

Our God whom we serve is able to deliver us (3:17): The same God who delivered the Israelites from the hand of the Egyptian Pharaoh (Exodus 18:10) could deliver the three youths from the hand of the Babylonian king. These three men may have been employed by Nebuchadnezzar (Daniel 2:49), but they did not serve the false gods of Babylon. They served only the one true God. And they had confidence that this one true God could deliver them.

We are again reminded of the First and Second Commandments, which were pivotal to the thinking of these Hebrew youths: "You shall have no other gods before me. You shall not make for yourself a carved image, or any likeness of anything that is in heaven above, or that is in the earth beneath, or that is in the water under the earth. You shall not bow down to them or serve them, for I the LORD your God am a jealous God" (Exodus 20:3-5).

Moreover, the three youths were fully aware that God not only has the power to deliver His people but also has promised to do so. We again recall what God said in Isaiah 43:1-2: "Fear not, for I have redeemed you; I have called you by name, you are mine. When you pass through the waters, I will be with you; and through the rivers, they shall not overwhelm you; when you walk through fire you shall not be burned, and the flame shall not consume you."

But if not, be it known to you (3:18): The Hebrew youths affirmed that God's deliverance was possible and even likely. They also recognized that martyrdom was possible. But one outcome was impossible from their perspective—come what may, they would never worship false gods. Regardless of the outcome, their commitment was to do God's will in all things. On that, they would not bend. They firmly believed that God would deliver them, and they would trust Him even if He didn't.

One is reminded of Joshua's attitude when he said to the Israelites, "Choose this day whom you will serve, whether the gods your fathers served in the region beyond the River, or the gods of the Amorites in whose land you dwell. But as for me and my house, we will serve the LORD" (Joshua 24:15). Like Joshua, the three Hebrew youths chose to follow and serve God alone.

The three Hebrew youths remind us of an important lesson—we should maintain faith in God even when our circumstances remain difficult. We are reminded of this truth in Habakkuk 3:17-19: "Though the fig tree should not blossom, nor fruit be on the vines, the produce of the olive fail and the fields yield no food, the flock be cut off from the fold and there be no herd in the stalls, yet I will rejoice in the LORD; I will take joy in the God of my salvation. GOD, the Lord, is my strength; he makes my feet like the deer's; he makes me tread on my high places."

Major Themes

1. *Belief in false gods.* Daniel and his associates knew that in reality the gods of Babylon were not true gods at all. Scripture consistently affirms that there is only one true God. God Himself affirmed, "Before me no god was

formed, nor shall there be any after me" (Isaiah 43:10). He said, "I am the Lord, and there is no other, besides me there is no God" (Isaiah 45:5). That there is only one God is the consistent testimony of Scripture (John 5:44; 17:3; Romans 3:29-30; 16:27; 1 Corinthians 8:4; Galatians 3:20; Ephesians 4:6; 1 Thessalonians 1:9; 1 Timothy 1:17; 2:5; James 2:19; 1 John 5:20-21; Jude 25). God understandably commands, "You shall have no other gods before me" (Exodus 20:3).

2. *Human arrogance*. Nebuchadnezzar was a sad example of unrestrained human arrogance—a character trait that God hates. Scripture reveals, "Pride and arrogance and the way of evil and perverted speech I hate" (Proverbs 8:13). God promises, "I will put an end to the pomp of the arrogant, and lay low the pompous pride of the ruthless" (Isaiah 13:11; see also 1 Samuel 2:3). Jeremiah 50:32 affirms, "The proud one shall stumble and fall, with none to raise him up." God promises, "The haughtiness of man shall be humbled, and the lofty pride of men shall be brought low, and the Lord alone will be exalted in that day" (Isaiah 2:17).

Digging Deeper with Cross-References

Human boasting—1 Samuel 17:10,44; Psalms 73:9; 75:4; Ezekiel 35:13; Daniel 3:15; Matthew 26:33,35; 1 Corinthians 4:7; Acts 8:9; Romans 1:30; 2 Timothy 3:2; James 3:5; 4:16; Jude 16; Revelation 13:5

Divine deliverance   Judges 8:34; 11:21; 1 Samuel 14:12; 17:37,46; 24:15; 2 Samuel 18:28; 22:2,18,49; 2 Kings 17:39; 19:19; 2 Chronicles 16:8; Psalms 18:2,17,43; 34:4,17; 54:7; 56:13; 68:20; 109:31; Jeremiah 1:8; Matthew 6:13; Luke 22:42; 2 Corinthians 1:10; 2 Timothy 3:11; 4:18; Hebrews 2:15

Life Lessons

1. *Courageous believers.* The three Hebrew youths were
   unbendingly courageous in the face of Nebuchadnezzar's
   threats. You and I can be bold and courageous as well.
   The early believers in the book of Acts prayed, "And now,
   Lord, look upon their threats and grant to your servants
   to continue to speak your word with all boldness" (Acts
   4:29). We are then told that "they were all filled with the
   Holy Spirit and continued to speak the word of God with
   boldness" (verse 31). We can be bold by the power of the
   Holy Spirit, just as the early believers were (see Psalm
   138:3; 2 Corinthians 3:12; 1 Thessalonians 5:14; 2 Timothy
   1:12). Deuteronomy 31:6 exhorts us, "Be strong and
   courageous...it is the LORD your God who goes with you.
   He will not leave you or forsake you." Stand strong for the
   Lord!

2. *Confidence in God.* Daniel and his friends were courageous
   because of their strong confidence in God. They seemed to
   have had the same confidence in God as portrayed in the
   psalms. The psalmist said, "The LORD is my light and my
   salvation; whom shall I fear? The LORD is the stronghold
   of my life; of whom shall I be afraid?" (Psalm 27:1). The
   psalmist goes on to say, "Though an army encamp against
   me, my heart shall not fear; though war arise against me,
   yet I will be confident" (verse 3). He affirms, "The LORD
   is a stronghold for the oppressed, a stronghold in times
   of trouble" (Psalm 9:9). He says to God, "My times are in
   your hand; rescue me from the hand of my enemies and
   from my persecutors!" (Psalm 31:15). God promises us, "I
   will never leave you nor forsake you" (Hebrews 13:5). You
   can be confident in God!

Questions for Reflection and Discussion

1. What stands out to you about Nebuchadnezzar's character in Daniel 3:13-15?

2. What inspires you most about the three Hebrew youths' response to the king in Daniel 3:16-18?

3. When was the last time you felt pressured to compromise your faith? How did you respond?

DAY 12

God Rescues Shadrach, Meshach, and Abednego from the Fiery Furnace

Daniel 3:19-30

Scripture Reading and Insights

Begin by reading Daniel 3:19-30 in your favorite Bible. As you read, never forget that God urges you to quickly obey His Word in all things (Psalm 119:60).

Yesterday we watched as Shadrach, Meshach, and Abednego remained unbendingly faithful to God by refusing to worship the golden image. Today we will witness God's glorious rescue of the three youths. With your Bible still accessible, consider the following insights on the biblical text, verse by verse.

Daniel 3:19-20

Filled with fury (3:19): Nebuchadnezzar had previously held these three youths in high regard (Daniel 1:20). But they had publicly defied his authority, and their continued defiance now brought public consequences. Burning them alive would provide a public example to anyone thinking about defying his authority in the future.

The expression of his face (3:19): So angry was the king that his countenance changed.

He ordered the furnace heated (3:19): So angry was the king that he ordered that the fiery furnace be heated as much as humanly possible ("seven times more"). He wanted the furnace to be intensely hot as an expression of his intense wrath. (See Major Themes.)

The mighty men of his army (3:20): As a show of his own personal strength, the king ordered that his strongest soldiers bind the youths and cast them into the furnace.

To cast them into the burning fiery furnace (3:20): Nebuchadnezzar's industrial-size oven had doors on top as well as a door on the side that allowed for ventilation. The king's strong men would cast the Hebrew youths into the fire through the top door, and the victims would be observed through the side door.

Daniel 3:21-23

Bound in their cloaks (3:21): Normally a person would be stripped naked before being cast into the flames of a furnace. In the present case, however, the three Hebrew youths remained fully clothed because the king had commanded an immediate execution.

The flame of the fire killed (3:22): A furnace burning at a lower temperature makes the victim suffer more as he or she takes longer to die. But in a furnace that is heated "seven times more," the temperature is so hot that victims are instantly incinerated. Nebuchadnezzar may not have anticipated that anyone near the top door of the superheated furnace would be incinerated as the hot flames burst up through the opening.

Fell bound into the burning fiery furnace (3:23): Apparently, once the top door of the furnace was opened, the explosive heat instantly killed the king's strong men, and the three Hebrew youths fell directly into the flames.

Daniel 3:24-25

Nebuchadnezzar was astonished (3:24): Though the main door was atop the furnace, there was also a secondary door on the side of the furnace, likely intended to provide ventilation for effective burning. Because of what he saw through this opening, Nebuchadnezzar "was astonished and rose up in haste," and asked those with him, "Did we not cast three men bound into the fire?" And they said, "True, O king."

I see four men unbound...the appearance of the fourth is like a son of the gods (3:25): The king now verbalized what astonished him. This fourth person was likely a preincarnate appearance of Jesus Christ (see Major Themes). Though Nebuchadnezzar had no personal knowledge of the Son of God (Jesus Christ), he witnessed what appeared to be a supernatural person or heavenly being who was saving the other three. The thing that must have stood out to Nebuchadnezzar as he witnessed all this was that none of Babylon's gods could have accomplished such a feat. He had earlier said to the three youths, "Who is the god who will deliver you out of my hands?" (verse 15). The answer was now clear. The God of Shadrach, Meshach, and Abednego had delivered them out of his hands.

Recall the New Testament teaching that the entire universe was created by Jesus Christ. John 1:3 says of Him, "All things were made through him, and without him was not any thing made that was made." Colossians 1:16 likewise says of Him, "For by him all things were created, in heaven and on earth, visible and invisible, whether thrones or dominions or rulers or authorities—all things were created through him and for him." Now, the same One who created the universe maintains absolute control over the elements in the universe, including fire. If Christ indeed made a preincarnate appearance in the burning furnace, His control of the effects of the fire would have been in perfect keeping with His divine power.

Daniel 3:26-28

Servants of the Most High God, come out, and come here (3:26): Earlier the Hebrew youths had informed the king, "Be it known to you, O king, that we will not serve your gods" (verse 18). Now the king looks into the furnace and recognizes that Shadrach, Meshach, and Abednego are servants of the Most High God, who was quite obviously more powerful than any of the gods Babylon offered. Earlier the king had referred to the youth's God as the "God of gods and Lord of kings" (2:47). Now he calls Him "the Most High God." This represented a major paradigm shift for Nebuchadnezzar. He had previously thought that Babylon's gods—and especially he himself—were more powerful than all other gods. Witnessing what transpired in the furnace was a game changer.

Nebuchadnezzar likely recalled the words of the Hebrew youths: "Our God whom we serve is able to deliver us from the burning fiery furnace, and he will deliver us out of your hand, O king" (verse 17). As requested, the three Hebrew youths exited the furnace—apparently through the side door—and came out to Nebuchadnezzar.

The fire had not had any power over the bodies (3:27): Nebuchadnezzar had ordered the furnace to be heated "seven times more," and yet their bodies were not burned, their hair was not singed, their clothes were not harmed, and no smell of fire was upon them. Nebuchadnezzar was not alone in witnessing this. Other government officials witnessed it as well. As Hebrews 11:34 describes it, in this miraculous act, God "quenched the power of fire."

Blessed be the God of Shadrach, Meshach, and Abednego (3:28): This carries the sense, "May the God of these three Hebrew youths be honored."

Who has sent his angel and delivered his servants (3:28): This was likely the "Angel of the Lord," or "Angel of Yahweh"—a preincarnate appearance of Christ. One is reminded of Psalm 34:7: "The angel of the LORD encamps around those who fear him, and delivers them."

Who trusted in him (3:28): Proverbs 3:5-6 affirms, "Trust in the LORD with all your heart, and do not lean on your own understanding. In all your ways acknowledge him, and he will make straight your paths"—including a straight path right out of the furnace.

And set aside the king's command (3:28): Nebuchadnezzar was apparently impressed that the three youths were so committed to their God that they were willing to yield up their bodies rather than serve and worship any god except their own God.

Daniel 3:29-30

I make a decree (3:29): Don't misunderstand Nebuchadnezzar. He was not here committing to following the Hebrew God alone. He was still a polytheist who believed in many gods. The king essentially added Yahweh to a large pantheon of deities. The purpose of his edict was to prevent anyone from criticizing the God of the Hebrews.

Nebuchadnezzar had still not learned his lesson. Recognizing

Yahweh as part of a pantheon of deities was grossly misguided. Nebuchadnezzar would soon learn that Yahweh is not one among many, but
is rather the unique and single God.

Torn limb from limb (3:29): Anyone who disobeyed this edict was
to be dismembered and suffer utter ruination.

There is no other god who is able to rescue in this way (3:29): Even
though Nebuchadnezzar still believed in many gods, he became convinced that no god could bring miraculous deliverance the way the
Hebrews' God did.

The king promoted Shadrach, Meshach, and Abednego (3:30): Nebuchadnezzar not only honored the one true God but also honored
Shadrach, Meshach, and Abednego by giving them a promotion.

Major Themes

1. *Heated seven times more.* Bible scholars have noted that the
   number seven in the Bible often indicates completeness or
   perfection (see Leviticus 26:18-28; Proverbs 6:31; 24:16).
   To heat the furnace "seven times more" than normal may
   just be a metaphorical way of saying, "as hot as it can get,"
   or "intensely." Notice that the more hotheaded the king
   became, the hotter he ordered the furnace to be heated.

2. *God's angel.* The one described as "a son of the gods" may
   have been the Angel of the Lord, an appearance of the
   preincarnate Christ. Scripture reveals that the Angel of the
   Lord—or more accurately, the Angel of Yahweh—*is* in fact
   Yahweh (Exodus 3:2-6). But the angel of Yahweh was also
   sent by Yahweh to minister to God's people (Judges 13:8-9),
   just as the Father sent Jesus in New Testament times. We
   begin to detect Trinitarian distinctions here. The Angel
   of Yahweh is often seen functioning as Sustainer and
   Rescuer of His people in Old Testament times (Genesis
   16:10-13; 22:15-18; Exodus 23:21; Joshua 5:14; Zechariah
   1:12-17).

Digging Deeper with Cross-References

> *The testing of faith*—Genesis 22:2; Matthew 9:28; 14:30; Mark
> 4:38; Luke 1:18; 5:5; John 4:50; Hebrews 11:8,17; James
> 1:3; 1 Peter 1:7
>
> *Divine preservation*—Genesis 7:23; 45:7; Deuteronomy 6:24;
> 8:4; Joshua 24:17; Nehemiah 9:6,21; Job 10:12; Isaiah 43:2;
> Jeremiah 39:18; Jonah 1:17; Acts 17:28; Colossians 1:17;
> Hebrews 1:3

Life Lessons

1. *Obedience to the point of death.* Daniel and his friends were
   obedient to God to the point of death—that is, they were
   willing to die rather than disobey God (Daniel 3:16-18).
   In the New Testament, Stephen was stoned to death
   because of his faithful testimony of Christ (Acts 7:54-60).
   Revelation 6:9 refers to those who were martyred because
   of their faithful witness to Christ. The apostle Paul was
   stoned and left for dead (Acts 14:19) though he survived.
   We do well to keep in mind the words of Jesus Christ:
   "Whoever would save his life will lose it, but whoever loses
   his life for my sake will find it" (Matthew 16:25). Those
   who die for Christ have eternal life waiting for them in
   heaven (see John 10:28; 2 Corinthians 5:8; Philippians
   3:21; Revelation 2:10).

2. *The incomparability of God.* Nebuchadnezzar said of God,
   "There is no other god who is able to rescue in this way." I
   noted previously that the Old Testament portrays God as
   being incomparably great. This is typically communicated
   with the declaration, "There is none like God," as well as
   the rhetorical question, "Who is like God?" The ancient
   Egyptians had earlier discovered this reality. Indeed, the
   Egyptian sun god (Ra) could not stop Yahweh from
   covering the land with darkness. Nor could the Egyptian
   river god (Nilus) prevent Yahweh from turning the

Nile—the lifeblood of Egypt—into real blood. Our God truly is incomparable (see Exodus 15:11; Numbers 33:4). Regardless of the mountain you are facing, our incomparably great God can always help you.

Questions for Reflection and Discussion

1. How does Psalm 25:2 reflect the attitude of the three youths in this passage?

2. How does Proverbs 19:21 relate to Nebuchadnezzar's intentions in this passage?

3. Is your faith presently being tested? What have you learned in this lesson that might help you?

Nebuchadnezzar Praises God and Has a Second Dream

Daniel 4:1-7

Scripture Reading and Insights

Begin by reading Daniel 4:1-7 in your favorite Bible. As you read, keep in mind that God desires for you not only to hear His Word but also to do it (James 1:22).

Yesterday we watched as God miraculously rescued Shadrach, Meshach, and Abednego from the fiery furnace. Today we will listen in as Nebuchadnezzar praises God in His awesomeness, and we will also touch on Nebuchadnezzar's second dream. With your Bible still accessible, consider the following insights on the biblical text, verse by verse.

Daniel 4:1

To all peoples (4:1): The events we read about in Daniel 4 took place some years after the three youths' episode in the fiery furnace. Notice that Daniel 4 begins (verses 1-3) and ends (verses 34-37) with Nebuchadnezzar offering praise to God. In between, Nebuchadnezzar narrates how God allowed him to suffer great humiliation to further teach him about God's greatness. This is the structure of the chapter:

1. I praise God for His greatness because

2. God put me through some humbling circumstances that thoroughly taught me about His greatness, and so, again,

3. I praise God for His greatness.

Nebuchadnezzar's praise of God is especially noteworthy in view of his earlier highly exalted view of his own greatness (see Daniel 3:1-7). Now Nebuchadnezzar understood that God is truly the Great One.

Nebuchadnezzar addressed his proclamation of God's greatness "to all peoples, nations, and languages, that dwell in all the earth." This form of opening was common in royal inscriptions (on a stela) as well as letters in ancient Persia and Babylon. It was also common in such inscriptions and letters to include a wish of well-being—a salutation. In the present case, Nebuchadnezzar says, "Peace be multiplied to you!" (compare with 1 Peter 1:2; 2 Peter 1:2).

Of course, not all "peoples, nations, and languages, that dwell in all the earth" even knew who Nebuchadnezzar was at that time. So in its initial context, the text is probably better understood as referring to all peoples, nations, and languages that were under the rule of Nebuchadnezzar. The proclamation was regional, not global.

There is another context, however, in which Nebuchadnezzar's words were, in fact, to "*all* peoples, nations, and languages, that dwell in all the earth." After all, Nebuchadnezzar's words are recorded in the Bible, and the Bible has global distribution.

Daniel 4:2-3

Show the signs and wonders (4:2): Nebuchadnezzar describes what he has witnessed of God as "signs and wonders." The word "sign" often carries the idea of a miracle with a message, whereas "wonder" refers to a miracle that evokes amazement (see Major Themes). As we will see, God's humbling of Nebuchadnezzar would be a miracle with a message (the message being that God is awesomely powerful and great), and the whole episode—including Nebuchadnezzar's restoration—would be amazing (see Deuteronomy 6:22; 7:19; 13:1-2; 26:8; Nehemiah 9:10; Isaiah 8:18).

Most High God (4:2): Notice again that Nebuchadnezzar refers to Yahweh as the Most High God. The one true God has no real competition, for all other alleged deities are false deities—that is, they are not deities at all.

How great are his signs (4:3): In Daniel 3, God gave Nebuchadnezzar a revelation of His awesome power by delivering the three Hebrew youths from the power of the burning flames in the fiery furnace. But God was not finished giving revelation to Nebuchadnezzar. He would give further revelation to the king by allowing him to go through some humbling circumstances for a period of time, after which he would recover. The new revelation Nebuchadnezzar learned through his experience was that God's signs are great, His wonders are mighty, His kingdom is eternal, and He reigns from generation to generation.

When Nebuchadnezzar said "great are his signs," it was with the recognition that signs always signal something. ("Sign" and "signal" come from the same root.) In this case, God performed miracles (signs) that signaled His identity as the only true God.

How mighty his wonders (4:3): God's miracles are "wonders" because they are amazing, astonishing, and unparalleled. Similar language was used to refer to God's great deliverance of the Jews from the Egyptian Pharaoh. Following this deliverance, Moses spoke to the people:

> Has any god ever attempted to go and take a nation for himself from the midst of another nation, by trials, by signs, by wonders, and by war, by a mighty hand and an outstretched arm, and by great deeds of terror, all of which the LORD your God did for you in Egypt before your eyes? To you it was shown, that you might know that the LORD is God; there is no other besides him (Deuteronomy 4:34-35).

As was the case in God's deliverance of the Jews from Egypt, God performed these signs and wonders in Babylon to demonstrate that "there is no other besides him."

An everlasting kingdom (4:3): Nebuchadnezzar realized that human kings can rise and fall. His experience of going mad and dwelling with animals, which he will recount in detail later in Daniel 4, is an example of a human king falling—though God would later restore him. So Nebuchadnezzar speaks from firsthand experience when he affirms that in contrast to temporal human kingdoms, God's kingdom is everlasting (see Daniel 2:44).

His dominion endures (4:3): Again, Nebuchadnezzar speaks from firsthand experience in affirming that in contrast to human kings, whose dominion lasts only as long as they are alive (and in their right mind, in Nebuchadnezzar's case), God—who Himself is eternal—has everlasting dominion as King of kings. Moreover, no human ruler possesses any authority except by God's permission. Human kings' authority is *derived* from God Himself. As Romans 13:1-2 puts it, "Let every person be subject to the governing authorities. For there is no authority except from God, and those that exist have been instituted by God."

Daniel 4:4-5

At ease in my house (4:4): Nebuchadnezzar now narrates the circumstances that led to his high praise of Yahweh. It all began with a dream. At the time of the dream, Nebuchadnezzar was prospering. All seemed to be going well. His earlier years had involved a lot of military conquest, but his vast domains were now resting in security. Wars were over, and he was enjoying the spoils of his conquests. As he was in this peaceful state, the dream seemed to come out of nowhere.

A dream that made me afraid (4:5): Nebuchadnezzar's sense of ease and prosperity was interrupted by a dream that frightened him. He had visions in his head that alarmed him. God was not about to allow him to remain in peace while his kingdom was filled with injustice and oppression (Daniel 4:27) and he remained full of pride (4:30). The serenity of the king's misguided life came to an abrupt halt.

Daniel 4:6-7

The wise men…brought before me (4:6): It was probably with a sense of dread that Nebuchadnezzar decreed that the wise men of Babylon be brought before him to interpret the dream. They failed miserably at their previous attempt. Perhaps the king thought that given another chance, they might be able to redeem themselves. Besides, because the king was afraid, he wanted any input he could get on the dream and its meaning.

They could not make known (4:7): This time Nebuchadnezzar revealed the dream to the wise men. Still, the magicians, the enchanters, the Chaldeans, and the astrologers were unable to interpret it (see Daniel 2:27). Daniel to the rescue (in the next lesson).

Major Themes

1. *God's signs and wonders.* In the Bible, the word "sign" often carries the idea of a miracle with a message. A sign is a miracle that attests to something (see Deuteronomy 6:22; 7:19; 13:1-2; 26:8; Nehemiah 9:10; Isaiah 8:18). We will see that King Nebuchadnezzar was greatly humbled for a period of time and then fully restored. He saw this as a sign that attested to the awesome power of God. This is the unspoken assumption: Where miracles are, deity is present. The miracle is also a wonder in the sense that it evokes astonishment or amazement in the beholder. In the New Testament, Jesus's miracles were signs and wonders that attested to His deity (John 2:11; 4:54; 6:2; 12:18).

2. *God's eternal kingdom.* Nebuchadnezzar affirmed that God's kingdom "is an everlasting kingdom, and his dominion endures from generation to generation" (Daniel 4:3). This is in contrast to human kingdoms, which rise and fall according to God's sovereign will (see Daniel 2; 7; Revelation 17:12-13). The central emphasis in the New Testament is on the Ruler of the eternal kingdom. The New Testament says of Jesus, "Of his kingdom there will be no end" (Luke 1:33). Indeed, "He shall reign forever and ever" (Revelation 11:15). Because the kingdom is eternal, nothing can injure or destroy it. We are therefore urged, "Let us be grateful for receiving a kingdom that cannot be shaken" (Hebrews 12:28).

Digging Deeper with Cross-References

God as the Most High—Genesis 14:22; Deuteronomy 32:8;
2 Samuel 22:14; Psalms 7:17; 9:2; 47:2; 57:2; 73:11; 83:18;
91:9; Acts 7:48

Blessing of peace—Genesis 43:23; Judges 6:23; 19:20; 1 Samuel
25:6; 1 Chronicles 12:18; Ezra 5:7; Luke 10:5; 24:36; John
20:21; Romans 1:7

Life Lessons

1. *God sovereignly reigns from heaven.* One lesson we
   encounter repeatedly in the book of Daniel is that God
   sovereignly reigns from heaven. In fact, this theological
   thread runs through the entire Bible from Genesis to
   Revelation. God Himself affirmed, "My counsel shall
   stand, and I will accomplish all my purpose" (Isaiah 46:10).
   The psalmist tells us that "his kingdom rules over all"
   (Psalm 103:19). Our God is "a great king over all the earth"
   (Psalm 47:2). First Chronicles 29:12-13 affirms of God,
   "You rule over all. In your hand are power and might, and
   in your hand it is to make great and to give strength to all.
   And now we thank you, our God, and praise your glorious
   name." We, too, should be thankful to God and praise
   Him for His sovereign oversight of our lives.

2. *Ruling and overruling.* God's desire is that human beings
   respond to His sovereign rule from heaven. When
   human beings choose not to respond to His rule, He
   often *overrules* them. By the time we get to Daniel 4,
   Nebuchadnezzar has seen plenty of evidence that Yahweh
   is the one true God, including the deliverance of the three
   Hebrew youths from the fiery furnace (Daniel 3). But
   Nebuchadnezzar remained a polytheist, acknowledging
   Yahweh as a powerful god in a pantheon of deities.
   Nebuchadnezzar should have responded to God's obvious
   rule from heaven. As we will see in the next two lessons,

God will overrule Nebuchadnezzar's reign and severely humble him so that he recognizes God's true greatness. Sometimes, God even has to overrule His own people. After all, God's people sometimes fail to respond to His rule, they go astray, and they fail to repent. In such cases, God overrules by bringing discipline—sometimes severe discipline—so His people will be motivated to return to the right path (Job 5:17; 33:19; Psalms 94:12; 118:18; 119:75; Proverbs 3:11-12). The best policy is to consistently submit to God's rule so He doesn't have to overrule us in our stubbornness.

Questions for Reflection and Discussion

1. Nebuchadnezzar was about to learn his lesson the hard way. Can you think of a time when God had to teach you a lesson the hard way?

2. Do you think God still does "signs and wonders" today? Why or why not?

3. What does it mean to you personally that God is the Most High God?

Nebuchadnezzar Reveals His Second Dream to Daniel

Daniel 4:8-18

Scripture Reading and Insights

Begin by reading Daniel 4:8-18 in your favorite Bible. As you read, stop and meditate on any verses that speak to your heart (Joshua 1:8; Psalm 1:1-3).

In yesterday's reading, Nebuchadnezzar praised God for His awesome signs and wonders, and he summoned the Babylonian wise men to interpret a second, more troubling dream. In today's lesson, Nebuchadnezzar reveals this dream to Daniel. With your Bible still accessible, consider the following insights on the biblical text, verse by verse.

Daniel 4:8-9

Belteshazzar (4:8): When the king originally invited wise men to interpret the second dream, Daniel was not among them. By now Daniel was in a position of significant governmental authority. He had risen far above the wise men of Babylon.

Daniel's assigned Babylonian name was Belteshazzar. This name means "Bel, protect his life," or "Bel, protect the king's life." Apparently, Bel had been Nebuchadnezzar's favorite Babylonian deity, because he referred to this deity as "my god." Nebuchadnezzar's continued use of this name indicates that despite Yahweh's open display of miracles, Nebuchadnezzar was somehow still a polytheist.

One wonders why Nebuchadnezzar did not summon Daniel at first. The other wise men of Babylon had a dismal track record. Perhaps the king was hoping to avoid hearing something from Daniel he did not want to hear. He may have expected the wise men to offer a more positive interpretation of the dream. Or perhaps, if the meaning was negative, they would soften it a bit rather than declare the hard truth, as Daniel would likely do.

In any event, our text tells us, "At last Daniel came in." One can almost hear Nebuchadnezzar breathing a sigh of relief. Whether the interpretation was positive or negative, at least the king would now know the meaning of the dream.

In whom is the spirit of the holy gods (4:8): Nebuchadnezzar was not affirming a belief that Daniel was filled by the Holy Spirit, the third person of the Trinity. He knew nothing of the Trinity. Rather, based on his earlier encounters with Daniel, Nebuchadnezzar appears to be acknowledging that the true God worked within Daniel, which made him capable of unraveling mysteries.

One must keep in mind that Nebuchadnezzar had recently been chastised in the fiery furnace episode (Daniel 3:24-30), and he affirmed that only Daniel's God was "a revealer of mysteries" (2:47). This being so, it is probably better to translate Daniel 4:8, "the Spirit of the holy God" instead of "the spirit of the holy gods." Some scholars argue against the plural (gods) because no pagans believed their deities were holy. This is something true only of the singular God of Daniel.

Chief of the magicians (4:9): Daniel did not call himself the "chief of the magicians." This was apparently a title ascribed to him by pagans in Babylon (compare with Daniel 2:48).

Another possibility is that Daniel was called "chief of the magicians" not because he was in authority over them but rather because he was wiser and more discerning than any other wise man in Babylon. In the same way, many have referred to Benjamin Warfield as "prince of theologians." Warfield had authority over no one, but he was a powerful theologian. Likewise, Daniel was a deeply insightful wise man.

No mystery is too difficult for you (4:9): Of course, Nebuchadnezzar got it wrong here. The truth of the matter is that no mystery is too difficult for *God*. God communicated the meaning of these mysteries to Daniel.

Daniel 4:10-12

A tree in the midst of the earth, and its height was great (4:10): We will focus attention on Daniel's interpretation of this dream in the next lesson. For now, we simply wish to investigate the details of the dream itself.

Nebuchadnezzar sees a tree of great height. The Bible often describes kingdoms or the realms of kings as trees. For example, we read of Assyria, "Behold, Assyria was a cedar in Lebanon, with beautiful branches and forest shade, and of towering height, its top among the clouds" (Ezekiel 31:3; see also 17:1-10,22-24; 2 Kings 14:9; Psalms 1:3; 37:35; 52:8; 92:12). (See Major Themes.)

Grew and became strong (4:11): The tree became powerful, sturdy, and abounding in strength.

Its top reached to heaven (4:11): This is a hyperbole, a purposeful exaggeration to make a point. This tree grew so tall that its top metaphorically reached into heaven. This same type of language was used to describe the tower of Babel: "Come, let us build ourselves a city and a tower with its top in the heavens, and let us make a name for ourselves, lest we be dispersed over the face of the whole earth" (Genesis 11:4).

Visible to the end of the whole earth (4:11): This was another hyperbole, intended to make the point that the tree was so tall that it could be seen from far away.

Food...shade (4:12): The tree not only grew large and powerful but also provided food and shelter for beasts and birds. It had abundant foliage and plenty of fruit.

Daniel 4:13-18

A watcher, a holy one (4:13): This is an angel from heaven commissioned by God to watch and observe. (See Major Themes.) One of the primary purposes of angels has always been to deliver messages to human beings on earth. The word translated "angel" actually means "messenger." This angel appears and issues instructions about what is to be done to the tree. The angel's message clearly points to impending judgment.

Chop down the tree (4:14): The angel instructed that the tree was to be cut down, its branches lopped off, its leaves stripped, and its fruit scattered. The beasts and the birds were to flee.

Leave the stump of its roots (4:15): The stump of the tree was to be left, with its roots still in the earth. This indicates that the tree, though stripped of its size and its greatness, is still alive and would one day be revived.

A band of iron and bronze (4:15): This protects the stump to ensure the tree's survival. The tree's "portion" would now be "with the beasts in the grass of the earth."

Let his mind be changed (4:16): The metaphorical nature of the tree now becomes clear. The tree is a man who will lose his sanity. His mental ability will not exceed that of an animal. Some scholars have suggested that Nebuchadnezzar's judgment involved the disease boanthropy, which causes a person to believe he or she is a bovine and to act accordingly.

Let seven periods of time pass over him (4:16): This state of being was to last for "seven periods," or seven years. Note that in the Bible seven is the number of completeness. Nebuchadnezzar would suffer a complete and thorough chastening from God through this experience.

The sentence is by the decree (4:17): Though the judgment is by the decree of the angels, one must not forget that the angels are here as representatives or ambassadors of God. Only God is sovereign King.

That the living may know (4:17): The purpose of this judgment on Nebuchadnezzar is stated plainly: "That the living may know that the Most High rules the kingdom of men and gives it to whom he will and sets over it the lowliest of men." More to the point, Nebuchadnezzar is finite and weak—the lowliest of creatures when compared to the unfathomable greatness of God. God can raise kings up. God can bring kings down.

Tell me the interpretation (4:18): Nebuchadnezzar no doubt suspected bad news, but he was bold enough to ask.

Major Themes

1. *Watcher angels.* Daniel 4:13 refers to angels who are called "watchers." Apparently these are angels who have been sent by God specifically to observe what is transpiring on the earth. The term suggests that these angels are especially vigilant. (The Aramaic word translated "watcher" communicates the idea of making sleepless watch.) We might consider the watchers to be God's reconnaissance agents. The watchers may relate to certain angels said to have many eyes. The cherubim, for example, are "full of eyes all around" (Ezekiel 1:18). The angels in Revelation 4:6 are "full of eyes in front and behind," and "full of eyes all around and within" (verse 8).

2. *Large, cosmic trees.* The idea of a large, cosmic tree at the center of the earth was common in ancient times.

   In the Myth of Erra and Ishum, Marduk speaks of the meshu tree, whose roots reach down through the great subterranean ocean to the underworld and whose top rises above the heavens. A sacred tree appears in various forms of Assyrian art.[2]

   The Bible refers to a great tree in Ezekiel 17, 31, and Daniel 4. In the next lesson, we will see that trees can also represent evil people. As we have seen, apocalyptic literature—including the books of Daniel and Revelation—often contains dreams, visions, and symbolic imagery.

Digging Deeper with Cross-References

General appearances of angels—Genesis 18:2; 22:11; Exodus 3:2; Daniel 8:15; 10:5; 12:5; Matthew 1:20; 2:13; 28:2; Luke 16:22; 22:43; Acts 5:19; 12:7; Hebrews 1:14; 13:2

Angels specifically coming down from heaven—Genesis 28:12;
Zechariah 14:5; Matthew 25:31; Jude 14; Revelation 19:14

Life Lessons

1. *The indwelling spirit.* Nebuchadnezzar referred to Daniel as one "in whom is the spirit of the holy gods" (Daniel 4:8). Though Nebuchadnezzar was not referring to the New Testament doctrine of the filling of the Holy Spirit, this is a doctrine we need to be aware of. Ephesians 5:18 instructs us, "Be filled with the Spirit." The word "filled" here is a present tense imperative verb. The present tense indicates continuing action. Moment by moment, you and I as Christians are to be filled with the Spirit. The imperative means it is a command from God. Being filled with the Spirit is not merely optional. As we are filled with the Holy Spirit, we will manifest the fruit of the Holy Spirit (Galatians 5:22-23).

2. *God deals with prideful leaders.* God knows what is in the human heart: "I the LORD search the heart and test the mind" (Jeremiah 17:10). "I am he who searches mind and heart" (Revelation 2:23). God "will bring to light the things now hidden in darkness and will disclose the purposes of the heart" (1 Corinthians 4:5). Looking into Nebuchadnezzar's heart, God saw unrestrained pride. The king could issue as many decrees as he wanted to (Daniel 2:13,15; 3:10,29; 6:7-13,15,26), but what really matters are heaven's decrees (Daniel 4:17,24; 9:24-27). Nebuchadnezzar was about to be humbled by the Almighty (see Psalm 103:19). God humbles you and me, too, if we maintain an attitude of pride (James 4:6).

Questions for Reflection and Discussion

1. Daniel was named Belteshazzar—a tribute to Nebuchad-nezzar's favorite god, Bel. You and I are called Christians, which means "belonging to Christ." Is it obvious to other people that you belong to Christ?

2. Do you have a healthy relationship with the Holy Spirit? Is it your goal to be controlled by the Holy Spirit in day-to-day living?

3. Daniel 4:17 tells us that God "rules the kingdom of men." Are there any areas of your life right now that you are not submitting to God's rule?

Daniel Interprets the Second Dream

Daniel 4:19-27

Scripture Reading and Insights

Begin by reading Daniel 4:19-27 in your favorite Bible. As you read, remember that God's Word is the true source of hope (Psalm 119:81).

In the previous lesson, Nebuchadnezzar revealed his second dream to Daniel. In today's lesson, Daniel interprets this second dream. With your Bible still accessible, consider the following insights on the biblical text, verse by verse.

Daniel 4:19

Daniel...was dismayed (4:19): Daniel did not get upset while interpreting Nebuchadnezzar's first dream (2:27-45). After all, in that dream, Nebuchadnezzar was portrayed as a head of gold. But this second dream was far different. It indicated that Nebuchadnezzar was to be greatly humiliated for an extended time as a form of divine discipline. Daniel became dismayed, perhaps because he had grown somewhat fond of the king—a surprising development because Nebuchadnezzar was the one who brought Daniel into captivity. Or perhaps Daniel was dismayed because bringing bad news to the king could result in his fall from the king's favor. At any rate, breaking this bad news to the king was difficult for Daniel.

Let not the dream...alarm you (4:19): The king could tell from Daniel's countenance that the news was not good. He nevertheless instructed Daniel not to be alarmed but to go ahead and share the meaning of the dream. Nebuchadnezzar's words might be paraphrased this way: "Speak out, and let the event be what it will."

May the dream be for those who hate you (4:19): Daniel prepared the king by confirming that the meaning of the dream was not good.

Daniel 4:20-22

The tree you saw...it is you, O king (4:20-22): Daniel got straight to the point. After repeating the description of the great tree, Daniel informed Nebuchadnezzar that the tree represented him. Daniel began tactfully, indicating that just as the tree had become great and strong, so Nebuchadnezzar's kingdom had also become great and strong. "Your greatness has grown and reaches to heaven, and your dominion to the ends of the earth" (verse 22).

Some Bible expositors have suggested that ancient Near Eastern kings were sometimes identified with the tree of life because they protected and sustained their people. If the king acted wickedly, however, the tree of life could become a tree of death, for protection and sustenance would vanish.

Daniel 4:23-25

It is a decree of the Most High (4:24): The judgment that was to fall on Nebuchadnezzar was a decree from the Most High God, who had rescued the three Hebrew youths from the fiery furnace. This decree was communicated through watcher angels.

You shall be driven from among men (4:25): Nebuchadnezzar was now to be removed from his position of authority in his own kingdom. He would no longer live in the palace, but would dwell among the wild animals and even act like one. As we saw in the previous chapter, some scholars have suggested that Nebuchadnezzar suffered from boanthropy, which causes a person to think he or she is a bovine and act accordingly.

Seven periods of time shall pass over you (4:25): This judgment—a decree from the Most High God—was to last for seven years, a significant portion of Nebuchadnezzar's life. For seven years, Nebuchadnezzar would live in a demented state like a wild animal. (Note that the word "times" is used again in Daniel 7:25, where it also refers to years.)

Till you know (4:25): The purpose of the judgment is now revealed. For years Nebuchadnezzar had been full of pride, acting like a god before the subjects of his kingdom. He apparently thought of himself as divine. Now Nebuchadnezzar must be shown the truth. The cutting down of the tree represents the breaking down of Nebuchadnezzar's pride. Nebuchadnezzar was to experience severe humiliation for an extended time in order to teach him "that the Most High rules the kingdom of men and gives it to whom he will." Indeed, it is God, not Nebuchadnezzar, who is the Lord of all the nations. No matter how powerful human beings may become, they are puny when measured against the infinite power and greatness of the Most High God.

Psalm 107:40 speaks of God's judgment on self-exalted rulers: "He pours contempt on princes and makes them wander in trackless wastes." The psalmist also tells us, "It is God who executes judgment, putting down one and lifting up another" (Psalm 75:7). God affirms, "It is I who by my great power and my outstretched arm have made the earth, with the men and animals that are on the earth, and I give it to whomever it seems right to me" (Jeremiah 27:5).

Daniel 4:26-27

Leave the stump of the roots of the tree (4:26): Despite the horror of such news, there was still hope for Nebuchadnezzar. The fact that the stump was left in the ground indicates that after his time of chastisement, Nebuchadnezzar would one day be restored to the throne. But that restoration to the throne would not take place until Nebuchadnezzar humbly acknowledged that God alone is the true Sovereign over humanity.

From the time that you know that Heaven rules (4:26): Daniel indicated that before Nebuchadnezzar came out of chastisement, he must come to understand that "Heaven rules." This phrase is a Jewish way of saying, "God rules," just as "kingdom of heaven" and "kingdom of God" are equated in the New Testament (see Matthew 5:3; Luke 6:20).

Break off your sins by practicing righteousness (4:27): With hopes of perhaps warding off such extended punishment, Daniel urged the king to break off sin and pursue righteousness. God typically withholds promised judgment when He sees repentance. The repentance of the Ninevites in the book of Jonah is a powerful example of this truth. When Daniel said, "Break off your sins by practicing righteousness," he was probably speaking of Nebuchadnezzar's prideful and self-exalted behavior. A key means of practicing righteousness is to live humbly before God. If Nebuchadnezzar did this one thing, it would affect everything else he did during his reign. Had Nebuchadnezzar been able to do this, he may have averted seven years of chastisement, and his kingdom would have been much better off. "Righteousness exalts a nation, but sin is a reproach to any people" (Proverbs 14:34).

Mercy to the oppressed (4:27): This is another aspect of practicing righteousness. Nebuchadnezzar's reign had been spent building a grand city that would be a monument to his greatness, and in the process, the poor were oppressed and uncared for. This must stop, Daniel said. God's Word speaks a great deal about a proper attitude toward the poor. Referring to the poor, God commanded His people, "You shall give to him freely, and your heart shall not be grudging when you give to him, because for this the Lord your God will bless you in all your work and in all that you undertake. For there will never cease to be poor in the land. Therefore I command you, 'You shall open wide your hand to your brother, to the needy and to the poor, in your land'" (Deuteronomy 15:10-11). Proverbs 29:14 exhorts, "If a king faithfully judges the poor, his throne will be established forever." Likewise, "Open your mouth, judge righteously, defend the rights of the poor and needy" (Proverbs 31:9).

A lengthening of your prosperity (4:27): By following Daniel's good advice, Nebuchadnezzar could have continued his prosperity. But being a prideful and thickheaded ruler, he refused and paid the consequences for it. In a test of wills, God will always win.

Major Themes

1. *Trees representative of evil people.* It is interesting to observe that evil people are sometimes metaphorically represented as trees. The psalmist affirmed, "I have seen a wicked, ruthless man, spreading himself like a green laurel tree" (Psalm 37:35). God raises some kings and brings down others: "All the trees of the field shall know that I am the LORD; I bring low the high tree, and make high the low tree, dry up the green tree, and make the dry tree flourish. I am the LORD; I have spoken, and I will do it" (Ezekiel 17:24). In the New Testament Jesus urged, "Even now the axe is laid to the root of the trees. Every tree therefore that does not bear good fruit is cut down and thrown into the fire" (Matthew 3:10; see also Luke 3:9).

2. *Seeking God to relent.* Daniel urged Nebuchadnezzar to repent of evil and turn to righteousness "that there may perhaps be a lengthening of your prosperity" (Daniel 4:27). Perhaps Daniel thought God might relent if Nebuchadnezzar repented. There is scriptural precedent for such an idea. The Ninevites repented at Jonah's preaching. "When God saw what they did, how they turned from their evil way, God relented of the disaster that he had said he would do to them, and he did not do it" (Jonah 3:10). This is in keeping with God's promise in Jeremiah 18:7-8: "If at any time I declare concerning a nation or a kingdom, that I will pluck up and break down and destroy it, and if that nation, concerning which I have spoken, turns from its evil, I will relent of the disaster that I intended to do to it" (compare with Acts 8:22).

Digging Deeper with Cross-References

God the sovereign King—Exodus 15:18; 1 Chronicles 16:31;
   2 Chronicles 20:6; Psalms 22:28; 47:7; 93:1; 95:3; Isaiah

6:5; 44:6,10; Romans 14:11; 1 Corinthians 15:23-28; Ephesians 1:11; 1 Timothy 1:17; Revelation 19:6

Examples of wise counsel—Genesis 41:35; Exodus 10:7; Numbers 13:30; Job 29:21; Proverbs 1:5; Ecclesiastes 9:17; Daniel 2:14; 4:27; Acts 5:35; Revelation 3:18

Life Lessons

1. *God brings down the proud.* God sovereignly decrees to
   bring low the mighty King Nebuchadnezzar (Daniel
   4:25). Corrie ten Boom offered a good word about pride.
   She said she was once asked if it was difficult for her to
   remain humble amid all the attention she was getting. She
   simply replied, "When Jesus rode into Jerusalem on Palm
   Sunday on the back of a donkey, and everyone was waving
   palm branches and throwing garments on the road, and
   singing praises, do you think that for one moment it ever
   entered the head of that donkey that any of that was for
   him?" Her point was, "If I can be the donkey on which
   Jesus Christ rides in His glory, I give Him all the praise and
   all the honor."[3] As we've affirmed previously in this book,
   Scripture says God not only exalts the humble (Luke
   1:52; James 4:10) but also humbles the proud (Isaiah 13:11;
   James 4:6; 1 Peter 5:5).

2. *Stop sinning and do what is right.* Daniel urged the king,
   "Break off your sins by practicing righteousness" (Daniel
   4:27). Daniel's comment was motivated by two spiritual
   realities: First, sin leads to destruction and death (Acts
   5:1-11; 1 Corinthians 5:5; 11:29-32; 1 John 5:16). Second,
   righteousness leads to blessing and long life (Deuteronomy
   4:40; 2 Kings 20:1-6; Proverbs 10:27; Ephesians 6:2-3).
   Daniel knew it was in the king's best interest to turn from
   sin and pursue righteousness. The same thing is true of
   you and me. God fervently desires to bless us. But before

that can happen, we must become "blessable" by turning
from evil and pursuing righteousness (Exodus 19:5;
Deuteronomy 4:40; Joshua 1:8; 1 Kings 2:3; Matthew
5:2-12).

Questions for Reflection and Discussion

1. Do you think you are presently a blessable person? If not, what changes do you need to make in your life?

2. Are you content to be a donkey on which Jesus rides in glory?

3. What impressed you most about today's Scripture reading?

Nebuchadnezzar Is Humiliated and Later Restored

Daniel 4:28-37

Scripture Reading and Insights

Begin by reading Daniel 4:28-37 in your favorite Bible. As you read, remember that great spiritual wisdom comes from studying God's Word (Psalm 119:98-104).

In yesterday's lesson, Daniel interpreted Nebuchadnezzar's second dream. Today we'll see this dream come to pass in Nebuchadnezzar's humiliation and restoration. With your Bible still accessible, consider the following insights on the biblical text, verse by verse.

Daniel 4:28-30

All this (4:28): Our text affirms plainly and simply, "All this came upon King Nebuchadnezzar." Everything God said would happen, did in fact happen. We recall Numbers 23:19: "God is not man, that he should lie." God made good on His word.

At the end of twelve months (4:29): It is significant that 12 months had passed since Daniel had given his exhortation to repent to Nebuchadnezzar. This was apparently a period of grace during which God gave Nebuchadnezzar the chance to repent. We are reminded of 2 Peter 3:9: "The Lord is not slow to fulfill his promise as some count slowness, but is patient toward you, not wishing that any should perish, but that all should reach repentance." God desired repentance, not suffering, for Nebuchadnezzar. But Nebuchadnezzar would not bend.

Had Nebuchadnezzar heeded Daniel's advice and repented (verse 27), he could have averted chastisement from God. But during this 12-month period, he proved he had no real interest in changing his self-exalting attitude. Apparently he completely ignored Daniel's advice. By the end of the 12 months, he was ripe for judgment.

Walking on the roof of the royal palace (4:29): Nebuchadnezzar had three palaces in Babylon. Some have suggested that he may have been walking on the top terrace of the famous hanging gardens at his main palace, considered one of the seven wonders of the ancient world.

My mighty power...the glory of my majesty (4:30): Nebuchadnezzar considered the glory of Babylon as a reflection of his own glory and majesty. The Aramaic phrase translated "which I have built" is more literally "which I myself have built." No credit is given to God as the Giver of all good gifts (see James 1:17). One recalls the words that the apostle Paul once spoke to the immature Corinthian believers: "What do you have that you did not receive? If then you received it, why do you boast as if you did not receive it?" (1 Corinthians 4:7). The same question could legitimately be asked of Nebuchadnezzar.

Daniel 4:31-32

While the words were still in the king's mouth (4:31): Nebuchadnezzar had been given a 12-month grace period to repent. He failed to repent, however, and there would now be no further delay in judgment. As the king was speaking his prideful words, judgment fell decisively and suddenly.

One is reminded of Jesus's warning in His parable of the rich fool. This fool said to himself, "Soul, you have ample goods laid up for many years; relax, eat, drink, be merry." But God said to him, "Fool! This night your soul is required of you, and the things you have prepared, whose will they be?" (Luke 12:19-20). Nebuchadnezzar, another rich fool, was unprepared for God's sudden chastisement even though he had been warned.

A voice from heaven (4:31): The source of the judgment was the Most High God (see Daniel 4:24).

To you it is spoken (4:31): This message of judgment was not communicated to Nebuchadnezzar through Daniel the prophet. Rather God spoke directly to Nebuchadnezzar.

The kingdom has departed from you (4:31): The Babylonian kingdom—which Nebuchadnezzar had just been pridefully gazing on—was immediately taken from him. What he had thought was a reflection of his own majesty and glory would now be a reminder of what he had lost.

Driven from among men…with the beasts of the field (4:32): Nebuchadnezzar had ruled over the people of Babylon for years, and he had exalted himself over them. Now he was no longer fit to live among them. He would live as a beast among other beasts.

Seven periods of time (4:32): This period of chastisement would last seven years. How ironic that the Babylonian king who took Israel into exile for seventy years now found himself in exile for seven years. Just as the seventy-year exile had a purifying effect on Israel, so this seven-year exile would have a purifying effect on Nebuchadnezzar.

Until you know that the Most High rules (4:32): Nebuchadnezzar was to remain in his beastly condition until he learned "that the Most High rules the kingdom of men and gives it to whom he will." God had communicated this truth to Nebuchadnezzar earlier in his life, but he wouldn't listen. Now Nebuchadnezzar would learn the lesson the hard way.

Daniel 4:33

Immediately the word was fulfilled (4:33): How sudden and unexpected judgment can fall! One minute the wicked can walk freely, feeling secure. The next minute—*bam!* Judgment falls.

During the time of Nebuchadnezzar's affliction, his counselors apparently carried out the administrative duties of the kingdom. Daniel would likely have played a critical role (see Daniel 2:48-49).

His body was wet…his hair grew…his nails were like birds' claws (4:33): Nebuchadnezzar apparently suffered boanthropy, a disease in which a person believes he or she is a bovine. This disease can actually result in the patient growing long, matted hair and thickened fingernails.

Like other beasts of the field, Nebuchadnezzar was unconcerned about bodily appearance. No longer was he groomed like a king. Instead of a royal appearance, he now had a barnyard appearance. Some have suggested that the king may have spent his time of insanity as a beast in one of the royal parks.

Daniel 4:34-35

At the end of the days (4:34): As stipulated by God, the chastisement ended after seven years.

My reason returned to me (4:34): No longer was Nebuchadnezzar insane. His reasoning ability returned to him.

I blessed the Most High (4:34): Nebuchadnezzar learned his lesson well. The first thing he did after his reason returned to him was to bless the Most High God.

Praised and honored him (4:34): Nebuchadnezzar praised and honored God as the one true God who manifested Himself in His mighty deeds. Notice that the king who had previously sought praise and honor for himself was now praising and honoring God. Notice also that the tenses of the verbs used here point to continued or habitual action. Nebuchadnezzar continued to praise and honor God.

His dominion...his kingdom (4:34): Nebuchadnezzar acknowledged that contrary to the temporal rule of finite earthly kings, God's dominion is everlasting, just as His kingdom is everlasting. Nebuchadnezzar also knew from firsthand experience how fast a finite, earthly king can fall from power.

Inhabitants of the earth (4:35): Nebuchadnezzar conceded that when compared to the Most High God, "all the inhabitants of the earth are accounted as nothing." Again, Nebuchadnezzar was speaking from firsthand experience. He knew that he himself, when compared to God, was as nothing.

He does according to his will (4:35): God accomplishes His sovereign will both in heaven and on earth. Nebuchadnezzar's seven-year chastisement and subsequent restoration was a manifestation of God's will on earth. Nebuchadnezzar was now a believer in God's authority and sovereignty.

None can stay his hand (4:35): Nebuchadnezzar reasoned that if he, the king of Babylon, could not stay God's hand, no one could. The Most High God truly is Almighty.

Or say to him, "What have you done?" (4:35): One is reminded of Isaiah 29:16: "You turn things upside down! Shall the potter be regarded as the clay, that the thing made should say of its maker, 'He did not make me'; or the thing formed say of him who formed it, 'He has no understanding'?" (see also Isaiah 45:9).

Daniel 4:36-37

Reason returned to me...splendor returned to me (4:36): God sovereignly restored Nebuchadnezzar's reason and his kingdom. God can exalt a person as easily as He can humble a person.

All his works are right and his ways are just (4:37): God's chastisement of Nebuchadnezzar was right and just.

Those who walk in pride he is able to humble (4:37): Nebuchadnezzar learned this lesson the hard way.

Major Themes

1. *God's sure word.* Things happened to Nebuchadnezzar just as God indicated they would. God's word is sure and trustworthy (see Genesis 21:1; 41:54; Exodus 7:13). No wonder we read of God, "Has he said, and will he not do it? Or has he spoken, and will he not fulfill it?" (Numbers 23:19). God said, "I will not...alter the word that went forth from my lips" (Psalm 89:34). God Himself proclaimed, "So shall my word be that goes out from my mouth; it shall not return to me empty, but it shall accomplish that which I purpose, and shall succeed in the thing for which I sent it" (Isaiah 55:11). He asserted, "I have spoken, and I will bring it to pass; I have purposed, and I will do it" (Isaiah 46:11). "The mouth of the LORD has spoken" (Isaiah 58:14).

2. *Judgment from God.* God is a God of judgment in the face of unrepentant sin. Judgment fell on Nebuchadnezzar

because of his relentless self-exaltation (Daniel 4:31-33). Judgment likewise fell on Adam and Eve because of their disobedience to God (Genesis 3). Judgment fell on the Jews for rejecting Christ (Matthew 21:42-44), on Ananias and Sapphira for lying to God (Acts 5), on Herod for self-exalting pride (Acts 12:21-23), and on Christians in Corinth for irreverence regarding the Lord's Supper (1 Corinthians 11:29-32). Christians will one day stand before the judgment seat of Christ (1 Corinthians 3:12-15; 2 Corinthians 5:10). Unbelievers will be judged at the great white throne judgment (Revelation 20:11-15).

Digging Deeper with Cross-References

Sudden reversals—Psalms 75:7; 147:6; Isaiah 22:25; 26:5; 40:23; Ezekiel 21:26; Daniel 4:31; Matthew 19:30; 20:16; Luke 1:52; 6:25; 16:25

God's voice—Genesis 3:8-9; 8:15-16; 9:8-11; Exodus 3:4; 19:19; Leviticus 1:1-2; Numbers 7:89; Deuteronomy 4:12,33,36; 5:22; 13:18; 26:14; 28:1; 1 Samuel 3:4; 2 Samuel 22:14; Job 37:2; Psalm 29:4; Isaiah 6:8; Ezekiel 10:5; Matthew 17:5

Life Lessons

1. *No one can hold back God's hand.* Once Nebuchadnezzar recovered from his affliction, he extolled God by saying, "None can stay his hand" (Daniel 4:35). We likewise read in Isaiah 14:27, "The LORD of hosts has purposed, and who will annul it? His hand is stretched out, and who will turn it back?" Job asks, "Who can turn him back?" (Job 9:12). Proverbs 21:30 assures us, "No wisdom, no understanding, no counsel can avail against the LORD." You can trust that God will surely do all that He has planned and promised to do!

2. *God can bring restoration.* God ultimately restored

Nebuchadnezzar's sanity and his kingdom (Daniel 4:36). Scripture reveals that God can restore people in many different ways. God can restore people spiritually: "The LORD is my shepherd; I shall not want. He makes me lie down in green pastures. He leads me beside still waters. He restores my soul" (Psalm 23:1-3). He can restore the joy of salvation: "Restore to me the joy of your salvation" (Psalm 51:12). God can restore us after we've experienced trials: "After you have suffered a little while, the God of all grace, who has called you to his eternal glory in Christ, will himself restore, confirm, strengthen, and establish you" (1 Peter 5:10; see also Psalm 71:20). If you are in need of restoration, turn to God without delay!

Questions for Reflection and Discussion

1. What is most striking to you about the fulfillment of Nebuchadnezzar's dream (Daniel 4:28-33)?

2. Do you think Nebuchadnezzar (a pagan king) became a part of God's family? Why or why not?

3. Do you sense any need for spiritual restoration? If so, what have you learned in this lesson that might help you?

Day 17

Belshazzar Parties It Up and Sees Handwriting on the Wall

Daniel 5:1-9

Scripture Reading and Insights

Begin by reading Daniel 5:1-9 in your favorite Bible. As you read, notice how the Word of God is purifying your life (John 17:17-18).

In the previous lesson, God humiliated Nebuchadnezzar for seven years and then restored him. In today's lesson, Belshazzar, another king, is partying it up when he suddenly sees handwriting on the wall. With your Bible still accessible, consider the following insights on the biblical text, verse by verse.

Daniel 5:1

King Belshazzar (5:1): The time span between Daniel 4:37 and Daniel 5:1 was about 23 years. After Nebuchadnezzar's death in 562 BC, a number of obscure kings reigned in Babylon until Nabonidus took the throne in 556 BC. Nabonidus then placed his son Belshazzar on the throne as coregent in about 553 BC. Belshazzar was in charge of the city while his father was reopening trade routes that Cyrus and the Persians had taken.

Belshazzar's name means "Bel protects [the king]" (Bel was a Babylonian deity). The name was a sign of wishful thinking because Babylon was now under siege by the Medo-Persian army, and a sense of doom permeated the city.

A great feast (5:1): Belshazzar may have sponsored this feast to allay the fears and boost morale of the people of Babylon in the face of impending defeat at the hands of the Medo-Persian army. It is noteworthy that two ancient Greek historians, Herodotus and Xenophon, document the all-night festivities and partying that transpired as Babylon was being taken over by the Medo-Persian army.

A thousand of his lords (5:1): Archaeologists have uncovered a royal room in ancient Babylon large enough to accommodate this group.

Daniel 5:2-4

Vessels of gold and of silver (5:2): These items were taken from Solomon's temple when Babylon overran Jerusalem and its temple. They were considered precious, holy instruments.

Nebuchadnezzar his father (5:2): While Belshazzar was the "son" of Nebuchadnezzar, the Aramaic term for a son could also refer to a grandson, descendant, or successor. Belshazzar was not the literal son of Nebuchadnezzar but was rather a descendant or royal successor of Nebuchadnezzar. In keeping with this, the Aramaic word for a father can refer to an ancestor or a predecessor.

The temple in Jerusalem (5:2): This was Solomon's temple. (See Major Themes.)

His wives, and his concubines (5:2): Belshazzar had many wives and concubines, though we are unsure about how many. Bible expositors suggest this feast may have been like an orgy.

We should note in passing that monogamy has always been God's will for human beings. From the very beginning, God set the pattern by creating a monogamous marriage relationship with one man and one woman, Adam and Eve (Genesis 1:27; 2:21-25). This God-established example of one woman for one man was the general practice of the human race (Genesis 4:1) until interrupted by sin (Genesis 4:23). The Law of Moses clearly commands that the king "shall not acquire many wives" (Deuteronomy 17:17). Our Lord affirmed God's original intention for one male and one female to be joined in marriage (Matthew 19:4). The New Testament stresses that "each man should have his own wife and each woman her own husband" (1 Corinthians 7:2). Belshazzar was clearly outside of God's will in his countless wives and concubines.

Drink from them...drank from them (5:2-3): Nebuchadnezzar had honored the true God toward the end of his life, but Belshazzar chose to show contempt for God by defiling these holy vessels. Instead of using them to honor the true God, he used them to dishonor the true God and to honor the false gods of Babylon (see verse 4). Belshazzar was apparently trying to undo Nebuchadnezzar's influence and undermine his positive words about the God of Israel. Though Belshazzar was unaware of it at the time, God's judgment on him would be swift and devastating. Belshazzar was about to lose his life.

Praised the gods of gold and silver, bronze, iron, wood, and stone (5:4): Perhaps the act of drinking wine with these holy vessels and then praising the gods of Babylon was a desperate attempt to invoke Babylon's deities to rescue them from impending doom at the hands of the Medo-Persians.

Daniel 5:5-6

The fingers of a human hand appeared and wrote (5:5): As Belshazzar was partying it up, things took an abrupt turn for the worse. Fingers of a human hand suddenly appeared and began writing on the plastered wall. The king witnessed it with his own eyes and was stunned. This was not a mystical vision that Belshazzar alone experienced. The handwriting was visible to everyone.

Notice the irony taking place here. At Belshazzar's command, Babylonian hands had taken hold of God's holy vessels, defiling and polluting them at a pagan feast, thereby showing utter contempt for God. Now the sovereign hand of the Most High God responds by writing words of judgment on the wall.

The king's color changed (5:6): The king was terrified when the divine hand began writing God's message on the wall. A doomsday pallor came to his face. His legs weakened and his knees shook. The party was over.

Daniel 5:7-9

Bring in the enchanters, the Chaldeans, and the astrologers (5:7): Belshazzar had no idea what the handwriting on the wall meant. He immediately summoned his occultists to help him decipher the meaning of the words. He promised that any who could interpret the strange words on the wall would be given splendid purple attire—*royal* attire. The successful interpreter would also become the third ruler in the kingdom, after Nabonidus and Belshazzar. The fact that Belshazzar promised such great reward is an indication of the great fear in his heart.

We recall that Pharaoh similarly rewarded Joseph. "Then Pharaoh took his signet ring from his hand and put it on Joseph's hand, and clothed him in garments of fine linen and put a gold chain about his neck. And he made him ride in his second chariot. And they called out before him, 'Bow the knee!' Thus he set him over all the land of Egypt" (Genesis 41:42-44). Such rewards seem to have been common among kings who lived in ancient times.

They could not read the writing (5:8): The Babylonian deities were impotent in helping these occultists, which is understandable because these deities did not really exist (see Daniel 2:4-11; 4:7; 5:15). Only Daniel, who depended on the one true God, would be able to help the king understand the mysterious words.

Greatly alarmed (5:9): "King Belshazzar was greatly alarmed, and his color changed, and his lords were perplexed." Though the king had no idea about the meaning of the words, he surmised that they did not bring good news.

Major Themes

1. *Solomon's temple*. Daniel 5:2 tells us that when the Jewish people went into Babylonian captivity, Nebuchadnezzar took precious items out of Solomon's temple in Jerusalem. This temple was rectangular, running east and west, and measured about 87 feet long, 30 feet wide, and 43 feet high. The walls of the temple were made of cedar wood, and carved into the wood were cherubim angels, flowers, and palm trees. The walls were overlaid with gold. The floor was made of cypress. This temple had a Holy Place

and a Most Holy Place. The Holy Place (the main outer room) housed the golden incense altar, the table of showbread, five pairs of lampstands, and utensils used for sacrifice. Double doors led into the Holy of Holies, where the ark of the covenant sat. This temple—the heart and center of Jewish worship—was destroyed by Nebuchadnezzar and the Babylonians in 587 BC.

2. *The finger of God.* The finger of God often symbolizes God's interaction with His creation in some way. When the Egyptian magicians could not mimic one of Moses's miracles, they acknowledged, "This is the finger of God" (Exodus 8:19). The two stone tablets containing God's Law that He gave to Moses were "written with the finger of God" (Exodus 31:18). Indeed, "The tablets were the work of God, and the writing was the writing of God, engraved on the tablets" (Exodus 32:16; see also Deuteronomy 9:10). When the psalmist looked up at the stars at night, he asked, "When I look at your heavens, the work of your fingers, the moon and the stars, which you have set in place, what is man that you are mindful of him?" (Psalm 8:3-4). The miraculous writing on the wall was also a manifestation of the finger of God, appearing as a human hand.

Digging Deeper with Cross-References

Feasts in the Bible—Leviticus 23:5-8,34-44; Exodus 5:1; 23:16; Deuteronomy 12:5-14; John 7:37-39; 1 Corinthians 11:23-26

Concubines—Genesis 16:1-4; 21:9-14; 25:6; 30:4; 35:22; 2 Samuel 3:7; 5:13; 1 Kings 11:1-4; 2 Chronicles 11:21; Daniel 5:3,23

Terror—Genesis 35:5; Leviticus 26:16; Job 9:34; 24:17; Psalm 91:5; Ezekiel 21:12; Luke 21:9; 24:37; Hebrews 12:21; 1 Peter 3:14

Life Lessons

1. *Rich apparel.* People often pay great attention to what
   they wear. Nothing is wrong with wearing nice clothes,
   but one must be on guard against impure motives. Jesus,
   for example, warned, "Beware of the scribes, who like
   to walk around in long robes and like greetings in the
   marketplaces" (Mark 12:38). In this case, fine clothing
   was a manifestation of arrogance and pride. James warned
   of the sin of showing favoritism toward those dressed
   better than others (James 2:3-4). We glean an important
   insight from the Lord's words in 1 Samuel 16:7. Israel was
   seeking a king to lead the people, but God told Samuel,
   "Do not look on his appearance or on the height of his
   stature...The Lord sees not as man sees: man looks on the
   outward appearance, but the Lord looks on the heart." In
   other words, God cares more about our hearts than our
   clothing. With this in mind, Paul exhorted Christians to
   "put on the Lord Jesus Christ" (Romans 13:14) and to "put
   on...compassionate hearts, kindness, humility, meekness,
   and patience" (Colossians 3:12).

2. *Turn from idolatry.* The guests at Belshazzar's feast "praised
   the gods of gold and silver, bronze, iron, wood, and
   stone" (Daniel 5:4). This is idolatry—the worship of other
   things in the place of the one true God. Pagan nations
   like Babylon typically believed in a plethora of gods who
   were often represented as statues of humans or animals.
   People would then worship these images. Some scholars
   have suggested that by promoting these idolatrous gods
   of Babylon, Belshazzar was attempting to undo any
   influence of Nebuchadnezzar's earlier honoring of the
   God of Israel (recall Daniel 4:34-35). The New Testament
   consistently urges Christians to avoid all forms of idolatry
   (1 Corinthians 5:11; 2 Corinthians 6:16; Galatians 5:19-21;
   Colossians 3:5; 1 John 5:21).

3. *The fear of the Lord.* Belshazzar was terrified at this
communication from God, and he had good reason
to be. Thankfully, you and I need not feel terror in our
relationship with God. But we are nevertheless called
to live in reverent fear of Him (1 Samuel 12:14,24;
2 Chronicles 19:9; Acts 10:35; 1 Peter 1:17; 2:17). Fear (or
reverence) of the Lord motivates obedience to God: "Fear
God and keep his commandments, for this is the whole
duty of man" (Ecclesiastes 12:13; see also Deuteronomy
5:29). It also fuels our desire to serve Him (Deuteronomy
6:13). In that sense, fearing God is a good thing.

Questions for Reflection and Discussion

1. Why might God have chosen to use visible fingers as a
means of communicating His message to Belshazzar?

2. What can you conclude about the character of Belshazzar
in Daniel 5:2-4?

3. How do you assess your own heart attitude regarding
external appearances versus inner beauty?

Belshazzar Requests Daniel to Interpret the Handwriting

Daniel 5:10-16

Scripture Reading and Insights

Begin by reading Daniel 5:10-16 in your favorite Bible. As you read, keep in mind that the Word of God brings spiritual maturity (1 Corinthians 3:1-2; Hebrews 5:12-14).

In yesterday's lesson, Belshazzar was partying it up when suddenly he saw fingers writing on the wall. In today's reading, Belshazzar asks Daniel to interpret the handwriting. With your Bible still accessible, consider the following insights on the biblical text, verse by verse.

Daniel 5:10-12

The queen (5:10): This was apparently the queen mother. All the wives of the king were present at the feast. However, this woman had easy access to the king as only a queen mother could. (See Major Themes.)

Because of the words of the king and his lords (5:10): The queen mother was on top of things. She was aware of the crisis facing the king. She heard the king and those under him strategizing on what to do next.

Came into the banqueting hall (5:10): Because of what she heard taking place, she decided to get involved. She had a solution to the king's problem and would now share it.

O king, live forever (5:10): As we have seen, this was apparently a common greeting of courtesy to kings in ancient times. The Chaldeans had earlier addressed Nebuchadnezzar this way (Daniel 2:4; see also

3:9; 6:6). Bathsheba used a similar phrase when addressing King David: "Bathsheba bowed with her face to the ground and paid homage to the king and said, 'May my lord King David live forever'" (1 Kings 1:31; see also Nehemiah 2:3; Daniel 3:9; 5:10; 6:21).

Let not your thoughts alarm you or your color change (5:10): The queen mother spoke to the king in motherly terms. In modern vernacular, she said something like this: "You're looking pale. Don't worry. Things will work out."

A man...in whom is the spirit of the holy gods (5:11): The queen mother described Daniel in terms similar to how he'd been described throughout his captivity in Babylon (Daniel 4:8-9,18). Some take this to be a claim that in some sense the gods of Babylon communicated their wisdom through Daniel. The phrase can also be translated, "the Spirit of the holy God," in which case it could refer to the one true God of Israel working in Daniel.

In the days of your father (5:11): Nebuchadnezzar died in 562 BC. The year was now 539 BC, more than 20 years later. By now, Daniel was about 80 years old. Perhaps as an old man he had retired. With the change in kings, Daniel might have faded in importance. Or perhaps the present administration simply distanced itself from both Daniel and Nebuchadnezzar because they both praised the one true God of Israel, and the present administration wanted to exalt Babylon's gods. In any event, the queen mother now indicated to the king that Daniel was the right man to solve the king's crisis.

Light and understanding and wisdom (5:11): Daniel's "light and understanding and wisdom" had enabled him to interpret Nebuchadnezzar's strange dreams. That being so, surely he would also be able to interpret the handwriting on the wall. The queen mother seemed to reason that a mystery is a mystery. Whatever form the mystery may take, Daniel would be able to figure it out.

Nebuchadnezzar...made him chief (5:11): To add a stamp of authority on Daniel, the queen mother reminded Belshazzar that Nebuchadnezzar had appointed Daniel to be "chief of the magicians, enchanters, Chaldeans, and astrologers." Daniel could thus succeed where the other wise men failed.

An excellent spirit, knowledge, and understanding (5:12): The queen mother continued to sing Daniel's praises. She said he had "an excellent spirit, knowledge, and understanding to interpret dreams, explain riddles, and solve problems." This was in dire contrast to Babylon's wise men, who were completely unable to solve such mysteries during Nebuchadnezzar's reign and now in Belshazzar's reign.

Daniel...Belteshazzar (5:12): It is interesting that the queen mother first referred to Daniel using his proper Hebrew name but also mentioned his Chaldean name. Belteshazzar means "Bel, protect his life," or "Bel, protect the king's life." (Bel was a Babylonian deity.)

He will show the interpretation (5:12): The queen mother urged the king to call for Daniel. There is a sense of immediacy to her words.

Daniel 5:13-14

You are that Daniel (5:13): The king took the queen mother's advice and summoned Daniel to appear before him. As soon as he arrived, the king said to him: "You are that Daniel, one of the exiles of Judah, whom the king my father brought from Judah." The king was seeking Daniel's help, but he was also putting Daniel in his place. Belshazzar is the king, whereas Daniel is a mere captive.

I have heard of you (5:14): The king said to Daniel, "I have heard of you that the spirit of the gods is in you, and that light and understanding and excellent wisdom are found in you." The king was issuing a challenge: "I've heard you're good at interpreting mysteries. Well, let's see how good you really are."

Daniel 5:15-16

The wise men...could not show the interpretation (5:15): Maintaining this sense of challenge, the king informed Daniel that Babylon's wise men had been brought in to interpret the handwriting on the wall, but they were unable to do so. He was implying, "Let's see if you can succeed where the others have failed."

Notice that the failure of the wise men has now become a recognizable pattern in the book of Daniel. They claimed to be empowered by Babylon's gods, but they consistently failed to interpret mysteries.

Daniel, a worshipper of the one true God, consistently succeeded in revealing the meaning of mysteries.

I have heard that you can give interpretations (5:16): We must not forget that Daniel consistently indicated that he had no special gift in himself. Rather, the one true God enabled him to decipher mysteries. Daniel 1:17 tells us, "God gave them [Daniel and his Hebrew buddies] learning and skill in all literature and wisdom, and Daniel had understanding in all visions and dreams." Daniel boasted of God, "He reveals deep and hidden things; he knows what is in the darkness, and the light dwells with him" (2:22). In keeping with this, Daniel informed Nebuchadnezzar, "There is a God in heaven who reveals mysteries" (2:28).

If you can read the writing (5:16): The king informed Daniel what would happen if he provided the proper interpretation of the words on the wall. "You shall be clothed with purple and have a chain of gold around your neck and shall be the third ruler in the kingdom." This is the same thing that had been earlier promised to Babylon's wise men if they were able to interpret the words. Purple attire is royal attire. A chain of gold held great monetary value. Becoming the third ruler in the kingdom would place Daniel right after Nabonidus and Belshazzar. This is similar to the type of reward Pharaoh had given Joseph (Genesis 41:42-44).

One cannot help but notice that Belshazzar's offer to Daniel would soon be absolutely worthless. Babylon was now under siege by the Medo-Persians. That very night Babylon would fall, so being given royal attire and being made "third ruler" in the kingdom would essentially amount to being third ruler over nothing.

Major Themes

1. *Divine communication through writing.* In today's Scripture passage, God used fingers writing on a wall to communicate revelation about impending judgment. This may seem a rather bizarre episode, but it reminds us that over and over again in the Bible, God instructs that His revelation be written down and preserved for coming

generations. "Moses wrote down all the words of the LORD" (Exodus 24:4). Joshua "wrote these words in the Book of the Law of God" (Joshua 24:25-26). Samuel "told the people the rights and duties of the kingship, and he wrote them in a book and laid it up before the LORD" (1 Samuel 10:25). God instructed Isaiah, "Take a large tablet and write on it in common characters" (Isaiah 8:1). Isaiah was told, "And now, go, write it before them on a tablet and inscribe it in a book, that it may be for the time to come as a witness forever" (Isaiah 30:8). Belshazzar was frightened (with good cause) by the fingers and their written message, but you and I should be thankful to God for going to such pains for us to have the written Word (the Bible).

2. *The queen.* The reference to the queen in our biblical text was actually the queen mother. Four reasons are offered in support of this view:

- She seems to be distinct from Belshazzar's many wives mentioned in Daniel 5:2-3.

- The queen freely and without restriction entered the king's presence as easily as a mother would enter in to see her son—something none of the common wives would dare do (5:10).

- Her personal knowledge that Daniel had been active "in the days of your father" (5:11) must mean she'd been around for a while and was therefore older than the common wives.

- She was influential—the king acted on her advice.

Digging Deeper with Cross-References

Men with wisdom—Deuteronomy 1:13; 1 Kings 3:12,28; 4:29; 5:12; 10:3,24; 2 Chronicles 9:22; Proverbs 28:2; Daniel 1:4,20; Acts 6:3

Spiritual discernment—Job 12:11; Psalms 82:5; 92:5-6; 119:125;
   Acts 17:11; Romans 3:11; 1 Corinthians 2:14-16; 1 John
   4:1-6; Revelation 2:2

Life Lessons

1. *An earthly perspective versus a divine perspective.* The queen
   mother, speaking from an earthly perspective, said to the
   king, "O king, live forever" (Daniel 5:10). But Daniel, who
   spoke for God, would soon inform the king that he was
   doomed. The king actually died that night (we'll address
   this in detail in the next lesson).

   You and I as Christians are called to maintain an
   eternal perspective, for we do not know how long we will
   live. In Colossians 3:1-2, we read, "If then you have been
   raised with Christ, seek the things that are above, where
   Christ is, seated at the right hand of God. Set your minds
   on things that are above, not on things that are on earth."
   The original Greek of this passage is intense, carrying the
   idea: "Diligently, actively, and single-mindedly pursue
   the things above." It is also a present tense, carrying the
   idea, "*Perpetually* keep on seeking the things above. Make
   it an ongoing process." Christians who maintain an eternal
   perspective are highly motivated to serve God.

2. *The importance of a good reputation.* Daniel had a stellar
   reputation, dating back to the reign of Nebuchadnezzar,
   who first took him into captivity. His good reputation not
   only brought him before kings but also brought him great
   honor throughout life. This reminds us of Proverbs 22:29:
   "Do you see a man skillful in his work? He will stand
   before kings" (see also Genesis 41:46). As Christians, we
   too ought to pursue a reputation of honesty and integrity,
   of being honorable, wise, and self-giving, like Daniel (see
   Proverbs 22:1; Ecclesiastes 7:1).

Questions for Reflection and Discussion

1. Do you have a good reputation before others, or could you
   stand to improve in this area? What steps might you take
   to improve?

2. Someone claimed that some Christians think about
   heaven so much that they are of no earthly good. Do you
   agree with that statement, or do you think the opposite
   may be true?

3. Would you say you are very wise, somewhat wise, not too
   wise, or unwise? How might you become more wise? (See
   Proverbs 1:1-7.)

Daniel Interprets the Words of Doom

Daniel 5:17-31

Scripture Reading and Insights

Begin by reading Daniel 5:17-31 in your favorite Bible. Read with the anticipation that the Holy Spirit has something important to teach you today (see Psalm 119:105).

Yesterday we saw Belshazzar ask Daniel to interpret the handwriting on the wall. In today's reading, Daniel interprets the words of impending doom. With your Bible still accessible, consider the following insights on the biblical text, verse by verse.

Daniel 5:17

Daniel answered and said before the king (5:17): King Belshazzar offered Daniel a reward for providing the interpretation of the handwriting on the wall: "You shall be clothed with purple and have a chain of gold around your neck and shall be the third ruler in the kingdom" (verse 16). Daniel responded, however, by asking the king to keep his gifts for himself and to give rewards to another. Abram responded the same way to the king of Sodom: "Abram said to the king of Sodom, 'I have lifted my hand to the LORD, God Most High, Possessor of heaven and earth, that I would not take a thread or a sandal strap or anything that is yours, lest you should say, "I have made Abram rich"'" (Genesis 14:22-23).

It is not wise to receive gifts from unworthy leaders for services rendered to them (see 2 Kings 5:15-16). Besides, Daniel had never been motivated by or impressed by material rewards. He was more interested in doing what was right. He was not trying to be disrespectful, but he had to remain true to his principles. Further, Daniel knew that the rewards and gifts—mostly pertaining to increased authority in Babylon—would soon be worth nothing, for Babylon was under siege from the Medo-Persians.

I will read the writing (5:17): Despite declining the gifts and rewards, Daniel nevertheless assured the king, "I will make known...the interpretation."

Daniel 5:18-21

The Most High God gave Nebuchadnezzar (5:18): Daniel first informed King Belshazzar of what God had given Nebuchadnezzar. By referring to God as "Most High God," Daniel was explicitly elevating Yahweh over all the false gods of Babylon, which Belshazzar worshipped (see Psalms 7:17; 9:2; 47:2; 57:2; 73:11; 83:18; 91:9). And by affirming that it was God who made Nebuchadnezzar great, glorious, and majestic, Daniel was pointing to God's sovereignty over human leaders. Daniel had earlier affirmed that God "removes kings and sets up kings" (Daniel 2:21). The psalmist likewise observed, "It is God who executes judgment, putting down one and lifting up another" (Psalm 75:7).

Because of the greatness that he gave him (5:19): Because of God's blessing on Nebuchadnezzar, people came to fear him and tremble before him. A single word from him could keep people alive or put them to death.

When his heart was lifted up (5:20): Daniel pointed to Nebuchadnezzar's life as a demonstration of the danger of pride and arrogance. Nebuchadnezzar remained prideful and did not humble himself before the true God, so God brought him down so he would be forced to learn humility.

He was driven from among the children of mankind (5:21): Nebuchadnezzar was removed from his throne, his glory was stripped from him, he was driven from among humans to live among animals, and he acted like an animal for seven years.

Until he knew that the Most High God rules (5:21): Nebuchadnezzar was forced to live this kind of existence until he recognized God's sovereignty. Belshazzar had failed to absorb this lesson from Nebuchadnezzar's experience.

Daniel 5:22-23

You...Belshazzar, have not humbled your heart (5:22): Belshazzar should have learned from Nebuchadnezzar's experience. He should have humbled himself before God, knowing the judgment that had fallen on Nebuchadnezzar. He failed to grasp the critical lesson that "whoever exalts himself will be humbled, and whoever humbles himself will be exalted" (Matthew 23:12).

You have lifted up yourself against the Lord of heaven (5:23): Instead of humbling himself, Belshazzar lifted himself up against God by defiantly using the holy vessels from the Jewish temple—the very house of God—for a wild orgy-like feast.

You have praised the gods of silver and gold, of bronze, iron, wood, and stone (5:23): Instead of submitting to the one true God, Belshazzar worshipped idols, "which do not see or hear or know" (compare with Jeremiah 10:5,15; 14:22: 50:38; 51:17).

But the God in whose hand is your breath (5:23): Belshazzar worshipped gods that had no true life in themselves, ignoring the God on whom his own life depended. Belshazzar had entrusted his life to dead idols—the height of folly.

Daniel 5:24-28

From his presence the hand was sent (5:24): Daniel informed the king that the one true God—the God who had severely chastened Nebuchadnezzar for his pride and arrogance—sent the hand to write on the wall. Daniel, of course, knew that the words brought judgment. But rather than softening the stern message of God's judgment when speaking with Belshazzar, he told the truth.

This is the writing that was inscribed (5:25): The writing on the wall was a direct message from God: "Mene, Mene, Tekel, and Parsin."

Mene *(5:26)*: This Aramaic word means "numbered" or "counted." It is doubled in the present context to bring emphasis. Because of Belshazzar's pride and wickedness, God had numbered his days and his kingdom. The invading Medo-Persian force would soon bring the kingdom to its demise.

Tekel *(5:27)*: This Aramaic word means "weighed" or "assessed." God is the one who weighs a person's actions and motives (see 1 Samuel 2:3; Psalm 62:9). He evaluates people as the divine Judge. Belshazzar had been weighed, and he and his kingdom were found to be ripe for judgment.

Peres *(5:28)*: This Aramaic word means "divided." Babylon was soon to be destroyed and taken over by the Medo-Persian Empire.

In short, God's message to Belshazzar was this: "You have grievously sinned. You have been defiant. You have not repented. You are terminated."

Daniel 5:29-31

Then Belshazzar gave the command (5:29): One might think that after hearing such words of judgment, Belshazzar might have put Daniel to death. Instead, the king gave the command to give Daniel the gifts and rewards he had promised. Again, however, the rewards were essentially useless because Babylon was about to fall to the Medo-Persian army.

That very night (5:30): That very night, King Belshazzar—who had pridefully and arrogantly exalted himself—forfeited his life through divine judgment at the hands of the invading Medo-Persian force.

We are reminded of the scriptural teaching that death often comes suddenly. We read in Ecclesiastes 9:12 that "man does not know his time. Like fish that are taken in an evil net, and like birds that are caught in a snare, so the children of man are snared at an evil time, when it suddenly falls upon them." In Proverbs 27:1 the wise man urged, "Do not boast about tomorrow, for you do not know what a day may bring." Each new day may bring the prospect of death. For this reason, the wise person—unlike Belshazzar—maintains a consistent awareness of his mortality so he will make good use of the time God has given. The psalmist therefore prayed, "O LORD, make me know my end and what is the measure of my days; let me know how fleeting I am" (Psalm 39:4). Those who maintain such an awareness live with great appreciation for each new day.

Darius the Mede (5:31): Darius was a popular name among Persian kings. The name is used most famously in reference to Darius the Mede. There has been much debate regarding Darius's actual identity. Three possibilities have been suggested:

- Darius could be an honored title for Cyrus.
- Darius could have been appointed by Cyrus to rule over Babylon.
- Darius may have been a son of Cyrus.

I believe the second option is probably best.

Major Themes

1. *Pride is predominant among human leaders.* Human leaders seem especially prone to pride and arrogance. Exodus 5:2 tells us that "Pharaoh said, 'Who is the LORD, that I should obey his voice and let Israel go? I do not know the LORD, and moreover, I will not let Israel go.'" Second Chronicles 26:16 says of Uzziah, "When he was strong, he grew proud, to his destruction. For he was unfaithful to the LORD his God." In the New Testament, Herod gave a speech, and the people shouted out, "The voice of a god, and not of a man!" Immediately following this, "an angel of the Lord struck him down, because he did not give God the glory, and he was eaten by worms and breathed his last" (Acts 12:22-23). Godly leaders, by contrast, are humble (see Luke 22:26).

2. *The vanity of worshipping idols.* Worshipping idols is the
   ultimate futility. This is a common theme in the book
   of Daniel. Daniel 5:23 reveals the obvious: The false
   gods of Babylon "do not see or hear or know." Jeremiah
   10:5 likewise tells us, "Their idols are like scarecrows in a
   cucumber field, and they cannot speak; they have to be
   carried, for they cannot walk." Jeremiah 51:17 affirms that
   "every goldsmith is put to shame by his idols, for his images
   are false, and there is no breath in them." Habakkuk
   2:18 warns, "What profit is an idol when its maker has
   shaped it, a metal image...Its maker trusts in his own
   creation when he makes speechless idols!" No wonder
   the apostle Paul declared, "An idol has no real existence"
   (1 Corinthians 8:4). Idolatry is sheer futility.

Digging Deeper with Cross-References

Sudden destruction—Genesis 19:24,28; Numbers 16:31-33;
   Deuteronomy 32:35; Psalm 35:8; Proverbs 6:14-15; Ecclesiastes 9:12; Isaiah 47:11; Jeremiah 15:8; Daniel 5:30; Luke
   17:27; 1 Thessalonians 5:3

Death as a penalty for sin—Genesis 6:5-7; 1 Chronicles 10:13;
   Job 27:8; Proverbs 2:22; 10:27; Luke 12:20-21; Acts 5:1-10;
   Romans 5:12; 6:23

Life Lessons

1. *Don't be enticed by what the world has to offer.* Notice that
   Daniel couldn't have cared less about the gifts the king
   offered. We should follow Daniel's lead. You and I must
   perpetually guard against the lure of what this world has to
   offer. "For all that is in the world—the desires of the flesh
   and the desires of the eyes and pride of life—is not from
   the Father but is from the world. And the world is passing
   away along with its desires, but whoever does the will of
   God abides forever" (1 John 2:16-17).

2. *The humble are often exalted at the hands of others.* We have
   already talked in this book about how God humbles the
   proud and exalts the humble. But notice that when God
   chooses to exalt one of His servants, He often does so
   by means of another powerful person. For example, in
   Egypt Joseph was elevated to a position of great authority
   by Pharaoh (Genesis 41:37-43). Daniel was exalted to a
   position of great authority by several kings (for example,
   Daniel 5:29). God can do the same today. God may use a
   president, a governor, a mayor, the president of a company,
   or some other person in authority to exalt one of His
   servants.

Questions for Reflection and Discussion

1. What does today's Scripture reading reveal about Daniel's
   character?

2. How would you characterize King Belshazzar's response to
   Daniel's words of impending judgment?

3. What is the most important spiritual lesson you learned
   from today's study?

A Plot Is Launched Against Daniel

Daniel 6:1-9

Scripture Reading and Insights

Begin by reading Daniel 6:1-9 in your favorite Bible. As you read, remember that the Word of God is alive and working in you (Hebrews 4:12).

In yesterday's reading, Daniel interpreted the words of doom written on the wall. King Belshazzar was killed, and King Darius came into power. In today's lesson, a devious plot is launched against Daniel. With your Bible still accessible, consider the following insights on the biblical text, verse by verse.

Daniel 6:1-2

120 satraps (6:1): Darius divided his kingdom into 120 provinces, each one governed by a single satrap (a lieutenant or viceroy). The territory of each satrap was called a satrapy.

Three high officials, of whom Daniel was one (6:2): These 120 satraps were under the oversight of three administrators, perhaps with 40 satraps under each administrator. The key character trait required of these three administrators was trustworthiness. Daniel was an obvious fit for this position. This system of government greatly aided Darius in his administrative responsibilities.

That the king might suffer no loss (6:2): The 120 satraps were responsible for the security of the provinces and for collecting the proper tributes. The three administrators were then responsible to ensure that the satraps didn't embezzle any money and that the tributes reached the king's treasury.

Daniel 6:3

Daniel became distinguished (6:3): Daniel was now more than 80 years old. He was working with people who were much younger than he was and had more vitality than he did, but they were not believers in the one true God who guided Daniel and gave him strength. Despite the age advantage of his younger workers, Daniel—with God's favor and blessing—proved himself much more capable than the others. For that reason, the king came to greatly respect him.

An excellent spirit was in him (6:3): This is one reason for Daniel's rise to prominence in Babylon. Recall from Daniel 1:17 that Daniel and his associates had "learning and skill in all literature and wisdom, and Daniel had understanding in all visions and dreams." As well, "an excellent spirit, knowledge, and understanding to interpret dreams, explain riddles, and solve problems were found in this Daniel" (5:12).

Bible expositors take the reference to "an excellent spirit" in various ways. Some take it as referring to the Babylonians' belief that their deities worked through Daniel. Others, however, say the phrase likely means that Daniel had a good character. He was a man of integrity. He was honest and faithful. He always accomplished his assigned task with a good attitude.

The king planned to set him over the whole kingdom (6:3): This would have made Daniel much like a prime minister. As noted previously in the book, when God exalts one of His own faithful children, He often does so through a powerful leader.

Daniel 6:4-5

A ground for complaint against Daniel (6:4): The satraps and other government officials in Babylon were apparently jealous and envious of Daniel's exaltation. They resented the king's favor toward him. They may have especially resented this favor being shown to Daniel since he was a Jew.

We learn elsewhere in Scripture that jealousy and envy are extremely dangerous. Jesus taught that negative emotions emerge from within the human heart: "What comes out of a person is what defiles him. For from within, out of the heart of man, come evil thoughts...coveting, wickedness, deceit...envy, slander, pride, foolishness" (Mark 7:20-22). James indicates that such negative attitudes are earthly and unspiritual: "If you have bitter jealousy and selfish ambition in your hearts...This is not the wisdom that comes down from above, but is earthly, unspiritual, demonic" (James 3:14-16; see also Galatians 5:19-21). The better policy, of course, is to ignore self-honor and seek God's honor in all things. But such thinking was entirely foreign to the officials who plotted against Daniel.

He was faithful (6:4): Daniel diligently accomplished every task assigned him. No one could impugn his faithfulness. Perhaps the best way to describe Daniel is that he persevered in faithfulness.

No error or fault (6:4): In terms of Daniel's work habits, he was faultless. He didn't arrive to work late or leave early, he didn't sleep on the job, he didn't waste time, he never daydreamed, he never settled for mediocrity...rather, his intent was to show excellence in accomplishing all his tasks.

The law of his God (6:5): These officials concluded, "We shall not find any ground for complaint against this Daniel unless we find it in connection with the law of his God." Their intent was to undermine Daniel based on his religious practices.

Don't miss the fact that Daniel's commitment to the one true God was well known among the pagans in Babylon. Daniel was not a secret-agent believer. He followed God openly and served Him regardless of the consequences.

Daniel 6:6-9

These high officials and satraps came by agreement (6:6): The plot was launched. These unscrupulous men appeared before Darius the king with evil intent. They began by buttering him up with words of respect: "O King Darius, live forever!" (recall Daniel 2:4; 3:9; 5:10).

All the high officials of the kingdom...are agreed (6:7): The officials who appeared before Darius lied. Not *all* agreed to their agenda— Daniel, one of the top three leaders, was certainly not consulted. All this was kept from Daniel, for the instigators knew that Daniel would not have agreed with this course of action. If a man of Daniel's high respect warned the king against this ordinance, the king probably would have declined. So the government officials kept all this hush-hush to ensure Daniel would not find out about it until it was too late.

The king should establish an ordinance (6:7): The government officials played on the king's ego: "Whoever makes petition to any god or man for thirty days, except to you, O king, shall be cast into the den of lions." Ancient kings were often worshipped as gods. The Egyptian Pharaoh was himself considered a god—the son of the sun god, Re. Likewise, emperor worship in Rome became common in New Testament times. Recall that Nebuchadnezzar had once spoken of himself in divine terms (see Daniel 3:1-7). Darius was no doubt greatly flattered by this course of action, and he consented.

The law of the Medes and the Persians (6:8): Medo-Persian custom dictated that once an injunction was signed into law, it could not be undone, even by the king. The leaders emphasized that an ordinance "cannot be changed, according to the law of the Medes and the Persians, which cannot be revoked." We also see this in Esther 1:19, where a royal order was "written among the laws of the Persians and the Medes so that it may not be repealed." To put it in modern vernacular, the injunction was set in concrete (see also Esther 8:8).

King Darius signed the document (6:9): The flattered king signed the document. By appealing to Darius's pride and vanity, the government officials were able to manipulate him into signing an irrevocable law that would put Daniel's life in jeopardy. The government officials knew Daniel would never compromise his commitment to God by praying to Darius, so he would be thrown into the lions' den. The government officials reasoned that they would finally be rid of Daniel.

Major Themes

1. *Human conspiracies.* Human conspiracies are common
   in the Bible. Joseph's brothers, in their jealousy and
   envy, conspired against him and sold him into slavery
   (Genesis 37:18-20). Korah and his associates engaged in
   a conspiracy against Moses (Numbers 16:1-35). Delilah
   and several Philistine leaders conspired against the mighty
   Samson (Judges 16:4-21). Jewish leaders conspired against
   the apostle Paul (Acts 23:12-15). And of Jesus we read,
   "The Pharisees went out and conspired against him, how
   to destroy him" (Matthew 12:14). The Jewish leaders
   "plotted together in order to arrest Jesus by stealth and kill
   him" (Matthew 26:4). Daniel thus finds himself in good
   company.

2. *People who lay snares.* Closely related to engaging in
   conspiracies is the laying of snares to entrap others—
   also common in Scripture. The psalmist lamented, "For
   without cause they hid their net for me; without cause
   they dug a pit for my life" (Psalm 35:7), and "The insolent
   have dug pitfalls for me; they do not live according to
   your law" (Psalm 119:85). "The arrogant have hidden a
   trap for me, and with cords they have spread a net; beside
   the way they have set snares for me" (Psalm 140:5). When
   one encounters such snares, the wisest policy is to obey
   God no matter what: "The wicked have laid a snare for
   me, but I do not stray from your precepts" (Psalm 119:110).
   One must maintain faith in God, for "He Himself will
   deliver you from the hunter's net...His faithfulness will be
   a protective shield" (Psalm 91:3-4 HCSB). One is also wise
   to pray to God, "Keep me from the trap that they have laid
   for me and from the snares of evildoers!" (Psalm 141:9).

Digging Deeper with Cross-References

Honor and promotion in the book of Daniel—Daniel 2:48-49;
3:30; 5:29

Examples of evil counsel—Numbers 31:16; 2 Samuel 16:21;
1 Kings 22:52; 2 Chronicles 22:3; Job 2:9; Psalms 1:1; 2:2;
Proverbs 12:5; Jeremiah 9:14; Nahum 1:11

Prayer should be to God alone—2 Chronicles 7:14; Daniel 6:10;
Matthew 6:5-15; Philippians 4:6-7

Life Lessons

1. *Good stewardship.* Daniel was consistently a good steward.
He proved this earlier during the reign of Nebuchadnezzar,
and now it was obvious to Darius. You and I are called
to be consistently good stewards as well. As Colossians
3:23 puts it, "Whatever you do, work heartily, as for the
Lord and not for men." Related to this, Jesus asked, "Who
then is the faithful and wise servant, whom his master has
set over his household?" (Matthew 24:45). The context
reveals that the faithful servant conscientiously fulfills his
responsibilities and obligations while his master is away.
He honors the stewardship entrusted to him. He pays
careful attention to the details of his assigned tasks and
avoids living carelessly and becoming lax in service. He
so governs his life that he is prepared whenever his master
returns. You and I are called to be good stewards, or good
servants of the Lord, until His coming (see 1 Peter 4:10).

2. *Faultless living.* God blessed Daniel because he lived
faultlessly before God and before other human beings
(Daniel 6:4). Faultless living is described for us in Psalm
119. The psalmist boasted, "Blessed are those whose way is
blameless" (verse 1). God blesses those who "seek him with
their whole heart, who also do no wrong" (verses 2-3). The

psalmist acknowledged to God, "You have commanded your precepts to be kept diligently" (verse 4). The psalmist then yearned, "Oh that my ways may be steadfast in keeping your statutes! Then I shall not be put to shame, having my eyes fixed on all your commandments" (verses 5-6). None of us is perfect, but we should all seek to be "Psalm 119" Christians.

Questions for Reflection and Discussion

1. Have you ever been victimized by others? If so, do you think God taught you any spiritual lessons in the experience?

2. Do you think Daniel exemplified Jesus's words in Matthew 5:11-12?

3. Have you ever thought of your Christian life as a stewardship involving service to Christ? If not, would you like to begin now?

Daniel Is Thrown into the Lions' Den

Daniel 6:10-17

Scripture Reading and Insights

Begin by reading Daniel 6:10-17 in your favorite Bible. As you read, remember that those who obey the Word of God are truly blessed (Psalm 119:2; Luke 11:28; Revelation 1:3).

In the previous lesson, a devious plot was launched against Daniel by some unscrupulous government officials. In today's lesson, we see the result of that plot—Daniel is thrown into the lions' den. With your Bible still accessible, consider the following insights on the biblical text, verse by verse.

Daniel 6:10-11

When Daniel knew (6:10): The injunction signed by the king became public knowledge. As soon as Daniel became aware of it, he did what he normally did when facing a crisis: He prayed to God. He knew that God is always the believer's first line of defense.

Toward Jerusalem (6:10): The windows in Daniel's upper chamber faced Jerusalem. The temple in Jerusalem was considered God's dwelling place. Exiled Jews often prayed toward Jerusalem. (See Major Themes.)

On his knees three times a day (6:10): Jewish people commonly prayed three times a day (see Psalm 55:16-17). Daniel consistently followed this tradition. Despite the threat of death in a lions' den, Daniel would not cease praying to the one true God. Notice that Daniel's intention was not to disobey the king but rather to obey the King of kings—the one true God. Daniel was obeying a higher authority (compare with Acts 5:29).

Gave thanks (6:10): Instead of complaining about the bad circumstances he now faced—circumstances that could lead to his death—Daniel began his prayer with thanksgiving. We are reminded of Psalm 95:2: "Let us come into his presence with thanksgiving." Psalm 100:4 also comes to mind: "Enter his gates with thanksgiving." Despite the present crisis, Daniel was thankful for God's continued goodness to him.

These men came by agreement (6:11): The conspiracy against Daniel continued to unfold. The group collectively sought to catch Daniel violating the king's injunction. One is reminded of Psalm 37:32-33: "The wicked watches for the righteous and seeks to put him to death. The LORD will not abandon him to his power or let him be condemned when he is brought to trial."

Found Daniel making petition and plea (6:11): Though Daniel began his prayer with thanksgiving, he also made "petition and plea" to God for help and guidance in the present situation. The conspirators now had the evidence they needed against Daniel to ensure his destiny in the lions' den.

Daniel 6:12-13

Did you not sign an injunction (6:12): Like adolescent tattletales, the conspirators rushed to the king and said, "O king! Did you not sign an injunction, that anyone who makes petition to any god or man within thirty days except to you, O king, shall be cast into the den of lions?" Because King Darius's injunction was according to the custom of the Medes and Persians, it was irrevocable, and the king could not negotiate on Daniel's behalf.

Daniel...pays no attention to you...or the injunction...but makes his petition (6:13): The conspirators' spin on the situation made Daniel look bad. The gist of their accusation was this: "Daniel is so defiant of you that he has disobeyed you not once, but thrice." Notice two things here. First, Daniel most certainly did pay attention to the king. But on a higher level, he paid a greater attention to the Most High King of kings. Second, Daniel never had any intention of doing wrong to the king. In verse 22 he affirms, "Before you, O king, I have done no harm."

Daniel 6:14

The king...was much distressed (6:14): The king "set his mind to deliver Daniel." He stayed up all night trying to think of a way to rescue Daniel. But it was to no avail.

Some Bible expositors suggest that the king's distress may have been twofold. Primarily, he was distressed that Daniel would end up in the den of lions. Beyond that, however, he may have been distressed at the sudden recognition that he had fallen prey to a plot against Daniel by the devious government officials.

Of course, had the king exercised foresight, he wouldn't have gotten himself into this dilemma in the first place. More specifically, had he remembered that Daniel was faithful to his God, he never would have gone along with this request from the satraps and other governmental officials. We learn an important lesson here. Before making decisions, we should always take the long look and evaluate the possible consequences. Proverbs warns against choosing too quickly: "Do you see a man who is hasty in his words? There is more hope for a fool than for him" (Proverbs 29:20; see also 19:2; 21:5).

Daniel 6:15-17

It is a law of the Medes and Persians (6:15): The devious government officials were not going to let the king off the hook. They reminded him that his injunction was irrevocable. Darius himself was bound by the very law he made.

Daniel was brought and cast into the den of lions (6:16): The king had no choice. He issued the command, and Daniel was cast into the den of lions. This brutal form of execution was one of several common among the Persians.

The Aramaic word translated "den" carries the idea, "to dig." Dens were therefore underground pits. Such pits often had two entrances.

There was an opening at the top for feeding the animals. People could also be lowered through this opening, if necessary. The lions would have entered through a second door, which likely was located on the side of a hill and led into the underground pit. Daniel was apparently lowered into the pit from above.

The king declared to Daniel (6:16): He said, "May your God, whom you serve continually, deliver you!" Notice the irony here. Daniel's commitment to the Most High God got him thrown into the lions' den as a result of the king's injunction. Now the king expresses his desire that the Most High God would rescue Daniel. The king's recognition that Daniel served God continually brings to mind the exhortation in 1 Corinthians 15:58: "Therefore, my beloved brothers, be steadfast, immovable, always abounding in the work of the Lord."

A stone was brought (6:17): A stone was "laid on the mouth of the den" so that Daniel could not escape.

The king sealed it with his own signet (6:17): A signet was typically worn on a chain around the neck and was engraved with the owner's name as well as a unique and distinct symbol. Anything imprinted with this signet carried the authority of the person who owned it. A modern counterpart might be a signature on a contract. The king's signet indicated that the door into the lions' den and the stone atop it were not to be tampered with.

Sometimes kings gave their signets to high officials who acted on their behalf, just as the Egyptian Pharaoh gave his signet ring to Joseph (Genesis 41:42).

That nothing might be changed concerning Daniel (6:17): The seal guaranteed that no one would tamper with the lions' den—not even the king himself.

Major Themes

1. *Facing Jerusalem in prayer.* There is no command in
   Scripture for Jews to face Jerusalem during their prayers.
   However, it became common for the Jews in Bible times
   to face Jerusalem during prayer when they were away from

Jerusalem. After all, it is the holy city, and in this holy city was the Jewish temple, the dwelling place of God. Facing Jerusalem amounted to facing God in prayer (see 1 Kings 8:29-45; 2 Chronicles 6:20-40). Even when the Jews went into captivity in Babylon, and Jerusalem and the temple were destroyed, the practice remained. Daniel's prayers toward Jerusalem were therefore in keeping with Jewish practices of the day.

2. *Praying three times a day.* This was another common practice among the Jews in Bible times. For example, in Psalm 55:17 the psalmist affirms, "Evening and morning and at noon I utter my complaint and moan, and he hears my voice." Scripture also makes individual references to morning prayers (Psalms 5:3; 88:13; 92:2), noontime prayers (Acts 10:9), and evening prayers (Psalm 141:2; Acts 3:1). In the New Testament we are instructed to "pray without ceasing" (1 Thessalonians 5:17). This means that believers can bring their prayers and petitions to God throughout the day as the need arises.

Digging Deeper with Cross-References

Thankfulness to God—1 Chronicles 23:30; Psalms 30:12; 35:18; 69:30; 95:2; 100:4; 116:17; Matthew 11:25; John 6:11; Ephesians 5:20; Philippians 4:6; Colossians 2:7; 3:15; 4:2; 1 Thessalonians 5:18; 1 Timothy 4:4

Kneeling and bowing before God—Exodus 4:31; 12:27; 34:8; 1 Kings 8:54; Ezra 9:5; Psalm 95:6; Isaiah 45:23; Acts 7:60; Ephesians 3:14

Slander—1 Samuel 24:9; Job 1:11; Psalm 50:20; Jeremiah 18:18; Luke 7:33; Romans 3:8; 2 Timothy 3:3

Malice—Leviticus 19:18; Psalms 38:19; 69:4; Proverbs 6:14,18-19; 21:10; Zechariah 8:17; John 8:44; Ephesians 4:31; Colossians 3:8; 1 Peter 2:1

Life Lessons

1. *Components of prayer*. Daniel prayed consistently and regularly. He sets a great example for each of us. As we peruse Scripture, we find that prayer should involve at least five key components.

   - thanksgiving (Psalms 95:2; 100:4; Ephesians 5:20; Colossians 3:15)
   - praise (Psalms 34:1; 103:1-5,20-22; Hebrews 13:15)
   - worship (Exodus 20:3-5; Deuteronomy 5:7; Psalm 95:6; Hebrews 12:28; Revelation 14:7)
   - confession (Proverbs 28:13; 1 John 1:9)
   - requests to God for specific things (Matthew 6:11; Philippians 4:6-7)

   Let's resolve to pray consistently and regularly, just as Daniel did.

2. *How to engage in effective prayer*. Scripture provides a number of principles for effective praying. Here are six of the most important:

   - All our prayers are subject to the sovereign will of God (1 John 5:14).
   - Prayer should be continual (1 Thessalonians 5:17).
   - Sin is a hindrance to answered prayer (Psalm 66:18).
   - Living righteously, by contrast, is a great benefit to prayer being answered (Proverbs 15:29).
   - We should pray in faith (Mark 11:22-24).
   - We should pray in Jesus's name (John 14:13-14).

3. *Trust in God even when things look their bleakest*. Sometimes our problems may be so severe and our future outlook so bleak that we feel like withdrawing and hiding from our difficulties. But God calls us to trust Him: "Call upon

me in the day of trouble; I will deliver you, and you shall glorify me" (Psalm 50:15). "Trust in him at all times...God is a refuge for us" (Psalm 62:8). "It is better to take refuge in the LORD than to trust in man" (Psalm 118:8). "Trust in the LORD with all your heart, and do not lean on your own understanding. In all your ways acknowledge him, and he will make straight your paths" (Proverbs 3:5-6). Remember, we may not know every single detail of what our future holds, but we do know the One who knows every single detail of our future. So let's make a daily habit of trusting Him!

Questions for Reflection and Discussion

1. What is the most significant thing you learned about prayer in today's lesson?

2. What is the most significant thing you learned about trusting God in this lesson?

3. Did Daniel have a good reason to trust in God's deliverance, based on his past experiences with God? How so?

God Protects Daniel

Daniel 6:18-23

Scripture Reading and Insights

Begin by reading Daniel 6:18-23 in your favorite Bible. As you read, keep in mind that just as we eat food for physical nourishment, so we need the Word of God for spiritual nourishment (1 Corinthians 3:2; Hebrews 5:12-14; 1 Peter 2:2).

In yesterday's lesson, Daniel was thrown into the lions' den. In today's reading, God protects Daniel throughout the night while he is in the lions' den. With your Bible still accessible, consider the following insights on the biblical text, verse by verse.

Daniel 6:18

The king went to his palace (6:18): We noted in the previous lesson that the king was troubled and upset on several levels. First, he was upset that Daniel would likely lose his life. This was especially irksome because the king knew that Daniel was an innocent and noble man. Second, he was upset that he had been duped by his own government officials. How dare they entrap him by his own law! They had pretended to seek his exaltation. In reality, their only interest was to injure Daniel and prevent the king from doing anything about it. The result was that the king couldn't sleep or eat.

Daniel 6:19-20

At break of day (6:19): So anxious was the king that at daybreak—the earliest allowable time—he got up and rushed immediately to the lions' den. He couldn't stand the anguish any further. He hoped against hope that Daniel was still alive, and accordingly made haste to the den.

At this juncture, one cannot help but remember the words spoken by Daniel's three Hebrew friends to Nebuchadnezzar when threatened with being thrown into the fiery furnace: "Our God whom we serve is able to deliver us from the burning fiery furnace, and he will deliver us out of your hand, O king" (Daniel 3:17). The same God who can deliver from fire can also deliver from lions.

Cried out in a tone of anguish (6:20): One can easily imagine the king panting and his heart racing. In modern vernacular, he was a bundle of nerves.

O Daniel (6:20): The king shouted out, "O Daniel, servant of the living God, has your God, whom you serve continually, been able to deliver you from the lions?" Notice that the king was well aware of Daniel's faithful service to God. The king likely reasoned that if Daniel's God did not deliver him, it was not because his God was displeased with Daniel, but rather because He was simply unable to help Daniel. That is why Darius asked if God had been able to rescue Daniel. Perhaps Darius's hopes were high because he had heard about what God had done for Daniel and his friends during the reigns of Nebuchadnezzar and Belshazzar.

Notice also that Darius referred to Daniel's God as "the living God." The term "living God" distinguishes Daniel's God from the lifeless idols and false gods of Babylon (see Deuteronomy 5:26; Joshua 3:10; Isaiah 37:17-18).

Daniel 6:21-22

My God sent his angel (6:22): Daniel immediately responded, "My God sent his angel and shut the lions' mouths, and they have not harmed me." This was probably another appearance of the "Angel of the

Lord"—the preincarnate Christ—who rescued Daniel's three friends in the fiery furnace (Daniel 3:25; see also Psalm 91:11; Hebrews 1:14). Recall Psalm 34:7: "The angel of the Lord encamps around those who fear him, and delivers them."

It is important to understand that God could have simply decreed that the lions' mouths would remain shut and not harm Daniel. Instead, he sent the Angel of the Lord. Daniel was rescued, and apparently the preincarnate Christ kept him company throughout the night, just as He remained with the three Hebrew youths during their fiery ordeal (Daniel 3:24-25).

Daniel was always quick to give God all the glory: "My God sent his angel…" We see this not only in our present passage but also in previous chapters in the book of Daniel (see, for example, Daniel 2:27-28). Daniel was consistently a God-exalting man.

What a relief Daniel's deliverance was to Darius. Despite the best efforts of the devious governmental leaders who sought Daniel's destruction, their plans were thwarted by God's intervention on Daniel's behalf. The king's back had been against the wall as a result of the law of the Medes and Persians, but the King of kings was watching out for Daniel. The king's law may have been irrevocable on earth, but it held no sway in heaven. Indeed, heaven overruled earth in this case.

One is immediately reminded of a truth spoken by the apostle Paul in the book of Romans: "If God is for us, who can be against us?" (8:31). We are also reminded of Proverbs 19:21: "Many are the plans in the mind of a man, but it is the purpose of the Lord that will stand."

I was found blameless (6:22): Daniel now gives the reasons that God chose to rescue him. Primarily, Daniel "was found blameless before him." Scholars have debated what this means. Some believe it refers to Daniel's flawless lifestyle. He avoided sin and did good works. Others believe that "found blameless" refers more narrowly to Daniel's deliberate trust in the Most High God while facing this singular dire situation. In this latter view, God saved Daniel not because of any good works but rather because of his strong faith in God.

Perhaps both views are correct—God rescued Daniel because he was righteous *and* because he trusted in God. One is reminded that

James in the New Testament not only spoke about the importance of a strong faith (James 2:14-26) but also said, "The prayer of a righteous person has great power as it is working" (5:16).

And also before you, O king (6:22): Daniel then noted a secondary reason God rescued him—he had "done no harm" before the king. The devious and conspiratorial government officials had harmed the king; Daniel had not.

Daniel 6:23

Exceedingly glad (6:23): King Darius was elated. He had sweat bullets all night and hadn't slept a wink. But now he was able to rest comfortably, knowing that God had indeed rescued Daniel. Daniel was immediately "taken up out of the den." Recall that the Aramaic word translated "den" carries the idea, "to dig." The den was likely an underground pit with an opening at the top for feeding the animals. It is through this top opening that Daniel was lifted out of the den.

Interestingly, this event—along with the rescue of Daniel's three friends from the fiery furnace—made it into faith's hall of fame in the New Testament. In Hebrews 11:33-34, we read about those "who through faith conquered kingdoms, enforced justice, obtained promises, stopped the mouths of lions, quenched the power of fire..."

No kind of harm (6:23): It would have been one thing for Daniel to have survived the night with scars all over his body. But our text tells us that "no kind of harm was found on him, because he had trusted in his God." This reminds us of how the three Hebrew youths were unharmed by the fiery furnace: "The fire had not had any power over the bodies of those men. The hair of their heads was not singed, their cloaks were not harmed, and no smell of fire had come upon them" (Daniel 3:27).

Bible expositors are careful to point out that while God completely delivered the three Hebrew youths in the fiery furnace and Daniel in the lions' den, there are other occasions in the Bible where God allowed His servants to suffer and even become martyrs. Such individuals are described for us in Hebrews 11:36-40 (see also Revelation 6:9-11). We must remain faithful and maintain our faith in God—even if our desired deliverance may not seem to be coming. Recall that the three Hebrew youths informed the king that even if God did not deliver them from the fiery furnace, they would not bow down to an idol (Daniel 3:18).

Major Themes

1. *Fasting.* The king was worried sick for Daniel's survival and spent the entire night fasting (Daniel 6:18). The word "fast" is rooted in a Hebrew word that means "cover the mouth"—thus indicating abstinence from food and/or drink. Ideally, fast days were to be a time of self-denial and repentance from sin. During fasts, people were to humble their souls before God while abstaining from food. They were also to reflect on their relationship with God and the need to fully obey His commandments. King Darius, on the other hand, apparently fasted because he was simply too worried to eat.

2. *Trials of ordeal in the ancient Near East.* It is interesting to observe that in the ancient Near East, "trials of ordeal" determined people's guilt or innocence by exposing them to dangerous situations. If they survived the jeopardy, it was assumed that their deity had intervened, and the person was deemed innocent. If the person did not survive the jeopardy, it was assumed that the deity purposefully chose not to intervene, and guilt was assumed. Some Bible expositors believe that Daniel's night in the lions' den illustrates this type of trial.

Digging Deeper with Cross-References

The protective ministry of angels—Genesis 18:22; 2 Kings 6:17; Psalm 91:11; Matthew 18:10; Acts 5:18-19

God is our shield in dangerous circumstances—Genesis 15:1;
  Deuteronomy 33:29; Psalms 33:20; 84:11; 115:9;
  Proverbs 30:5

Life Lessons

1. *Servants of God.* Darius addresses Daniel as "servant of
   the living God" (Daniel 6:20). Many servants of God are
   mentioned in Scripture. Abraham was a servant of God
   (Psalm 105:6,42), as were Moses (Deuteronomy 34:5;
   Joshua 1:1,13,15; Psalm 105:26) and Joshua (Joshua 24:29;
   Judges 2:8). The prophets were God's servants (Ezra 9:11;
   Jeremiah 7:25; Daniel 9:6; Amos 3:7). The apostles and
   their fellow workers were bondservants of God (Romans
   1:1; Colossians 4:12; Titus 1:1; James 1:1; 2 Peter 1:1; Jude 1;
   Revelation 1:1). Even Nebuchadnezzar, whom God used
   as His whipping rod to chastise Israel, was called God's
   servant (Jeremiah 27:6; 43:10). You and I are called to be
   servants of God as well (1 Peter 2:16).

2. *Trusting God.* Our text says of Daniel, "No kind of harm
   was found on him, because he had trusted in his God"
   (Daniel 6:23). Trusting God is a common theme in
   Scripture. A great verse that applies to Daniel's situation is
   Proverbs 3:5-6: "Trust in the LORD with all your heart, and
   do not lean on your own understanding. In all your ways
   acknowledge him, and he will make straight your paths."
   According to his own understanding, Daniel could not
   possibly have survived a night in the lions' den. But Daniel
   didn't lean on his own understanding. He trusted God
   with all his heart, and God gave him a "path" right out of
   the lions' den. In keeping with this, Psalm 37:5 affirms,
   "Commit your way to the LORD; trust in him, and he will
   act." Daniel trusted God, and God acted (see also Psalms
   40:4; 50:15; 62:8; 118:8; John 14:1; Hebrews 10:35).

Questions for Reflection and Discussion

1. Are you facing any crises right now in which you need to trust *not* in your own understanding but rather in the Lord?

2. Daniel's name literally means "God is my judge." How is this name illustrated in today's passage of Scripture?

3. Who rested more comfortably throughout the night—King Darius or Daniel? Why?

The God of Daniel Is Exalted

Daniel 6:24-28

Scripture Reading and Insights

Begin by reading Daniel 6:24-28 in your favorite Bible. As you read, remember that storing God's Word in your heart can help you to avoid sinning (Psalm 119:9,11).

In yesterday's reading, God protected Daniel while he was in the lions' den. Today we'll see the king exalt God as a result of this miraculous deliverance. With your Bible still accessible, consider the following insights on the biblical text, verse by verse.

Daniel 6:24

Those men who had maliciously accused Daniel (6:24): Now that Daniel was safe, it was time to mete out justice to the unscrupulous governmental leaders who launched this deadly scheme against Daniel. The wicked destiny they had planned for Daniel would now become their own destiny. (See "Justice" in Major Themes.)

They, their children, and their wives (6:24): The wives and children of these wicked men were also thrown into the lions' den. This reminds us of Hosea 8:7: "They sow the wind, and they shall reap the whirlwind." These men had committed a great evil but would now suffer a catastrophically greater evil in that both they and their families would pay the ultimate price. Greek historian Herodotus indicates that executing an entire family for a single family member's crime was a common practice among the Persians (*Histories*, 3.119). This was intended as a deterrent against criminal acts. Of course, one must keep in mind that the Bible records many events that it does not condone.

The lions overpowered them (6:24): Death came quickly. Unlike our modern justice system, ancient rulers often rendered justice with extreme rapidity.

Daniel 6:25-27

King Darius wrote to all the peoples (6:25): Darius testified of God's greatness. We recall what Nebuchadnezzar said earlier: "I make a decree: Any people, nation, or language that speaks anything against the God of Shadrach, Meshach, and Abednego shall be torn limb from limb, and their houses laid in ruins, for there is no other god who is able to rescue in this way" (Daniel 3:29; see also 4:34-37). Daniel had lived such a godly and uncompromising lifestyle and had exhibited such open trust in God that two kings were impacted with the truth.

I make a decree (6:26): A decree was an order or a declaration from a person in high authority. Royal decrees were common in biblical times (see, for example, Ezra 4:19,21; 5:3,9,13).

Tremble and fear (6:26): Darius instructed that throughout his entire kingdom, people were to tremble and fear before the God of Daniel. Darius's words reflect the sentiment in a number of psalms: "Serve the LORD with fear, and rejoice with trembling" (2:11). "Let all the earth fear the LORD; let all the inhabitants of the world stand in awe of him!" (33:8). "The LORD reigns; let the peoples tremble! He sits enthroned upon the cherubim; let the earth quake! The LORD is great in Zion; he is exalted over all the peoples. Let them praise your great and awesome name!" (99:1-3). "My flesh trembles for fear of you, and I am afraid of your judgments" (119:120).

The living God (6:26): Darius discovered a pivotal truth that is emphasized all through the book of Daniel. The God of Daniel truly is the "living God," unlike the many inanimate idols of Babylon. The living God is portrayed in Scripture as continually being among His people, and this is certainly true in the lives of Daniel and his three Hebrew friends. (See Life Lessons.)

Enduring forever (6:26): Darius acknowledged that Daniel's God endures forever. This is a contrast to the temporal, false deities of Babylon and other pagan cultures. The Bible often recognizes God as eternal. He has always existed and is beyond time altogether. He is the King eternal (1 Timothy 1:17) who alone is immortal (6:16). The psalmist affirmed, "From everlasting to everlasting you are God" (Psalm 90:2).

His kingdom shall never be destroyed (6:26): We recall that Nebuchadnezzar had earlier said that God's kingdom "is an everlasting kingdom, and his dominion endures from generation to generation" (Daniel 4:3). This is in contrast to human kingdoms, which rise and fall (see Daniel 2:1-49; 7:1-28; Revelation 17:12-13).

His dominion shall be to the end (6:26): We learn elsewhere in Scripture of Christ's central role in exercising dominion forever and ever. The New Testament says of Jesus, "Of his kingdom there will be no end" (Luke 1:33). Indeed, "he shall reign forever and ever" (Revelation 11:15). Because the kingdom is eternal, nothing can injure or destroy it. We are therefore urged, "Let us be grateful for receiving a kingdom that cannot be shaken" (Hebrews 12:28).

He delivers and rescues (6:27): The book of Daniel offers undeniable empirical evidence for this fact. God had earlier delivered and rescued the three Hebrew youths from the fiery furnace (Daniel 3:8-30). Now God had delivered and rescued Daniel from the lions' den (6:16-23). The implication is that if God can rescue His people from these dire circumstances, He can rescue His people in any situation.

Signs and wonders (6:27): We have noted that in the Bible, the word "sign" often carries the idea of a miracle with a message. It attests to something (see Deuteronomy 6:22; 7:19; 13:1-2; 26:8; Nehemiah 9:10; Isaiah 8:18). In the present context, God attested that He is the one true, living God by delivering Daniel from the jaws of death in the lions' den. The word "wonder" is appropriate because God's miracles often have a jaw-dropping effect on people. Recall that Nebuchadnezzar had earlier said, "It has seemed good to me to show the signs and wonders that the Most High God has done for me" (Daniel 4:2).

Who has saved Daniel from the power of the lions (6:27): Darius here memorialized God's deliverance of Daniel. Everyone throughout his kingdom would now become aware of it.

Daniel 6:28

Daniel prospered (6:28): This section closes with the recognition of Daniel's prosperity during the reigns of Darius and Cyrus. God prospers those who are committed and obedient to Him. Daniel was definitely a Psalm 1 kind of man: "Blessed is the man who walks not in the counsel of the wicked, nor stands in the way of sinners, nor sits in the seat of scoffers; but his delight is in the law of the LORD, and on his law he meditates day and night. He is like a tree planted by streams of water that yields its fruit in its season, and its leaf does not wither. In all that he does, he prospers."

We witness parallels between Daniel and Joseph, who was another Psalm 1 kind of man: "The LORD was with Joseph, and he became a successful man" (Genesis 39:2). When Joseph was unjustly thrown in prison, "the LORD was with Joseph and showed him steadfast love and gave him favor in the sight of the keeper of the prison" (verse 21). "Whatever he did, the LORD made it succeed" (verse 23). As it was with Joseph, so it was with Daniel. God prospered Daniel because, like Joseph, he was a faithful and obedient servant of God.

Major Themes

1. *God is eternal.* Darius recognized that Daniel's God
   endures forever (Daniel 6:26). The eternal nature of God
   is a common theme in the Bible. Indeed, Scripture teaches
   that God transcends time altogether. As an eternal being,
   He has always existed. God is the King eternal (1 Timothy
   1:17), who alone is immortal (6:16). God is the "Alpha and
   the Omega" (Revelation 1:8), who affirms, "I am the first
   and I am the last" (Isaiah 44:6; 48:12). God exists "from
   everlasting to everlasting" (Psalms 41:13; 90:2) and lives
   forever (Psalm 102:12,27; Isaiah 57:15).

2. *Justice.* The king was aware that unscrupulous governmental officials had wronged Daniel and himself. He therefore brought about justice by having them executed. Indeed, they suffered the same fate they had intended for Daniel. This brings to mind Proverbs 11:8: "The righteous is delivered from trouble, and the wicked walks into it instead." We also recall Proverbs 26:27: "Whoever digs a pit will fall into it." We see this type of thing quite often in Scripture. Recall that Pharaoh had ordered the death of the Hebrew male babies, but ultimately the Egyptian firstborn died. He gave the order for Jewish newborns to be drowned in the Nile, but later his own army drowned in the Red Sea (Exodus 14–15). The evil Haman was hanged on the very gallows he had made to execute the righteous Mordecai (Esther 7:9-10; 9:25).

Digging Deeper with Cross-References

God's awesome signs and wonders—Deuteronomy 6:22; Nehemiah 9:10; Psalms 105:26-36; 135:9; Jeremiah 32:20-21; Daniel 3:28-29; 4:3; 6:27

Justice—Psalms 99:4; 106:3; 112:5; Proverbs 29:4; Leviticus 19:15; Isaiah 9:7; 61:8; Luke 18:7-8; Acts 17:31; Revelation 19:11

Life Lessons

1. *The living God.* Darius referred to Daniel's God as "the living God" (Daniel 6:26). This is a common ascription used of God throughout Scripture (see Deuteronomy 5:26; 1 Samuel 17:26-36; Psalm 84:2). The living God is "among" His people (Joshua 3:10). This is certainly illustrated in the life of Daniel, for God was with both Daniel and his three friends in their times of trouble. The

term "living God" is often used in contexts that contrast
the Lord with lifeless idols (see Deuteronomy 5:26; Joshua
3:10; Isaiah 37:17-18). In his wonderful book *The Living
God*, Bible scholar R.T. France explains how the ancients
viewed God as living.

> Watch the hand of this living God intervening, in
> answer to His people's prayers, working miracles,
> converting thousands, opening prison doors, and
> raising the dead, guiding His messengers to people
> and places they had never thought of, supervising the
> whole operation and every figure in it so as to work out
> His purpose in the end. Is it any wonder they prayed,
> constantly, not in vague generalities, but in daring
> specific requests? To them, God was real; to them He
> was the living God.[4]

You and I have the privilege of interacting with the living
God.

2. *Salvation.* The king affirmed that God "saved Daniel from
   the power of the lions" (Daniel 6:27). This illustrates for
   us that there are different nuances of the words "saved"
   and "salvation." We most often think of being saved as
   it pertains to our eternal salvation in heaven (see John
   3:14-17; 5:24; 6:29,47; Ephesians 2:8-9). Our text in
   Daniel, however, indicates that God can also temporally
   save a person from earthly danger. A person can also be
   saved from sickness (James 5:15-16). Salvation can refer to
   God delivering His people from oppressors (Exodus 14:13)
   and rescuing a person from trouble (Exodus 15:2; Psalm
   62:2). Salvation can also take place as a local church works
   out its internal problems (Philippians 2:12). Let us never
   forget that God can save in many different ways.

Questions for Reflection and Discussion

1. List at least five reasons you are thankful that God is a living God.

2. Are you facing any tough circumstances right now in which you need the salvation of the Lord (Exodus 14:13; 2 Chronicles 20:17; Lamentations 3:26)? What have you learned in today's lesson that can give you confidence in this regard?

3. What impacted you most in Darius's words about God after Daniel's deliverance?

Daniel's First Vision, Part 1

Daniel 7:1-8

Scripture Reading and Insights

Begin by reading Daniel 7:1-8 in your favorite Bible. As you read, trust God to open your eyes so you can discover wondrous things from His Word (Psalm 119:18).

In yesterday's reading, King Darius exalted God following Daniel's mighty deliverance in the lions' den. In today's lesson, Daniel receives his first vision from God. With your Bible still accessible, consider the following insights on the biblical text, verse by verse.

Daniel 7:1-3

The first year of Belshazzar king of Babylon (7:1): We've been talking about King Darius, who reigned after Belshazzar, so this must represent a flashback to 14 years prior to the fall of Babylon (about 553 BC). This means that the events described in Daniel 7 actually predate those described in Daniel 5–6. Daniel must therefore have had this vision when he was about 68 years old.

Daniel saw a dream (7:1): In Bible times many people had visions during their waking hours. Daniel, however, had this vision while he was asleep.

Daniel had helped kings solve mysteries, whether they related to dreams or to handwriting on the wall. Now, however, Daniel himself had a prophetic dream and visions.

The four winds of heaven (7:2): This phrase (or something similar) is sometimes used of God's providential acts among human beings or their nations (see Jeremiah 23:19; 49:36; 51:16; Zechariah 6:1-6; 7:14; Revelation 7:1-3). The word "sea" often represents nations and peoples (compare with Isaiah 17:12-13; 57:20). So Daniel's vision focuses on God's providential actions among the Gentile nations.

Four great beasts (7:3): These four beasts represent four kingdoms that play an important role in the unfolding of biblical prophecy. Notice that these nations were previously identified in Nebuchadnezzar's dream (Daniel 2:31-35) and that they are increasingly violent.

Daniel 7:4

The first was like a lion and had eagles' wings (7:4): However, Daniel said, "its wings were plucked off." This imagery apparently represents Babylon, its lionlike quality indicating power and strength. It is interesting to observe that winged lions guarded the gates of Babylon's royal palaces (see Jeremiah 4:7,13). Also, some biblical passages represent Nebuchadnezzar as a lion (see Jeremiah 4:7; 49:19; 50:17,44). The wings on the lion indicate rapid mobility, while the plucking of the wings indicate a removal of mobility—perhaps a reference to Nebuchadnezzar's insanity or to Babylon's deterioration following his death.

Daniel 7:5

Behold, another beast, a second one, like a bear (7:5): This animal of great strength represents the kingdom of Medo-Persia. The fact that the bear was "raised up on one side" indicates that the Persians maintained the higher status in the Medo-Persian alliance. The bear "had three ribs in its mouth between its teeth; and it was told, 'Arise, devour much flesh.'" The ribs are vanquished nations—apparently Lydia (conquered 546 BC), Babylon (conquered 539 BC), and Egypt (conquered 525 BC). Medo-Persia was well known for its strength and fierceness in battle (see Isaiah 13:17-18).

Daniel 7:6

Another, like a leopard (7:6): The third beast had "four wings of a bird on its back. And the beast had four heads, and dominion was given to it" (Daniel 7:6). The leopard was known for its swiftness, cunning, and agility. This imagery represents Greece under Alexander the Great (born in 356 BC). The four heads are the four generals who divided the kingdom following Alexander's death, ruling Macedonia, Asia Minor, Syria, and Egypt.

Daniel 7:7

A fourth beast, terrifying and dreadful and exceedingly strong (7:7): The fourth beast was more powerful than the three preceding beasts. The wild imagery refers to the Roman Empire, which existed in biblical times but fell apart in the fifth century AD.

It had ten horns (7:7): This empire will be revived in the end times. It will apparently be comprised of ten nations ruled by ten kings (ten horns). It is noteworthy that Rome has never consisted of a ten-nation confederacy with ten corulers. If it hasn't happened yet, this means this prophecy must deal with the future. (See Major Themes.)

Daniel 7:8

Another horn, a little one (7:8): Speaking of the prophetic future, Daniel now refers to an eleventh horn—a little horn (the antichrist) who seems insignificant at first but grows powerful enough to uproot three of the existing horns (kings). The antichrist will emerge from apparent obscurity. By his profound diplomatic skills, however, he will win the admiration of the political world and compel others to follow his lead. Though he will begin his political career as just a "little horn," his brilliant statesmanship will catapult him into global fame and power. He will quickly ascend to the topmost rung of the political world. Once he gains ascendancy, none will challenge his political power. His political domain will eventually be global. All other political leaders will be pawns in his hands.

The antichrist, of course, will be energized by none other than Satan, who is pictured in Revelation 12:3 as a "great red dragon." The color red may imply bloodshed, which would be expected because Satan has always been a murderer (John 8:44). This dragon (Satan) is pictured with "seven heads and ten horns, and on his heads seven diadems." From similar descriptions in Daniel 7:7-8,24 and Revelation 13:1, we infer that this terminology points to Satan's control over world empires during the tribulation period, apparently through the antichrist.

The ten horns apparently represent the ten kings of Daniel 7:7 and Revelation 13:1, over whom the antichrist—empowered by Satan—will gain authority. The ten countries headed by the ten kings will form the nucleus of the antichrist's (and thus Satan's) empire. The seven heads and seven crowns apparently refer to the principal rulers of the empire.

The eyes of a man (7:8): This idiom refers to intelligence, shrewdness, or powers of observation. This intelligence and shrewdness will enable the antichrist to come into world dominion in the end times.

A mouth speaking great things (7:8): The antichrist will apparently be an oratorical genius—a master of the spoken word (see also verse 20). He has "a lion's mouth" (Revelation 13:2), which Bible interpreters believe means that his oratorical skills will be majestic and awe-inspiring. Most world dictators have been persuasive speakers, able to motivate the masses to support their political agenda. The antichrist will mesmerize the world through his words.

Most Bible expositors believe that the "great things" spoken by the antichrist will include self-exalting things. Revelation 13:5 tells us, "The beast [antichrist] was given a mouth uttering haughty and blasphemous words." Indeed, "it opened its mouth to utter blasphemies against God, blaspheming his name and his dwelling, that is, those who dwell in heaven" (verse 6). The antichrist's blasphemous words are in keeping with his blasphemous nature (see 2 Thessalonians 2:3-11). The root meaning of the Greek and Hebrew words for blasphemy carries the idea of injuring the reputation of another. It can range from a lack of reverence to utter contempt for God (Leviticus 24:16; Matthew 26:65; Mark 2:7). It can also involve making claims of divinity for oneself, as the antichrist will do (compare with Mark 14:64; John 10:33).

Major Themes

1. *Horns.* Animals use horns as weapons. For this reason, the horn came to be seen as a symbol of power and might. As an extension of this symbol, horns in biblical times were sometimes used as emblems of dominion, representing kingdoms and kings, as is the case in the books of Daniel and Revelation (see Daniel 7–8; Revelation 12:13; 13:1,11; 17:3-16).

2. *The connection between Daniel 2 and Daniel 7.* According to Daniel 7, in the end times, the antichrist will come into absolute power and dominance over a revived Roman Empire. This will likely occur about midpoint in the future tribulation period.

   In Daniel 2 we read of Nebuchadnezzar's prophetic dream, in which this end-times Roman Empire was pictured as a mixture of iron and clay (see verses 41-43). Daniel, the great dream interpreter, saw this as meaning that just as iron is strong, so this latter-day Roman Empire would be strong. But just as iron and clay do not naturally mix with each other, so this latter-day Roman Empire would have some divisions. There would not be complete internal cohesion in the empire.

3. *Identifying this end-times Roman Empire.* Many modern biblical interpreters see the present European Union as a primary prospect for the ultimate fulfillment of this prophecy. This confederacy is currently characterized by both unity and some division. It appears that the stage is even now being set for the fulfillment of Daniel 2 and 7. Once the antichrist emerges into power in a revived Rome, it is just a matter of time before he comes into complete global domination.

Digging Deeper with Cross-References

> *Visions*—Genesis 46:2; Numbers 12:6; Psalm 89:19; Daniel
> 2:19; 4:5,13; 10:7; Hosea 12:10; Joel 2:28; Luke 1:22; Acts
> 2:17; 10:3; 11:5; 16:9; 18:9; 2 Corinthians 12:1
>
> *The four winds of heaven*—Daniel 8:8; 11:4; Jeremiah 49:36;
> Ezekiel 37:9; Zechariah 2:6; Revelation 7:1
>
> *Ten horns*—Daniel 7:20; Revelation 12:3; 13:1; 17:12

Life Lessons

1. *The primacy of Scripture.* When interpreting biblical
   prophecy, we must always be cautious to maintain the
   primacy of Scripture. Be careful not to use current events
   to interpret the Scriptures. Rather, use Scriptures to
   interpret current events. In other words, we must never
   force current events into biblical prophecy. The better
   policy is to first learn what the prophetic Scriptures teach
   and then observe the world to watch for any legitimate
   correlations between world events and biblical prophecy.
   We are not to be sensationalistic in studying prophecy.
   Rather, as 1 Peter 4:7 puts it, "The end of all things is at
   hand; therefore be self-controlled and sober-minded."

2. *God's sovereignty and human fear.* The description of
   this final earthly kingdom sounds a bit scary. But when
   we remember that God is sovereign over the nations,
   Christians never need to be afraid. In the book of Job we
   read, "He makes nations great, and he destroys them; he
   enlarges nations, and leads them away" (Job 12:23). We
   are told that "from one man he created all the nations
   throughout the whole earth. He decided beforehand
   when they should rise and fall, and he determined their
   boundaries" (Acts 17:26 NLT). Daniel 2:21 tells us that "it
   is He who changes the times and the epochs; He removes

kings and establishes kings" (NASB). So regardless of what happens in earthly kingdoms, we can rest in the comfort of knowing that God is in absolute control.

Questions for Reflection and Discussion

1. Are you ever fearful of world events—especially those that are related to terrorism? What have you learned in this lesson that comforts you?

2. Do you think we are living in the end times? Why or why not?

3. Has your study of biblical prophecy bolstered your faith in God and your confidence in the Bible? If so, how?

Daniel's First Vision, Part 2

Daniel 7:9-14

Scripture Reading and Insights

Begin by reading Daniel 7:9-14 in your favorite Bible. As you read, allow the Word of God to bring revival to your soul (Psalm 119:25,93,107).

In the previous lesson, we were introduced to Daniel's first vision. In today's lesson, we continue to explore it. With your Bible still accessible, consider the following insights on the biblical text, verse by verse.

Daniel 7:9

Thrones were placed (7:9): One of these would be occupied by the Ancient of Days—the Most High God.

Ancient of Days (7:9): God's names in the Bible reveal something about His nature. God's name Yahweh, for example, indicates that He is eternally self-existing and that He is the faithful covenant-keeping God of His people. The name *Elohim* indicates that God is a mighty God. The ascription *Adonai* indicates that God is Lord and is sovereign over all things in the universe. Many biblical scholars believe the descriptive phrase "Ancient of Days" indicates that God is an eternal being. Others believe it points to God as the divine Judge. If this latter view is correct, the idea is that the Most High God not only assigns power to the kingdoms of humankind but will also judge those kingdoms in the end. (See Major Themes.)

His clothing was white as snow, and the hair of his head like pure wool (7:9): This apparently points to the infinite wisdom, holiness, and purity of the Most High God (compare with Psalm 51:7; Revelation 1:14).

His throne was fiery flames (7:9): This affirmation reflects God's incredible glory and purity. Revelation 4:5 says of God's throne, "From the throne came flashes of lightning." We are elsewhere told that God "dwells in unapproachable light" (1 Timothy 6:16). The psalmist says of God, "You are clothed with splendor and majesty, covering yourself with light as with a garment" (Psalm 104:2).

Interestingly, in Isaiah 6:1-6 we read of seraphim (angels) surrounding the throne of God and constantly affirming, "Holy, holy, holy is the LORD of hosts." These seraphim had six wings each. With two of these wings they cover their faces. This seems to communicate that even the holy angels cannot look at the full, unveiled glory of God on His glorious throne.

Its wheels were burning fire (7:9): This apparently pictures God as sitting on a chariot-like throne from which He issues His sovereign decrees. This recalls God's fiery throne-chariot with wheels in Ezekiel 10:2-6.

Daniel 7:10

A stream of fire (7:10): From the burning bush that Moses saw at Horeb (Exodus 3:3) to the pillar of fire that guided the Israelites through the wilderness (Exodus 13:21), fire often represents the presence of God. Fire is also pictured as going before God as a preparation for His coming: "Our God comes...before him is a devouring fire" (Psalm 50:3). Indeed, "fire goes before him" (Psalm 97:3).

A thousand thousands served him (7:10): This is a reference to the countless angels who render service to God. We have seen that God's angels are countless. Luke 2:13 refers to "a multitude of the heavenly host" (see Psalm 68:17). Their number is elsewhere described as "myriads of myriads and thousands of thousands" (Revelation 5:11).

Ten thousand times ten thousand stood before him (7:10): While the "thousand thousands" serving God are His countless angels, the "ten thousand times ten thousand" standing before him are apparently those being judged in God's divine court. Daniel witnessed God judging virtually millions who were standing before Him.

The court sat in judgment, and the books were opened (7:10): This is similar to the language of judgment in Revelation 20:12: "I saw the dead, great and small, standing before the throne, and books were opened. Then another book was opened, which is the book of life. And the dead were judged by what was written in the books, according to what they had done." These books point to the reality that God keeps accurate records and will use these as a basis for the future judgment (compare with Exodus 32:32; Psalms 69:28; 139:16; Malachi 3:16; Philippians 4:3; Revelation 20:12,15; 21:27).

Of course, all people will one day stand in judgment before God. Unbelievers will face Christ at the great white throne judgment, after which they will be cast into the lake of fire (Revelation 20:11-15). Christians will not appear at this judgment, for their salvation is already secure. Rather, they will receive or lose rewards at a separate judgment—the judgment seat of Christ (Romans 14:8-10; 1 Corinthians 3:11-15)—and spend eternity with Christ.

Daniel 7:11-12 (Meanwhile, on earth...)

The great words that the horn was speaking (7:11): The "little horn"—the antichrist—was boasting and speaking blasphemous words against God (compare with verse 8; see also 2 Thessalonians 2:4).

The beast was killed (7:11): The fourth beast—referring to the Roman Empire, revived in the end times and led by the antichrist—would be "killed," or destroyed, not by another nation, but rather as a result of divine judgment (compare with Luke 21:24-27; Revelation 19:20). The empire and its wicked leader, the antichrist, will be divinely terminated. The antichrist will be destroyed at Christ's second coming (see Revelation 19:20; 20:10; compare with Daniel 2:35,45).

This event will put an end to what is called "the times of the Gentiles" (Luke 21:24,27). This phrase refers to the Gentile domination of Jerusalem. This period began with the Babylonian captivity that started in 606 BC. This time will last all the way through the seven-year future tribulation period (Revelation 11:2), finally ending with the second coming of Jesus Christ.

The rest of the beasts (7:12): The remaining three kingdoms (or some part of their cultures) would remain in some form—but only as faint reflections of their former prominence and power—until Christ's messianic kingdom is initiated. No longer would these three kingdoms have any kind of dominance.

Daniel 7:13-14 (Back in heaven...)

There came one like a son of man (7:13): While "the Ancient of Days" is a reference to the Father, the first person of the Trinity, "a son of man" is a messianic title of Jesus Christ, the second person of the Trinity (see Matthew 24:30; 25:31; 26:24; Mark 13:26; Luke 21:27; John 12:34). The "clouds of heaven" that accompany His appearance apparently refer to divine glory (see Exodus 16:10; 40:34-35; Numbers 16:42; 1 Kings 8:10-11; Isaiah 6:4).

He came to the Ancient of Days (7:13): The second person of the Trinity appears before the first person of the Trinity. Jesus, the divine Messiah, appears before the heavenly Father. Scripture consistently portrays Jesus in submission to the heavenly Father: "I have come down from heaven, not to do my own will but the will of him who sent me" (John 6:38; see also John 4:34; 5:19; 14:31; 16:28).

To him was given dominion (7:14): The four beasts (or four earthly kingdoms headed up by powerful human leaders) had sought dominion on earth. They are now destroyed, and Jesus the Messiah is given global dominion. All the authority, glory, and sovereign power that had been sought by the earthly rulers is at last conferred on Christ so that He is sovereign over "all peoples, nations, and languages." This represents a fulfillment of the promise the Father had earlier made to the Son: "I have set my King on Zion, my holy hill...I will make the nations your heritage, and the ends of the earth your possession" (Psalm 2:6-8). This will take place at the second coming of Jesus Christ (see Matthew 24:30; 25:31; Revelation 11:15).

Everlasting dominion (7:14): Christ's kingdom will be everlasting. It will never be conquered by another. This reign will be established in the future millennial kingdom (Revelation 20:1-6). Following that, Christ's reign continues forever in the eternal state (1 Corinthians 15:24-28).

Major Themes

1. *The Son of Man*. Daniel in his vision witnessed "one like a son of man" (Daniel 7:13). The term "son of man" is an important messianic title. We see the term not only in Daniel but also in the Gospels (see Matthew 8:20; 20:18; 24:30). The title is often used in contexts of Christ's deity. For example, the Bible says that only God can forgive sins (Isaiah 43:25; Mark 2:7). But as the Son of Man, Jesus had the power to forgive sins (Mark 2:10). Likewise, after the tribulation period, "then will appear in heaven the sign of the Son of Man, and then all the tribes of the earth will mourn, and they will see the Son of Man coming on the clouds of heaven with power and great glory" (Matthew 24:30).

2. *The Ancient of Days*. Daniel in his vision witnessed the Ancient of Days. This is a reference to Yahweh, the God and divine Judge of the universe (Daniel 7:9,13,22). The portrayal of the Ancient of Days is awesome and majestic, for "his clothing was white as snow, and the hair of his head like pure wool; his throne was fiery flames" (verse 9). Indeed, "a stream of fire issued and came out from before him; a thousand thousands served him" (verse 10). The great age of this majestic individual is not intended to communicate that God actually ages. Rather, this is a symbolic representation that God is eternal (see Exodus 3:6,14; Isaiah 9:7). This is in obvious contrast to the temporal, finite rulers of earth.

Digging Deeper with Cross-References

> *Throne of God*—Psalms 45:6; 103:19; Isaiah 66:1; Revelation
> 20:11
>
> *Messianic prophecies*—Genesis 3:15; 12:3; 49:10; Deuteronomy
> 18:15; Psalms 2:2; 69:21; 110:1; 118:22; 132:11; Isaiah 7:14;
> 9:6-7; 11:10; 25:8; 61:1; Jeremiah 23:5; Daniel 7:13; Micah
> 5:2; Zechariah 11:12; 12:10

Life Lessons

1. *God's countless angels.* Daniel 7:10 says that "a thousand
   thousands" served God. Scripture elsewhere refers to "a
   multitude of the heavenly host" (Luke 2:13). Their number
   is also described as "myriads of myriads and thousands of
   thousands" (Revelation 5:11). The word "myriad" means
   "vast number" or "innumerable." Job 25:3 understandably
   asks, "Is there any number to his armies?" Scripture never
   specifies for us the exact number of God's angels. But one
   thing is certain: There are more than enough angels to
   serve as "ministering spirits" for Christians (Hebrews 1:14).

2. *God's books.* Our passage tells us that "the books were
   opened" (Daniel 7:10). The opening of God's books
   implies that God keeps an accurate record, which He will
   use as the basis of His future judgment of humankind.
   Recall that Moses interceded in prayer on behalf of the
   Israelites and asked that they be forgiven. If not, he said,
   "Please blot me out of your book that you have written"
   (Exodus 32:32). The psalmist urged that the wicked "be
   blotted out of the book of the living" (Psalm 69:28). The
   psalmist conceded that his entire life was recorded in God's
   book: "In your book were written, every one of them,
   the days that were formed for me, when as yet there was
   none of them" (Psalm 139:16). The apostle Paul spoke
   of his coworkers, "whose names are in the book of life"
   (Philippians 4:3). At the future judgment, God's books

will be opened (Revelation 20:12,15; 21:27). You and I ought to rejoice that our names are recorded in the book of life!

Questions for Reflection and Discussion

1. What strikes you most regarding the description of God as the Ancient of Days?

2. What do you learn from Matthew 24:30 about the Son of Man, who is coming "on the clouds of heaven"? How about Matthew 26:24? Mark 13:26? Acts 1:9-11?

3. Does the reality that your name is in God's book impact the way you live? Do you want to make any midcourse corrections in your life?

Daniel's Vision Interpreted, Part 1

Daniel 7:15-22

Scripture Reading and Insights

Begin by reading Daniel 7:15-22 in your favorite Bible. As you read, never forget that God urges you to quickly obey His Word in all things (Psalm 119:60).

In the previous two lessons, we were introduced to Daniel's first vision. Now let's zero in on the interpretation of this vision. With your Bible still accessible, consider the following insights on the biblical text, verse by verse.

Daniel 7:15

My spirit within me was anxious (7:15): Daniel was troubled. He indicated this in two ways: His spirit was anxious, and the visions alarmed him. He understood that judgment was coming on his people as a result of sin, and this made him sad. A bit later, after Daniel understands the full meaning of his dream, we read, "As for me, Daniel, my thoughts greatly alarmed me, and my color changed" (verse 28).

A pattern we see emerging in the book of Daniel is that dreams cause alarm. We recall that when Nebuchadnezzar had a dream, "his spirit was troubled, and his sleep left him" (Daniel 2:1). Sometime later, we read that when Daniel became aware of Nebuchadnezzar's second dream, "Daniel, whose name was Belteshazzar, was dismayed for a while, and his thoughts alarmed him" (4:19).

Daniel 7:16

I approached one of those who stood there (7:16): On previous occasions, Daniel had interpreted other people's dreams and the handwriting on the wall. With God's empowerment, Daniel was gifted at deciphering mysteries. Presently, however, Daniel's interpretive abilities escaped him. He did not know what his own dream and visions meant.

For this reason, Daniel "approached one of those who stood there and asked him the truth concerning all this." This may well have been the angel Gabriel. After all, in Daniel 8:16, Gabriel is instructed, "Gabriel, make this man understand the vision." A bit later, Daniel said, "While I was speaking in prayer, the man Gabriel, whom I had seen in the vision at the first, came to me in swift flight at the time of the evening sacrifice" (9:21).

One is reminded that God used Gabriel to bring other important revelations to humankind. For example, in the New Testament—some 500 years after the time of Daniel—Gabriel told Zechariah about the birth of John the Baptist, and he also announced the birth of Jesus to the Virgin Mary (Luke 1:11-17,26-38).

Daniel 7:17-18

Four great beasts (7:17): Gabriel explained to Daniel, "These four great beasts are four kings who shall arise out of the earth." We have already noted the identity of the four kingdoms. The nation that was "like a lion and had eagles' wings" (verse 4) was Babylon. The nation "like a bear" (verse 5) was Medo-Persia. The nation "like a leopard" (verse 6) was Greece. The nation that was "terrifying and dreadful and exceedingly strong" (verse 7) was the Roman Empire. The "kings" of these kingdoms were, respectively, the four most notable leaders: Nebuchadnezzar, Cyrus, Alexander the Great, and the so-called "little horn" (the antichrist).

The saints of the Most High (7:18): Gabriel then revealed that "the saints of the Most High shall receive the kingdom and possess the kingdom forever, forever and ever." The word "saints" means "holy people." These people are not intrinsically holy, but rather are made holy as a result of trusting in Christ's work of salvation on the cross (compare with Romans 1:7; 12:2; 1 Corinthians 14:33; 2 Corinthians 5:17; Hebrews 12:1; Revelation 5:8; 8:3; 14:12).

Christians debate over what group of people is meant by the term "saints." Some say it refers to all of God's people throughout all ages. Others say it refers specifically to the church. Still others say it refers to believing Jews. Because Daniel's book deals only with the Jews, and the church is not created until New Testament times (see Matthew 16:18), it seems likely that Daniel is indeed referring to Jews—more specifically, to Jews who become redeemed in the end times.

Armageddon seems to be the historical context in which Israel finally becomes converted (Zechariah 12:2–13:1). In terms of chronology, Israel's restoration will include the confession of Israel's national sin (Leviticus 26:40-42; Jeremiah 3:11-18; Hosea 5:15), and then the remnant of the Jews will be saved, thereby fulfilling Paul's prophecy of Israel in Romans 11:25-27. In dire threat from the antichrist at Armageddon, Israel will plead for their newly found Messiah to return and deliver them (they will "mourn for him, as one mourns for an only child"—Zechariah 12:10; see also Isaiah 53:1-9; Matthew 23:37-39), at which point their deliverance will surely come (see Romans 10:13-14). Israel's leaders will finally have realized the reason why the tribulation has fallen on them—perhaps due to the Holy Spirit's enlightenment of their understanding of Scripture, or the testimony of the 144,000 Jewish evangelists, or perhaps the testimony of the two (Jewish) prophetic witnesses. These redeemed Jews will enter into Christ's millennial kingdom, where the land promises of the Abrahamic covenant (Genesis 12:1-3; 15:18-21) and the throne promises of the Davidic covenant (2 Samuel 7:12-13) will finally be fulfilled.

Of course, the fact that the Jews will "possess the kingdom" doesn't rule out the church's role in the millennial kingdom. Christ will rule from the throne of David, and previously raptured believers will reign with Christ. Revelation 5:10 reveals that believers have been made "a kingdom and priests to our God, and they shall reign on the earth." Likewise, Revelation 20:6 affirms, "Blessed and holy is the one who shares in the first resurrection! Over such the second death has no power, but they will be priests of God and of Christ, and they will reign with him for a thousand years."

Daniel 7:19-22

The truth about the fourth beast (7:19): Daniel seemed to have understood what he needed to know about the first three kingdoms—Babylon, Medo-Persia, and Greece. But he wanted to know more about the Roman Empire. He especially wanted to know more about "its teeth of iron and claws of bronze," and how it "devoured and broke in pieces and stamped what was left with its feet," and "the ten horns that were on its head," and "the other horn...that had eyes and a mouth that spoke great things" (Daniel 7:19-20). Gabriel would shortly tell Daniel all he needed to know about the Roman Empire (7:23-27).

Made war with the saints (7:21): At this juncture, Gabriel simply informed Daniel that the little horn "made war with the saints and prevailed over them." As noted previously, this little horn is none other than the antichrist, who will rise to power in the future seven-year tribulation period. He seems to emerge from insignificance to absolute control and dominance over a revived Roman Empire. As a ruler, he starts out small but eventually becomes the greatest of all (compare with 2 Thessalonians 2:3-10; Revelation 13:1-10).

As in verse 18, the "saints" in verse 21 are apparently the nation of Israel. The antichrist will launch great persecution against the Jewish people during the tribulation period (compare with Matthew 24:15-22; 2 Thessalonians 2:4). In the next lesson, we will see that Daniel 7:25 affirms that the antichrist "shall wear out the saints of the Most High...and they shall be given into his hand for a time, times, and half a time." "A time" is a year, "times" is two years, and "half a time" is half a year. This comes to three and a half years—the second half of the tribulation period (see also Matthew 24:16-31; Revelation 12:4-6).

Until the Ancient of Days came (7:22): The Ancient of Days is the indescribably glorious heavenly Father, who, through the Mediator Jesus Christ, overrules the agenda of the antichrist. At His second coming, Christ rescues the newly reborn Jewish remnant, and the antichrist is defeated and thrown into the lake of fire. The saved Jews then enter into Christ's millennial kingdom—the messianic kingdom promised in the Abrahamic and Davidic covenants (see Genesis 12:1-3; 15:18-21; 2 Samuel 7:12-13). God is a promise keeper, and the Jews will finally be in possession of all that God promised so long ago.

Major Themes

1. *Human kingdoms versus God's kingdom.* Our passage describes four human kings and their kingdoms that will rise and fall. These kingdoms are Babylon, Medo-Persia, Greece, and a future revived Roman Empire that will rise under the leadership of the antichrist but then fall by God's judgment. In contrast to these temporal human kingdoms, God's kingdom is eternal. This is good news for God's saints. We are told, "The saints of the Most High shall receive the kingdom and possess the kingdom forever, forever and ever" (Daniel 7:18). The Most High's "kingdom shall be an everlasting kingdom, and all dominions shall serve and obey him" (verse 27).

2. *God is the Most High.* In our passage God is referred to as the Most High (Daniel 7:18,22). The title is also used elsewhere in Scripture (Genesis 14:18; Numbers 24:16; Deuteronomy 32:8-9; Psalm 73:11; Isaiah 14:14). The term carries several nuances of meaning. Foundationally it indicates God's universal authority over all things. The confession of God as the Most High by a pagan, such as Nebuchadnezzar (Daniel 3:26), carries the idea that Yahweh is absolutely supreme over all other gods (Daniel 4:2,17,34). To a Jew, the title means that Yahweh is the only true God, and all other acclaimed gods are false gods (see Daniel 4:24-32; 5:18,21; 7:18-27).

Digging Deeper with Cross-References

> *The antichrist*—Matthew 24:4-5; 2 Thessalonians 2:1-11;
> 1 John 2:18,22; 4:3; 2 John 1:7-11; Revelation 13:1-10; 19:20
> *God's saints exalted in the book of Revelation (which parallels*
> *some of Daniel's prophecies)*—Revelation 2:26; 3:9,21; 4:4;
> 5:10; 11:12; 20:4

Life Lessons

1. *Trusting God's control over the prophetic future.* One of the purposes of Bible prophecy is to bring comfort to God's people. The book of Revelation is a good example. The recipients of the book of Revelation were suffering persecution, and some of them were even being killed (Revelation 2:13). John therefore wrote this book to give his readers a strong hope that would help them patiently endure amid relentless suffering (see Revelation 21–22). The same is true of the book of Daniel. The Jewish captivity in Babylon was not the end of the story. As we noted in the introduction, common themes in apocalyptic literature (such as Daniel) include the promise that our sovereign God will intervene and overcome all evil. God's people are therefore called to live righteously and to patiently endure their trials, knowing that restoration will soon come. Today, in the midst of a world that often seems out of control, we too can trust that God will intervene, overcome evil, and deliver us.

2. *Casualties of war.* In Daniel's dream about the future tribulation period, the antichrist "made war with the saints and prevailed over them" (Daniel 7:21). Many of these will be martyred for their faith (see Revelation 6:9-11). Scripture seems to teach that Christians will be raptured

before the tribulation begins (1 Thessalonians 1:9-10; 5:9; Revelation 3:10) and therefore will escape encounters with the antichrist. But they may still encounter persecution, and some may even forfeit their lives (Galatians 3:4; 1 Thessalonians 3:4; 2 Timothy 3:12; Hebrews 10:32; 1 Peter 3:14; 4:12; 3 John 1:10). Even today, Christians in various parts of the world suffer martyrdom (compare with Matthew 10:21,39). Let us therefore never forget the words of Jesus: "Do not fear what you are about to suffer...Be faithful unto death, and I will give you the crown of life" (Revelation 2:10).

Questions for Reflection and Discussion

1. Do you think war is being made on the saints in our own day? How so?

2. Have you ever been persecuted for your faith in Christ? How did you handle it?

3. What does it mean to you personally that you will one day possess God's kingdom "forever, forever and ever" (Daniel 7:18)?

Daniel's Vision Interpreted, Part 2

Daniel 7:23-28

Scripture Reading and Insights

Begin by reading Daniel 7:23-28 in your favorite Bible. As you read, ask God to help you understand His Word (Psalm 119:73).

Yesterday we began our study of the interpretation of Daniel's visions. Now let's further explore the interpretation of these visions. With your Bible still accessible, consider the following insights on the biblical text, verse by verse.

Daniel 7:23

Different from all the kingdoms (7:23): This last of the four kingdoms will be different in two key ways. First, it will be different in its leadership, for the leader will expressly be against (anti) Christ and will be energized by Satan (2 Thessalonians 2:9). Second, it will be different in its scope, not embracing a single geographical territory but rather engulfing the entire world.

Shall devour the whole earth (7:23): The antichrist, who will rule over this kingdom, will "devour the whole earth, and trample it down, and break it to pieces." The antichrist will be an unparalleled military ruler. Revelation 6:2 tells us that the antichrist will come out "conquering, and to conquer." People living during that time will say, "Who is like the beast, and who can fight against it?" (Revelation 13:4). His military exploits will not be regional, but global.

Daniel 7:24

The ten horns (7:24): Previously in the book I noted that because animals use horns as weapons, the horn is a symbol of power and might. As an extension of this symbol, horns in biblical times were sometimes used as emblems of dominion, representing kingdoms and kings. The ten horns of verse 24 indicate that the revived Roman Empire will be comprised of ten nations ruled by ten kings.

Another shall arise after them (7:24): An eleventh horn—a little horn (the antichrist)—seems to emerge from insignificance to absolute control and dominance over this revived empire. As a ruler, he starts out small but becomes the greatest of all (see 2 Thessalonians 2:3-10; Revelation 13:1-10).

Shall put down three kings (7:24): The antichrist starts out in an insignificant way, but he nevertheless grows powerful enough to uproot (defeat) three of the existing horns (or rulers) who resist his rise to power. He eventually rises to total dominion over the entire revived Roman empire.

Daniel 7:25

Shall speak words against the Most High (7:25): The antichrist will be an oratorical genius—a master of the spoken word. Verse 8 reveals that he will have "a mouth speaking great things" (see also verse 20). He has "a lion's mouth" (Revelation 13:2), which Bible interpreters believe means that his oratorical skills will be majestic and awe-inspiring.

Much that comes from the mouth of the antichrist will be blasphemous. As we have seen, the root meaning of the Greek and Hebrew words for blasphemy carries the idea of injuring the reputation of another. Biblically, the meaning can range from a lack of reverence for God to an extreme contempt for God or a sacred object (see Leviticus 24:16; Matthew 26:65; Mark 2:7). It can involve speaking evil against God (Psalm 74:18; Isaiah 52:5; Romans 2:24; Revelation 13:1,6; 16:9,11,21). It can also involve showing contempt for the true God by making claims of divinity for oneself (see Mark 14:64; John 10:33).

The most heinous blasphemy found in the pages of Scripture relates to the antichrist. The apostle John tells us, "I saw a beast rising out of the sea, with ten horns and seven heads, with ten diadems on its horns and blasphemous names on its heads" (Revelation 13:1). The antichrist "was given a mouth uttering haughty and blasphemous words, and it was allowed to exercise authority for forty-two months. It opened its mouth to utter blasphemies against God, blaspheming his name and his dwelling, that is, those who dwell in heaven" (verses 5-6; see also 17:3). The antichrist's blasphemous words are in keeping with his blasphemous nature (see 2 Thessalonians 2:3-11).

Shall wear out the saints (7:25): The antichrist will persecute, oppress, and even kill the Jewish people. As the one who is against (anti) Christ, he is certainly against the race that gave birth to the Christ.

Shall think to change the times and the law (7:25): The antichrist will set up laws in keeping with his own evil agenda instead of God's agenda.

Shall be given into his hand for a time, times, and half a time (7:25): A comparison with other prophetic verses indicates that this is the last three and a half years of the tribulation. We know, for example, that the antichrist's persecution of the saints begins at the midpoint of the tribulation (verse 21; Revelation 13:7-10). This persecution will continue for "a time, times, and half a time"—three and a half years—until the "time came when the saints possessed the kingdom"—that is, until Christ's millennial kingdom begins, following the second coming of Jesus Christ (see Zechariah 14:1-9; Revelation 19:11–20:6).

We should note that the last three and a half years of the tribulation period is called the *great* tribulation because it is especially intense. Some have claimed there is a contradiction between saying that the second half of the tribulation is three and a half years long and Jesus's end-time affirmation recorded in Matthew 24:21-22: "Then there will be great tribulation, such as has not been from the beginning of the world until now, no, and never will be. And *if those days had not been cut short,* no human being would be saved. But for the sake of the elect *those days will be cut short.*"

Was Jesus saying He would make the great tribulation shorter than three and a half years, or was He saying that He would shorten it to three and a half years?

To answer this question, we turn to the parallel verse in Mark 13:20: "And if the Lord had not cut short the days, no human being would be saved. But for the sake of the elect, whom he chose, he shortened the days." Greek scholars note that the two verbs in this verse—"cut short" and "shortened"—express action that was *taken by God in the past*. In this view, God in eternity past sovereignly decreed a limitation on the length of the great tribulation. In other words, God in the past already shortened the great tribulation. He did so in the sense that in the past He sovereignly decreed to cut it off at a specific time rather than let it continue indefinitely. In His omniscience, God knew that if the great tribulation were to continue indefinitely, all humanity would perish. To prevent that from happening, God in eternity past sovereignly set a specific time for the great tribulation to end—that is, when it had run its course for three and a half years.

Daniel 7:26-28

The court shall sit in judgment (7:26): The one true God, the divine Judge, will judge the antichrist and take away his power. The antichrist will be utterly destroyed at Christ's second coming. As we read in 2 Thessalonians 2:8, "The lawless one will be revealed, whom the Lord Jesus will kill with the breath of his mouth and bring to nothing by the appearance of his coming." In Revelation 19:20 we read of the antichrist's end: "The beast was captured, and with it the false prophet who in its presence had done the signs by which he deceived those who had received the mark of the beast and those who worshiped its image. These two were thrown alive into the lake of fire that burns with sulfur."

The kingdom and the dominion (7:27): At the second coming of Jesus Christ, the armies gathered against God will be destroyed (Revelation 19:17,21), the beast (antichrist) and the false prophet will be cast into the lake of fire (19:20), and Satan will be bound (20:1-3). Christ will then set up His millennial kingdom, and at long last, God's covenant promises to Israel will be fulfilled (Genesis 12:1-3; 15:18-21; 2 Samuel 7:12-13).

My thoughts greatly alarmed me (7:28): All of this was a phenomenal amount to take in. The prophecies of Israel in the tribulation period were particularly burdensome to Daniel.

Major Themes

1. *The earth.* Daniel 7:23 and the verses that follow speak of the earth as the arena of an end-times conflict between evil and good. In view of the sheer vastness of the stellar universe, it is truly amazing that God sovereignly chose our tiny planet as the center of divine activity. Relatively speaking, the earth is but an astronomical atom among the whirling constellations, only a tiny grain of sand among the ocean of stars and planets in the universe. To the naturalistic astronomer, the earth is but one of many planets in our small solar system, all of which are in orbit around the sun. But the earth is nevertheless the center of God's work of salvation in the universe. On this little planet God made unconditional covenants, God's Son became incarnate, and God's Son died on the cross. To this earth God's Son will one day return. The centrality of the earth is also evident in the creation account, for God created the earth before He created the rest of the planets and stars.

2. *God the Judge.* Many verses in the Bible refer to God as the divine Judge. Psalm 50:6 affirms, "God himself is judge." In Genesis 18:25 Abraham asks, "Shall not the Judge of all the earth do what is just?" (This points to God as the perfectly fair Judge.) In Psalm 96:13 we are told, "He comes to judge the earth. He will judge the world in righteousness." Such verses indicate that God's judgment of the antichrist will be just (compare with John 5:22; 2 Corinthians 5:10; 2 Timothy 4:1).

Digging Deeper with Cross-References

> *Blasphemy against God*—Exodus 20:7; Leviticus 19:12; 22:32;
> Deuteronomy 5:11; 2 Chronicles 32:17; Psalm 73:9; Mat-
> thew 12:31-32; 2 Thessalonians 2:4
> *God's universal kingship*—Numbers 14:21; Psalms 47:7; 59:13;
> 65:5; 67:7; 68:31; 72:8,11; 82:8; 102:22; 103:19; 108:9; Isa-
> iah 54:5; Jeremiah 3:17; Micah 5:4; Zechariah 9:10; 14:9

Life Lessons

1. *Patiently enduring persecution.* God calls His people
   to patiently endure in the midst of their trials and
   tribulations. The book of James emphasizes this: "Blessed
   is the man who remains steadfast under trial, for when he
   has stood the test he will receive the crown of life, which
   God has promised to those who love him" (James 1:12).
   We are urged, "Be patient, therefore, brothers, until the
   coming of the Lord...Be patient. Establish your hearts, for
   the coming of the Lord is at hand...The Judge is standing
   at the door" (James 5:7-9; see also 1 Peter 1:6-7).

2. *God's control of time.* Our passage makes reference to "a
   time, times, and half a time" (Daniel 7:25). Scripture says
   a lot about time. Regardless of what comes our way in
   life, our times are in God's hands (Psalm 31:15). Therefore
   we are to "trust in him at all times" (Psalm 62:8). We are
   urged to make "the most of every opportunity, because
   the days are evil" (Ephesians 5:16 NIV). We are to "walk in
   wisdom toward outsiders, making the best use of the time"
   (Colossians 4:5). And because God is in sovereign control
   of the universe, we must ever be mindful that our use of
   time tomorrow is subject to God's will (James 4:13-17).
   Our goal should be to constantly be about the business of
   doing what is right, day in and day out (Psalm 106:3).

Questions for Reflection and Discussion

1. Why might Daniel have kept the matter in his heart?

2. Have you ever thought about God's gift of time to each of us? Do you think you are a good steward of time?

3. What impacted you most about this lesson?

Daniel Has Another Vision

Daniel 8:1-14

Scripture Reading and Insights

Begin by reading Daniel 8:1-14 in your favorite Bible. As you read, never forget that you can trust everything that is recorded in the Word of God (Matthew 5:18; John 10:35).

Yesterday we completed our study of the interpretation of Daniel's first vision in a dream. In today's lesson and the lesson that follows, we will investigate an entirely different vision that provides Daniel (and us) details on the rise of Antiochus Epiphanes, the cruel persecutor of the Jews and diabolical forerunner of the antichrist. With your Bible still accessible, consider the following insights on the biblical text, verse by verse.

Daniel 8:1-2

The third year of the reign of King Belshazzar (8:1): This would have been about 551 BC, some two years after the dream and visions in Daniel 7 but before Babylon's fall in 539 BC. At this time Daniel would have been close to 70 years old.

Daniel no doubt included this material here because these latter chapters in Daniel focus exclusively on Israel during the times of the Gentiles. Accordingly, the text changes from Aramaic back to Hebrew. Recall that the phrase "times of the Gentiles" refers to the extended time of Gentile domination over Jerusalem. This period began in

606 BC with the Babylonian captivity and will not end until the second coming of Jesus Christ.

I was in Susa the citadel (8:2): In the vision, Daniel saw himself in Susa, the chief city of the Medo-Persian Empire, some 250 miles east of Babylon. (See Major Themes.) The Ulai canal was apparently a man-made canal.

Daniel 8:3-4

A ram standing on the bank of the canal...two horns (8:3): As in previous visions in the book of Daniel, the animals in this vision represent world kingdoms. Daniel first saw a ram, which represented the Medo-Persian Empire. (This becomes clear in the next section of Daniel, which we will explore in the next lesson.) The two horns on the ram represent the Medes and the Persians respectively. One of the horns was longer than the other even though it came up after the other horn. This larger horn represents Persia, which was originally the weaker of the two nations but eventually became dominant.

Charging westward and northward and southward (8:4): Daniel said, "No beast could stand before him, and there was no one who could rescue from his power. He did as he pleased and became great." This indicates that the Medo-Persian Empire dominated all the territory it moved against. No nation could withstand it. The empire became great, and its dominion was irresistible, regardless of which direction the empire expanded.

Daniel 8:5-7

A male goat came from the west...a conspicuous horn (8:5): This goat represents the Greek Empire, and the conspicuous horn represents Alexander the Great. Its movement across the earth without touching the ground represents Alexander's speedy conquest of Asia Minor, Syria, Egypt, and Mesopotamia in a mere three years (334–331 BC). History reveals that Alexander had an army of 35,000 soldiers.

Came to the ram (8:6): The goat, full of wrath, ran against the ram with two horns. This means that Alexander the Great's Greek army attacked the Medo-Persian Empire.

Struck the ram (8:7): The Medo-Persian Empire was powerless in the face of Alexander's massive onslaught. The ram's two horns—the Medes and the Persians—broke. Alexander "trampled" the Medes and the Persians. Previously no nation could withstand the Medo-Persian Empire. Now, even the Medo-Persian Empire could not withstand the Greek Empire.

Daniel 8:8-12

The goat became exceedingly great (8:8): The Greek Empire became exceedingly great and powerful as a result of the conquests of Alexander the Great.

Great horn was broken...four conspicuous horns (8:8): The Greek Empire was seemingly invincible. But then Alexander the Great died in 323 BC at the young age of 32 and at the height of his power, perhaps of malaria or typhoid fever. His empire was then divided among four of Alexander's prominent generals. These four generals are pictured as "four conspicuous horns." Cassander took over Macedonia and Greece. Lysimachus governed Thrace and Asia Minor. Seleucus ruled Syria and Babylon. Ptolemy reigned in Egypt.

A little horn (8:9): This little horn is not the little horn of Daniel 7:8. The contexts are entirely different. In Daniel 7, the little horn is the antichrist and emerges in a future revived Roman Empire. The little horn in Daniel 8:9 emerged out of Greece and refers to Antiochus Epiphanes. Our text tells us that Antiochus "grew exceedingly great toward the south, toward the east, and toward the glorious land." This means that he conquered territories to the south and the east, but also dominated the glorious land of Israel.

It grew great (8:10): Antiochus ruled the Seleucid Empire from 175 BC until his death in 164 BC. History reveals that Antiochus opposed the worship of Yahweh, defiled the Jewish temple by slaughtering a pig in the Most Holy Place, set up a graven image of himself, and treated the Jews cruelly.

Some of the host and some of the stars (8:10): Antiochus Epiphanes threw these to the ground and trampled on them. There is no small controversy among Bible expositors as to what this terminology means.

However, a consensus has emerged among many that the terms "host" and "stars" likely refer to the Jewish people, so this metaphorical language apparently describes Antiochus's relentless persecution of the Jewish people. Keep in mind that "stars" often refer to the Jewish people. For example, recall Joseph's dream: "Behold, I have dreamed another dream. Behold, the sun, the moon, and eleven stars were bowing down to me" (Genesis 37:9). In this dream, the sun (Joseph's father), the moon (Joseph's mother), and the 11 stars (Joseph's 11 brothers) would one day bow before him. These astronomical terms refer to the whole clan of Israel. Likewise, in Revelation 12:1 we encounter a metaphorical description of Israel as a woman with a "crown of twelve stars." The 12 stars represent the 12 tribes of Israel. We conclude, then, that Antiochus's trampling of the "host" and the "stars" refers to his trampling of the Jewish people. History reveals that Antiochus brutally persecuted the Jewish people from 170 to 164 BC.

As great as the Prince of the host (8:11): Our text tells us that Antiochus "became great, even as great as the Prince of the host." In other words, he set himself up as being great as the Most High God. This, of course, is not the first time in Daniel that a human leader imagined himself to be God. Recall how Nebuchadnezzar spoke of himself in divine terms (Daniel 2:1-7). Darius, too, was prayed to as a god for a time (6:6-9).

The regular burnt offering was taken away (8:11): Antiochus stopped the daily sacrifices in the Jewish temple, thereby halting Israel's religious practices, and also defiled the temple by slaughtering a pig in the Most Holy Place. He was apparently seeking to destroy the Jewish faith.

A host will be given over to it (8:12): This verse is difficult to interpret. The opening clause seems to indicate that Antiochus's activities against God and His people were divinely permitted by the Most High God—but only for a time (see verse 14). His rebellious stand against God and His people included prohibiting the daily sacrifices in the Jewish temple, apparently substituting some form of paganized worship, thus bringing great transgression against God.

It will throw truth to the ground (8:12): Antiochus trashed the Law of Moses, which was communicated to Moses by God. This act essentially amounted to trashing God. Speaking of Antiochus, 1 Maccabees 1:56-57 informs us, "The books of the law which they found they tore in pieces and burned with fire. Where the book of the covenant was found in the possession of anyone, or if anyone adhered to the law, the decree of the king condemned them to death."

It will act and prosper (8:12): Antiochus prospered in all his plans—but only for a time, according to the divine timetable (verse 14).

How long (8:13-14): One of God's angels—a "holy one"—announced that Antiochus's defiling of Israel and her temple would last only 2300 evenings and mornings—from 171 BC to 165 BC. In 164 BC, the temple would be rededicated by Judas Maccabeus.

Major Themes

1. *Susa.* Susa was a strategic diplomatic and administrative city in the Medo-Persian Empire, about 250 miles east of Babylon (Nehemiah 1:1; Esther 2:8; 3:15). The city's name comes from the word *shushan* ("lily") and refers to the abundance of lilies in the area. Ancient Susa was located in modern Iran. It was a well-developed city with a fortress. In the vision, Daniel saw himself in this city even though he wasn't there physically (just as Ezekiel had a vision of Jerusalem's temple even though he wasn't there physically—Ezekiel 8–11). Susa is the site where the Code of Hammurabi, an ancient law code, was discovered.

2. *The heavenly host.* One might initially be inclined to interpret the host of heaven as the realm of angels, for elsewhere in Scripture the angels are called the heavenly host (2 Chronicles 18:18; Psalm 148:2; Luke 2:13). In the present context, however, the host of heaven refers to God's people, the Jews, who were being horribly persecuted by Antiochus (see Genesis 15:5; Daniel 12:3). The stars being thrown to the ground metaphorically represents the fall of God's people under persecution. This

attack against God's people (the host of heaven) amounts to an attack against heaven itself.

Digging Deeper with Cross-References

The wicked resist the truth—Isaiah 59:4; Jeremiah 9:5; 2 Thessalonians 2:10; 1 Timothy 6:5; 2 Timothy 3:8

Rebellion—Deuteronomy 9:24; Psalm 32:1-2; 1 Samuel 15:23; 2 Thessalonians 2:3

Life Lessons

1. *Prolonged trials.* God's people sometimes go through sustained trials. This reality is especially reflected in the psalms: "My soul also is greatly troubled. But you, O LORD—how long?" (Psalm 6:3). "How long, O LORD? Will you forget me forever? How long will you hide your face from me?" (13:1). "How long, O Lord, will you look on? Rescue me from their destruction, my precious life from the lions!" (35:17; see also 74:10; 79:5; 80:4; 89:46; 90:13; 94:3; 119:84). The solution is for believers to patiently endure in the midst of the trials regardless of how long they last, knowing that even in our suffering, God is working good in our lives. Meditate on Deuteronomy 8:2,16; Psalms 66:10; 119:71; Isaiah 1:25; Ezekiel 14:11; John 15:2; 2 Corinthians 4:17; 12:7; Hebrews 12:5; 1 Peter 1:7.

2. *God's Word endures forever.* Daniel 8:12 tells us that one of Antiochus's transgressions was that truth was thrown to the ground, meaning that Antiochus destroyed some copies of Scripture—more specifically, scrolls of the Torah (see 1 Maccabees 1:56-57). (The Torah refers to the first five books of the Old Testament, all written by Moses.) Regardless of such acts, the Word of God cannot be destroyed. "The grass withers, the flower fades, but the word of our God will stand forever" (Isaiah 40:8). "The

word of the Lord remains forever" (1 Peter 1:25). Jesus affirmed, "Heaven and earth will pass away, but my words will not pass away" (Matthew 24:35). Aren't you thankful that God's Word is always with us?

Questions for Reflection and Discussion

1. What might be the reason God gave people visions that featured animals?

2. In what way do people "throw truth to the ground" today (Daniel 8:12)?

3. Why is God's absolute truth so important?

Details on Daniel's Vision

Daniel 8:15-27

Scripture Reading and Insights

Begin by reading Daniel 8:15-27 in your favorite Bible. As you read, notice how the Word of God is purifying your life (John 17:17-18).

Yesterday we considered some basic details of Daniel's vision relating to the rise of Antiochus Epiphanes. Today we will learn more about this disconcerting vision, which Daniel received during the third year of the reign of King Belshazzar. With your Bible still accessible, consider the following insights on the biblical text, verse by verse.

Daniel 8:15-16

I sought to understand it (8:15): In earlier years, Daniel had been the one to interpret mysteries of God to others. He interpreted two dreams for Nebuchadnezzar (Daniel 2:31-45; 4:19-27) and the handwriting on the wall for Belshazzar (5:13-31). But Daniel needed help interpreting his own dreams and visions.

One having the appearance of a man (8:15): Gabriel appeared to Daniel in the form of a man. This reminds us of Hebrews 13:2: "Do not neglect to show hospitality to strangers, for thereby some have entertained angels unawares." Angels can appear so realistically as human beings that they may actually be taken for human beings.

Gabriel (8:16): The angel Gabriel helped Daniel understand the vision. Gabriel is portrayed in Scripture as one who brings revelation to the people of God regarding God's purpose and program (Daniel 9:21; Luke 1:11-19,26-38).

Daniel 8:17-19

The vision is for the time of the end (8:17): "The time of the end" cannot refer only to the last days, when the antichrist emerges during the tribulation period. The vision also relates more immediately to Antiochus Epiphanes. This has led many Bible expositors to conclude that "the time of the end" has both a near and far fulfillment—near as it pertains to Antiochus Epiphanes, but far as it pertains to the antichrist and the last days.

I fell into a deep sleep (8:18): Daniel became weak in the presence of Gabriel—a common occurrence during heavenly visitations. (See Major Themes.)

He touched me (8:18): When Daniel became weak in Gabriel's presence, Gabriel touched him and made him stand up. One of the ministries of angels is to strengthen humans when there is a need. Psalm 91:11-12 promises that God's angels "will bear you up." Jesus experienced this in the Garden of Gethsemane, when He struggled under the tremendous weight of what was ahead of Him at the cross. After He prayed to the Father, an angel appeared from heaven and strengthened Him (Luke 22:43).

The appointed time of the end (8:19): God's plan of the ages unfolds according to a divine timetable (see, for example, Psalm 31:15; Ecclesiastes 3:1; John 7:6; Galatians 4:4).

Daniel 8:20-22

The ram...with the two horns (8:20): This is the Medo-Persian Empire. Recall from the previous lesson that one of the horns was longer than the other even though it came up after the other horn. This larger horn represents Persia, originally the weaker of the two nations but eventually the more dominant (see verse 3). Note that this is the same empire represented by the bear raised up on one side (7:5).

The goat (8:21): The goat represents Greece. (See notes on Daniel 8:5-7.)

The great horn (8:21): The large horn on the goat is the first king of Greece—Alexander the Great, who rapidly conquered the Medo-Persians and many others.

The horn that was broken, in place of which four others arose (8:22): Following Alexander's death, the Greek Empire was divided among four of Alexander's prominent generals. After some 22 years of fighting, Cassander ruled in Macedonia and Greece, Lysimachus reigned in Thrace and Asia Minor, Seleucus governed Syria and Babylon, and Ptolemy took over Egypt.

Daniel 8:23-25

A king of bold face (8:23): A bold and fierce Antiochus took the throne through deceit and guile. Note that some Bible expositors believe Antiochus was a *type* of the coming antichrist. A type is an Old Testament institution, event, person, object, or ceremony that has reality and purpose in biblical history but also by divine design foreshadows something yet to be revealed. Antiochus set himself up as God and defiled the Jewish temple, and the antichrist will do the same in the future tribulation period (see 2 Thessalonians 2:4). Antiochus was a fierce persecutor of the Jews, just as the antichrist will be.

His power shall be great (8:24): Antiochus's power was manifest in his conquests and subjugation of others.

But not by his own power (8:24): This comes through loud and clear in our passage: God is sovereign over and controls the nations of the world and their leaders. Psalm 113:4 tells us, "The LORD is high above all nations." "Kingship belongs to the LORD, and he rules over the nations" (Psalm 22:28). In Job 12:23 we read, "He makes nations great, and he destroys them; he enlarges nations, and leads them away." Jehoshaphat affirmed to God, "In your hand are power and might, so that none is able to withstand you" (2 Chronicles 20:6; see also Jeremiah 27:5-6). God, for His own sovereign purposes, allowed Antiochus to rise to power. God would also bring him down.

He shall cause fearful destruction (8:24): Antiochus intended to destroy not only the Jewish religion but also the Jews themselves.

He shall make deceit prosper (8:25): Antiochus was deceitful, cunning, full of guile, treacherous, and unscrupulous.

He shall destroy many (8:25): Many of those destroyed were Jewish people. In this way, Antiochus foreshadows the future antichrist.

He shall even rise up against the Prince of princes (8:25): As a pagan king who claimed divinity, Antiochus raised himself up against Israel's king, the Most High God, the Ruler of heaven and earth.

He shall be broken—but by no human hand (8:25): Just as Antiochus came into power according to God's divine providence, so he would be destroyed by God's hand. God is sovereign over the day a person dies. Job said to God, "[Man's] days are determined, and the number of his months is with you, and you have appointed his limits that he cannot pass" (Job 14:5; see also Psalm 139:16; Acts 17:26). Scripture also reveals that God sometimes inflicts premature death as a judgment (see Acts 5:1-10; 12:23; 1 Corinthians 11:30; 1 John 5:16).

Daniel 8:26-27

The evenings and the mornings (8:26): Antiochus would defile Israel and her temple for 2300 evenings and mornings—from 171 to 165 BC. In 164 BC, the temple would be rededicated by Judas Maccabeus.

Seal up the vision (8:26): Why did God tell Daniel, "Seal up the vision, for it refers to many days from now"? Some interpret this as meaning that Daniel shouldn't share the vision during Belshazzar's reign because some people might accuse Daniel of treason or insurrection. Others believe it means to "put away for safekeeping" (for future generations). Others say it means, "Keep the vision confidential for now because it pertains to the distant future and has little relevance for the present moment." Still others say the word simply means, "Conclude the vision."

I, Daniel, was overcome (8:27): Daniel said, "I was appalled by the vision and did not understand it." Daniel was sickened because he loved his fellow Jews, and he was saddened to become aware of the future that awaited them.

Major Themes

1. *Fainting with fear during heavenly encounters.* When Gabriel came near to Daniel, Daniel said, "I was frightened and fell on my face...I fell into a deep sleep with my face to the ground" (Daniel 8:17-18). We often witness men of God becoming weak-kneed and falling down in the presence of heavenly beings. It happened to Abram (Genesis 17:3), to Moses and Aaron (Numbers 16:22), to Ezekiel (Ezekiel 1:28), to John (Revelation 1:17), and to the apostle Paul (Acts 9:4).

2. *The prosperity of the wicked.* Scripture reveals that the evil Antiochus will seem to prosper for a time. This brings to mind the words of the psalmist: "I saw the prosperity of the wicked...They are not in trouble as others are; they are not stricken like the rest of mankind. Therefore pride is their necklace...They set their mouths against the heavens" (Psalm 73:3-9). If this were the end of the story, then all would be vanity. But the truth is, the wicked fall hard in the end. The psalmist affirmed to God, "You make them fall to ruin. How they are destroyed in a moment, swept away utterly by terrors" (verses 18-19). Antiochus may have prospered for a time, but he fell hard and permanently.

Digging Deeper with Cross-References

The time of the end—1 Timothy 4:1; 2 Timothy 3:1–4:5; James 5:3; 2 Peter 3:3; Jude 18

Self-exaltation—Proverbs 3:34; 8:13; 16:5,18-19; 18:12; 21:4; Isaiah 13:11; Ezekiel 28:2; Daniel 4:37; Matthew 23:12; Luke 18:11; 20:46; Romans 12:16; Philippians 2:3; 2 Timothy 3:2; James 4:6; 1 Peter 5:5

The persecution of the saints—Proverbs 29:27; Matthew 5:10,44; 10:21; Luke 6:22-23; Acts 8:1-4; 11:19; 2 Corinthians 6:5; 11:23; 1 Thessalonians 2:14-15; 2 Timothy 1:12; 2:9; 3:12; 1 Peter 3:17; 1 John 3:13; Revelation 2:10

Life Lessons

1. *The full measure of sin.* Daniel 8:23 refers to transgressors who "have reached their limit." This reminds us of the scriptural teaching that once the fullness of sin has come about in a person or a nation, God takes action. In Genesis 15:16, God explained why He did not judge the Amorites immediately: "The iniquity of the Amorites is not yet complete." First Peter 3:20 reveals that before the worldwide flood, the wicked "did not obey, when God's patience waited in the days of Noah." God's patience lasted only so long, and then He acted. In Revelation 2:21 we read Christ's assessment of Jezebel: "I gave her time to repent, but she refuses to repent of her sexual immorality." As Christians, we all ought to repent and confess sin as soon as we become aware of it in our lives (Psalm 32:1-5; 1 John 1:9).

2. *God's purpose for futuristic prophecy.* Out of the 23,210 verses in the Old Testament, 6641 (28.5 percent) are prophetic. The New Testament contains 7914 verses, and 1711 (21.5 percent) are prophetic. Merging the Old and New Testaments together, 8352 of the Bible's 31,124 verses are prophetic. That comes to 27 percent of the Bible—more than one-fourth—being prophecy. God did not give us all this prophecy so we'd have mere head knowledge of what the future holds. Rather, there are underlying themes in prophecy that are life-changing. For example, prophecy demonstrates that God is sovereign over human history. It assures us that God will triumph over evil. Prophecy causes us to yearn for the soon coming of Jesus Christ. It gives us a powerful hope for reuniting with our Christian loved ones in heaven. It gives us an exalted view of Jesus Christ. Prophecy gives us a strong sense of the trustworthiness of the Bible.

Questions for Reflection and Discussion

1. What do you learn about God's awesome sovereignty in our passage?

2. What have you learned about God's patience toward human sin in this lesson?

3. Can you relate to how Daniel reacted to the vision?

Daniel Prays for His People, Part 1

Daniel 9:1-7

Scripture Reading and Insights

Begin by reading Daniel 9:1-7 in your favorite Bible. As you read, remember that God's Word is the true source of hope (Psalm 119:81).

Yesterday we concluded our study of Daniel's second vision, which indicated hard times are ahead for the Jewish people. In today's reading, Daniel prays for his people. With your Bible still accessible, consider the following insights on the biblical text, verse by verse.

Daniel 9:1-2

In the first year of Darius the son of Ahasuerus (9:1): This was the first year of the reign of Darius the Mede, which would have been about 538 BC. This was about 67 years after Daniel had been taken captive in Babylon along with his three Hebrew friends. Daniel would have been more than 80 years old at this time.

I, Daniel, perceived in the books (9:2): Daniel is referring specifically to the book of Jeremiah, completed about a generation prior to the events described in Daniel 9. The prophet Daniel recognized from Jeremiah 25:11-13 and 29:10 that Jerusalem's desolation was to last only 70 years. The first wave of Jews were taken captive in 605 BC, and it was now 538 BC, so the 70-year period was almost over. The Jews in Babylon would soon be free.

We can make an interesting observation here. The book of Jeremiah had not been written for very long, but Daniel already considered it to be Scripture. This goes against the modern liberal allegation that the books of Scripture were not determined until much later by various councils.

Daniel 9:3

Prayer and pleas (9:3): Because his people were about to be released from captivity, Daniel sought the Lord "by prayer and pleas for mercy." After all, Daniel wanted his people not only to be released from bondage to Babylon but also to be fully restored to God. He wanted his people to make a fresh start with God, which would necessarily include repentance of sin. No doubt recalling the Law of Moses, Daniel knew that obedience to God brings blessing from God, whereas disobedience to God brings discipline from God (compare with Deuteronomy 28:48-57,64-68). Daniel desired to see an end to the present discipline from God.

Daniel's prayer was accompanied by fasting, sackcloth, and ashes— Hebrew means of expressing grief and contrition for the sins of his people (see Genesis 37:34; Nehemiah 9:1-2; Job 2:12-13). We will see that throughout the prayer, Daniel did not separate himself from his people, but rather included himself in the prayer of confession.

Daniel 9:4-5

Made confession (9:4): The first step in restoration to God is the confession of sin. Though the Jews had rebelled against God and had consequently landed themselves in captivity as a divine discipline, God has a long track record of showing mercy to those who confess their sins. Proverbs 28:13 tells us, "Whoever conceals his transgressions will not prosper, but he who confesses and forsakes them will obtain mercy." Deuteronomy 4:31 reminds us, "The LORD your God is a merciful God." As we discover in Lamentations 3:22-23, "The steadfast love of the LORD never ceases; his mercies never come to an end; they are new every morning." Following a great sin, David prayed, "Have mercy on me, O God, according to your steadfast love; according to your abundant mercy blot out my transgressions" (Psalm 51:1).

O Lord, the great and awesome God (9:4): God had repeatedly demonstrated just how awesome He was among the Jews in captivity. Highlights included God's rescue of the three Hebrew youths from the fiery furnace (Daniel 3:23-26) and His rescue of Daniel in the lions' den (6:16-28).

God, who keeps covenant and steadfast love (9:4): The Old Testament consistently emphasizes that God, in His faithful covenant love, will ultimately restore and bless His wayward people. He will eventually turn away His anger and shower love upon them. His people had been unfaithful, but God Himself is always faithful.

Those who love him and keep his commandments (9:4): Notice the strong connection between love for God and obedience to Him. In Exodus 20:5-6 God said, "I the LORD your God am a jealous God...showing steadfast love to thousands of those who love me and keep my commandments." In Deuteronomy 7:9 God affirmed, "Know therefore that the LORD your God is God, the faithful God who keeps covenant and steadfast love with those who love him and keep his commandments, to a thousand generations." He also affirmed to His people, "Because you listen to these rules and keep and do them, the LORD your God will keep with you the covenant and the steadfast love that he swore to your fathers" (Deuteronomy 7:12). Nehemiah referred to God as "the great and awesome God who keeps covenant and steadfast love with those who love him and keep his commandments" (Nehemiah 1:5). (See Life Lessons.)

We have sinned (9:5): Notice two things here. First, as noted previously, Daniel included himself in the confession of sin even though his personal behavior had been praiseworthy. Daniel was identifying with his people in order to more effectively intercede on their behalf before God. Second, notice the comprehensive description of the Jews' wrongdoing: "We have sinned and done wrong and acted wickedly and rebelled, turning aside from your commandments and rules."

The word "sin" carries the idea of "missing the mark." The target was God's Law contained in God's Word, but the Jews had consistently missed the mark by a wide margin. The phrase "done wrong" carries the idea of committing a bent or twisted act. Instead of walking the straight and narrow path, they had deviated from God's requirements. The phrase "turning aside from your commandments and rules" carries the idea of scorning God's commandments and rules. In short, the Jewish people had woefully rebelled against God (compare with Psalm 106:6; Isaiah 53:6).

Daniel 9:6

We have not listened (9:6): Daniel conceded that his people had not listened to the prophets, who were God's servants. We are reminded of Jeremiah 7:25-26, where God lamented, "From the day that your fathers came out of the land of Egypt to this day, I have persistently sent all my servants the prophets to them, day after day. Yet they did not listen to me or incline their ear, but stiffened their neck." God's lament is also recorded for us in Psalm 81:13: "Oh, that my people would listen to me, that Israel would walk in my ways."

The word "prophet"—from the Hebrew word *nabi*—refers to a spokesman for God who either declares God's message regarding a contemporary situation to humankind, or foretells God's actions based on divine revelation. The predictive role is often stressed, but the Bible equally emphasizes the teaching function. Both aspects require communication from God to the prophet (see 2 Samuel 7:27; Jeremiah 23:18). In the present context, God's prophets call Israel to repentance as well as prophesy about her future.

Daniel 9:7

To you, O Lord, belongs righteousness (9:7): Righteousness is among the most important attributes of God. The Scriptures portray God as singularly righteous, with no hint of unrighteousness. We read, "Righteous are you, O LORD" (Jeremiah 12:1). "The LORD is righteous; he loves righteous deeds" (Psalm 11:7). "He loves righteousness and justice" (Psalm 33:5). "Righteousness and justice are the foundation of your throne" (Psalm 89:14). Daniel acknowledged to God that He had been perfectly righteous and just in disciplining the Jews, for the Jews had been utterly rebellious against God. Daniel knew that his people got just what they deserved.

But to us open shame (9:7): This carries the idea of public shame of face—that is, one is so shamed by something that one has a look of embarrassment and humiliation on his or her face, a shame that others witness firsthand. We might translate it "public shame." The New Living Translation puts it nicely: "Our faces are covered with shame."

The lands to which you have driven them (9:7): The Lord had earlier warned His people that if they turned from His law and rebelled against Him, "The LORD will bring you and your king whom you set over you to a nation that neither you nor your fathers have known...You shall father sons and daughters, but they shall not be yours, for they shall go into captivity...because you did not obey the voice of the LORD your God, to keep his commandments and his statutes that he commanded you" (Deuteronomy 28:36-45; see also verses 49-68). God had given them plenty of time to repent, but they remained hard-hearted against Him.

Treachery (9:7): This word carries the idea of disloyalty. God had previously called His people to be loyal to His covenant. Instead, they were disloyal and therefore treacherous.

Major Themes

1. *Expressions of mourning.* Daniel's "sackcloth and ashes" were expressions of intense mourning (Daniel 9:3). Mourners often wore sackcloth and put ashes on their heads (see Genesis 37:34; Nehemiah 9:1; Esther 4:1,3; Isaiah 58:5; Jeremiah 49:3; Ezekiel 7:18; Joel 1:8; Matthew 11:21). Daniel's mourning was rooted in the sins of his people. He knew these sins had brought judgment from God.

2. *God is a promise keeper.* This is a thread that runs through this passage and, in fact, all of Scripture. Numbers 23:19 asserts, "God is not a man, that he should lie, or a son of man, that he should change his mind. Has he said, and will he not do it? Or has he spoken, and will he not fulfill it?" Prior to his death, an aged Joshua declared, "Now I am

about to go the way of all the earth, and you know in your hearts and souls, all of you, that not one word has failed of all the good things that the LORD your God promised concerning you. All have come to pass for you; not one of them has failed" (Joshua 23:14). Solomon later proclaimed, "Blessed be the LORD who has given rest to his people Israel, according to all that he promised. Not one word has failed of all his good promise, which he spoke by Moses his servant" (1 Kings 8:56; see Joshua 21:45).

Digging Deeper with Cross-References

The importance of searching God's Word—Deuteronomy 17:19; Isaiah 34:16; Matthew 19:4; 22:31; Luke 10:26; John 5:39; Acts 8:28; 17:11; Romans 15:4; 1 Timothy 4:13; Revelation 22:19

The shame of sin—Genesis 3:7,10; Ezra 9:6; Job 8:22; Psalm 44:15; Proverbs 13:18; Jeremiah 3:25; Ezekiel 7:18; Luke 15:19

Confession of sin—Psalms 32:3,5; 38:18; 51:4; Proverbs 28:13; 1 John 1:9

Life Lessons

1. *Prayer and fasting.* Previously in the book I noted that the word "fast" is rooted in a Hebrew word that means "cover the mouth," thus indicating abstinence from food and/or drink. During fasts, people were to humble their souls before God while abstaining from food. Fasting goes hand in hand with fervent prayer. This was the case with Daniel (Daniel 9:3). He so wanted to intercede on his people's behalf that he denied himself food. You and I, too, can engage in prayer and fasting on occasion, especially when facing a major crisis (see Exodus 34:28; 1 Samuel 7:6; 2 Samuel 3:35; Matthew 4:2; 6:16).

2. *Love and obedience.* Daniel refers to those "who love him and keep his commandments" (Daniel 9:4). Scripture often draws a connection between love for God and obedience to Him. In the New Testament, Jesus informed His followers, "If you love me, you will keep my commandments...Whoever has my commandments and keeps them, he it is who loves me" (John 14:15,21). Closely related to this, 1 John 2:3 tells us, "By this we know that we have come to know him, if we keep his commandments" (compare with John 15:10).

Questions for Reflection and Discussion

1. Do you make a habit of expressing your love to God by obeying Him?

2. Have you ever fasted during a crisis? If so, did you find it fruitful?

3. Did today's lesson motivate you to deal with any sin that may yet linger in your life?

Daniel Prays for His People, Part 2

Daniel 9:8-19

Scripture Reading and Insights

Begin by reading Daniel 9:8-19 in your favorite Bible. As you read, remember that great spiritual wisdom comes from studying God's Word (Psalm 119:98-104).

In yesterday's reading, we were introduced to Daniel's prayer for his people. In today's lesson, we continue our study of Daniel's prayer. With your Bible still accessible, consider the following insights on the biblical text, verse by verse.

Daniel 9:8

Open shame (9:8): When something is repeated in consecutive verses in the Bible, the author is strongly emphasizing a point. Recall that in the previous verse, Daniel said to God, "To you, O Lord, belongs righteousness, but to us open shame." He repeats himself in verse 8: "To us, O Lord, belongs open shame." The repetition indicates that Daniel was lamenting and grieving over the dire state of his people.

To our kings, to our princes, and to our fathers (9:8): No one is exempt from condemnation. Guilt for sin ranges from the top leadership down to the common person. All are liable before God. There is none righteous. (See Major Themes.)

Daniel 9:9-10

Mercy and forgiveness (9:9): When used of God, the term "mercy" indicates God's compassion and kindness. It includes the withholding of deserved punishment. Daniel knew his people were guilty of gross sin, so he appealed to God to withhold the judgment they deserved. He appealed to God's mercy.

Mercy is closely connected to forgiveness. Again, Daniel knew his people were guilty. That is why they had been subjected to captivity in Babylon. Now that the captivity was coming to an end, Daniel appealed to God to forgive the Jews. Daniel desired for his people to begin anew with a clean slate from God.

Have not obeyed the voice of the LORD *(9:10)*: How were God's voice and His laws communicated? Through God's prophets, who were His mouthpieces in Old Testament times. But the Jews predominantly ignored the warnings of the prophets.

> The LORD warned Israel and Judah by every prophet and every seer, saying, "Turn from your evil ways and keep my commandments and my statutes, in accordance with all the Law that I commanded your fathers, and that I sent to you by my servants the prophets." But they would not listen, but were stubborn, as their fathers had been, who did not believe in the LORD their God. They despised his statutes and his covenant that he made with their fathers and the warnings that he gave them (2 Kings 17:13-15).

Daniel 9:11-15

All Israel has transgressed (9:11): When Daniel said, "All Israel has transgressed your law and turned aside," we are reminded of what Daniel said just previously: "To us, O LORD, belongs open shame, to our kings, to our princes, and to our fathers" (verse 8). All Israel—from the top of the social ladder to the bottom—had sinned against God.

The curse and oath (9:11): As a result of their unrepentant sin, the Jews suffered the "curse and oath that are written in the Law of Moses" (see Leviticus 26:21-42; Deuteronomy 28:15-68). The Jews had the choice of obedience or disobedience. Their continued disobedience caused them to suffer the curse. Had they rendered obedience to God, they would have experienced great blessings (see Leviticus 26:3-13; Deuteronomy 28:1-14). This illustrates the age-old maxim that choices have consequences—sometimes severe consequences.

We should note that God offered grace even in the midst of His chastisement of the Jews. If His people would only repent, He would bring upon them renewed blessing (Leviticus 26:40-42).

We should also be mindful that the purpose of God's chastising of His people was never to get even. Rather it was to cause His people to repent and turn back to Him. God's chastisement is like a divine form of parental discipline.

He has confirmed his words (9:12): God had promised His people that if they sinned against Him and refused to repent, they would experience captivity at the hands of foreign nations as well as other manifestations of the curse (Leviticus 26:21-39; Deuteronomy 28:15-68). God "confirmed his words" by sending His people into captivity in Babylon.

A great calamity (9:12): Daniel lamented, "Under the whole heaven there has not been done anything like what has been done against Jerusalem." God's disciplinary act of using the Babylonians as His whipping rod against Israel during the captivity was unique in all of history. God dealt with the Jews as no other people had ever been dealt with.

As it is written in the Law of Moses (9:13): The main point here is that Israel had been warned. God, through the Law of Moses, had instructed His people about the connection between behavior and consequences: Obey God and be blessed, or disobey God and be cursed. Despite God's clear instructions and warnings, the Jews chose not to remain faithful to God and fell into gross sin.

Yet we have not entreated the favor of the LORD our God (9:13): To add insult to injury—that is, to add to their earlier sins—Israel had now failed to turn to God in prayer. Despite God's chastising judgment, there had been no repentance, no revival, and no restoration to God. The people simply persisted in their evil ways. Daniel recognized that because the people had spurned the mercy of God, God had no other recourse than to bring discipline upon Israel. This is why, in the verses that follow, Daniel pled for mercy and forgiveness for his people.

The LORD has kept ready the calamity (9:14): God's disciplinary hand has always been at the ready to deal with His rebellious child, Israel.

The LORD our God is righteous (9:14): Daniel repeated the contrast between God's righteousness and Israel's disobedience. God dealt with Israel with justice. There had been no unfair treatment.

Who brought your people out of the land of Egypt (9:15): Recall from verses 4-5 that Daniel had spoken of "the great and awesome God" and then acknowledged the great sin of His people Israel. Daniel now essentially repeats all this, affirming that God delivered His people from Egyptian bondage with a mighty hand and admitting, "We have sinned, we have done wickedly." God is great, but we have sinned! The idea is this: "God, you have honored Yourself by delivering us from Egypt, but now we have dishonored You by our sin."

Daniel 9:16-19

Let your anger and your wrath turn away (9:16): Daniel appealed to God's faithful mercies to turn from His displeasure with Israel because of her sins. After all, the neighboring nations were mocking and laughing at Israel's suffering under her load of guilt. These nations were also apparently mocking Israel's God, claiming He was impotent, utterly unable to deliver the Jews from Babylonian bondage. Daniel appealed to God to forgive Israel and to vindicate Himself in the eyes of neighboring nations.

Listen to the prayer of your servant (9:17): There is a strong sense of urgency in Daniel's prayer here and in the following verses. "Incline your ear and hear" (verse 18). "O Lord, hear; O Lord, forgive. O Lord, pay attention and act" (verse 19). Don't miss the passion in Daniel's voice. He is crying out to the Lord on behalf of his people.

For your own sake, O Lord (9:17): This carries the idea, "Renew Your honor in the eyes of neighboring pagan nations, who think of You as weak and unable to help us."

Open your eyes and see (9:18): In other words, "Open Your eyes with a view to moving Your mighty hand on our behalf."

Your great mercy (9:18): Daniel's appeal is not based on Israel being deserving of God's response. Rather it's based entirely on God's mercy and compassion (compare with Exodus 34:6; Jonah 4:1-3; Micah 6:8).

Pay attention and act. Delay not (9:19): By God's providence, it was not long after this that King Cyrus issued a decree allowing the Jewish people to return to Judea (see Ezra 1:1-4). A new temple was built, completed by 515 BC. God answered Daniel's prayer on behalf of his people.

Major Themes

1. *Universal sin.* In Daniel's confession, he says to God, "All Israel has transgressed your law and turned aside" (Daniel 9:11). Scripture consistently teaches the universality of sin. "All we like sheep have gone astray; we have turned—every one—to his own way" (Isaiah 53:6). "Surely there is not a righteous man on earth who does good and never sins" (Ecclesiastes 7:20). "If we say we have no sin, we deceive ourselves, and the truth is not in us" (1 John 1:8). This obviously includes you and me.

2. *Just retribution.* In the context of God punishing Israel for her sins, Daniel affirmed, "The Lord our God is righteous in all the works that he has done, and we have not obeyed his voice" (Daniel 9:14). God brought just retribution on the sinful Jewish people. God's just retribution is a common theme in Scripture. In Isaiah 42:24 we read, "Who gave up Jacob to the looter, and Israel to the plunderers? Was it not the LORD, against whom we have sinned, in whose ways they would not walk, and whose law they would not obey?" God had promised, "Thus says the Lord GOD: I will deal with you as you have done" (Ezekiel 16:59). God also says, "I the LORD search the heart and test the mind, to give every man according to his ways, according to the fruit of his deeds" (Jeremiah 17:10).

Digging Deeper with Cross-References

Impenitence—1 Samuel 15:23; Psalms 52:7; 78:8; 81:11-12; 95:8; 106:25; Proverbs 1:24; Isaiah 48:4,8; Jeremiah 5:21; 7:13; 16:12; 44:10; Hosea 4:17; Acts 7:51; Hebrews 3:8

God's delays according to the psalms—Psalms 6:3; 13:1; 40:17; 69:3; 70:5; 119:82

Life Lessons

1. *God's forgiveness.* A popular Old Testament passage on the forgiveness of sins is Psalm 103:11-12: "For as high as the heavens are above the earth, so great is his steadfast love toward those who fear him; as far as the east is from the west, so far does he remove our transgressions from us." There is a definite point that is north and another that is south—the North and South Poles. But there are no such points for east and west. Regardless of how far one goes to the east, one will never arrive where east begins because by definition east is the opposite of west. The two never meet. They never will meet and never could meet because they are defined as opposites. To remove sins "as far as the east is from the west" is by definition to put them where no one can ever find them. That is the kind of forgiveness Daniel sought for his people Israel.

2. *Urgency in prayer.* Notice the sense of urgency in Daniel's prayer. "Now therefore, O our God, listen to the prayer of your servant and to his pleas...incline your ear and hear...pay attention and act. Delay not" (verses 17-19). This brings to mind James 5:16: "The urgent request of a righteous person is very powerful in its effect" (HCSB). The word "urgent" in this verse carries the idea of "earnest" or "heartfelt." You and I, too, ought always to offer up earnest and heartfelt prayers to God.

Questions for Reflection and Discussion

1. What did you learn about prayer that most impacted you from today's lesson?

2. Does God's just retribution scare you or comfort you?

3. Do you intellectually agree that God has forgiven you? Do you actually *feel* forgiven? What did you learn from Psalm 103:11-12 that could help you connect your understanding and your emotions?

Daniel Prophesies About the 70 Weeks

Daniel 9:20-27

Scripture Reading and Insights

Begin by reading Daniel 9:20-27 in your favorite Bible. As you read, remember that reading Scripture can strengthen your faith in God (Romans 10:17).

In the previous lesson, we finished our study of Daniel's intercessory prayer for his people. In today's lesson, we zero in on Daniel's prophecy of the 70 weeks. With your Bible still accessible, consider the following insights on the biblical text, verse by verse.

Daniel 9:20-21

While I was speaking and praying...the man Gabriel...came to me in swift flight (9:20-21): The amazing thing about this text is how fast Daniel's prayer was answered. Daniel was still praying—confessing Israel's sins and petitioning God for the restoration of his people—when the angel Gabriel suddenly appeared. Of course, Daniel had just requested God, "Delay not" (verse 19). And now Gabriel arrives "in swift flight."

We are reminded of what God said in Isaiah 65:24: "Before they call I will answer; while they are yet speaking I will hear." God likewise affirmed in Isaiah 58:9, "Then you shall call, and the LORD will answer; you shall cry, and he will say, 'Here I am.'"

Notice that the angel Gabriel is called a man in this text because he took on the appearance of a man (compare with Daniel 8:16; Hebrews 13:2).

The holy hill of my God (9:20): This refers to Jerusalem. Recall God's words in Psalm 2:6: "As for me, I have set my King on Zion, my holy hill." Jerusalem's temple rested on a hill. Because the temple itself was holy, the hill was therefore considered holy as well.

At the time of the evening sacrifice (9:21): The Mosaic Law required both a morning and an evening sacrifice (Exodus 29:39-40; Numbers 28:3-4). The Jewish temple had been destroyed, making these sacrifices impossible. Daniel nevertheless reserved this time for prayer to God, thereby indicating his reverence for God. This was likely one of the three times Daniel prayed each day (see Daniel 6:10).

Daniel 9:22-23

I have now come out to give you insight and understanding (9:22): Gabriel came to inform Daniel what lay ahead in the immediate and distant future for his people. Recall that Gabriel is often portrayed in Scripture as bringing revelation to God's people regarding God's purpose and program. This is the second time he appeared to Daniel (see 8:16). Five hundred years later he told Zechariah about the upcoming birth of John the Baptist, and soon after that he announced the birth of Jesus to the Virgin Mary (Luke 1:11-17,26-38).

At the beginning of your pleas (9:23): Gabriel informed Daniel, "At the beginning of your pleas for mercy a word went out, and I have come to tell it to you." Bible expositors have suggested two possibilities as to what this word was. The word may have related to God's sovereign decree to end Israel's exile and allow the Jews to return to Jerusalem. Or the word may simply have been God's instruction to Gabriel to appear to Daniel and explain the future to him. The latter view seems to best fit the context.

You are greatly loved (9:23): The phrase "greatly loved" is rich in the original Hebrew. The Holman Christian Standard Bible translates it, "You are treasured by God." The New Living Translation renders it, "You are very precious to God." The Amplified Bible renders it, "You are greatly beloved."

Daniel 9:24

Seventy weeks are decreed about your people and your holy city (9:24): Gabriel gave a real mouthful of revelation to Daniel in this verse. He provided Daniel a prophetic timetable for the nation of Israel. It was divided into 70 groups of 7 years, totaling 490 years. At the end of these 490 years, six things will occur.

1. Israel's apostasy will end at the second coming of Jesus Christ, when she repents of her rejection of Jesus Christ as divine Messiah.

2. Israel's sin will be removed, now having trusted in Jesus Christ (see Ezekiel 37:23; Romans 11:20-27).

3. As Israel repents of her rejection of Jesus Christ at the second coming, the atonement He wrought at the cross will bring salvation to the Jews.

4. Christ will bring about perfect righteousness in His covenant people in the millennial kingdom (see Isaiah 60:21; Jeremiah 23:5-6).

5. All the covenant promises to Israel in the Old Testament will be "sealed"—that is, fully realized in the millennial kingdom. (In this context, an "unsealed" prophecy is an unfulfilled prophecy.)

6. The Most Holy Place in the millennial kingdom will be consecrated (see Ezekiel 41–46).

Daniel 9:25-26

Seven weeks...sixty-two weeks (9:25-26): Gabriel provided some rather complex details about both the immediate future and the more distant end-times future. Here is the gist of what is important to grasp: Gabriel informed Daniel about 70 weeks of years. A week of years is 7 years, so 70 weeks of years comes to a total of 490 years.

Gabriel spoke of 7 weeks of years followed by 62 weeks of years. Seven weeks plus 62 weeks adds up to 69 weeks of years. And what is

69 weeks of years? It comes to 483 years (69 multiplied by 7). Here is the important point: Gabriel indicated that there was to be a 483-year period from the issuing of a decree to rebuild Jerusalem to the time the Messiah comes (that is, the first coming of Jesus Christ, not the second coming). The day Jesus rode into Jerusalem on a donkey to proclaim Himself Israel's Messiah was 483 years to the day after the command to restore and rebuild Jerusalem had been given.

After the sixty-two weeks (9:26): At the coming of the Messiah, God's prophetic clock was to stop. Daniel described a gap between these 483 years and the final 7 years of Israel's prophetic timetable.

Several events were to take place during this gap, according to Daniel 9:26:

1. The Messiah will be killed (or "cut off").

2. The city of Jerusalem and its temple would be destroyed (which occurred in AD 70).

3. The Jews would encounter difficulty and hardship from that time on.

Daniel 9:27

He shall make a strong covenant (9:27): The final week of seven years will begin for Israel in the end-times future when the antichrist confirms a covenant for seven years. When this peace pact is signed, the tribulation period will begin. That signature marks the beginning of a seven-year countdown to the second coming of Christ, which follows the tribulation period.

For half of the week he shall put an end to sacrifice and offering (9:27): Scripture reveals that the Jews will rebuild their temple during the first part of the seven-year tribulation period (Daniel 9:27; 12:11; Matthew 24:15-16). The Jewish sacrificial system will be reinstated. But in the middle of the tribulation period, the antichrist will put a stop to Jewish sacrifices. From then on, no one on earth will be permitted to worship anyone but the antichrist. The antichrist will set himself up as deity and demand worship from all on earth (see 2 Thessalonians 2:4).

In this way, the antichrist will take on the character of Satan, who energizes him (see Isaiah 14:12-17; Ezekiel 28:11-19; 2 Thessalonians 2:9).

One who makes desolate (9:27): Later, in Daniel 11:31, we read of the antichrist, "Forces from him shall appear and profane the temple and fortress, and shall take away the regular burnt offering. And they shall set up the abomination that makes desolate." We find further clarity on this "abomination that makes desolate" in the New Testament. It will take place at the midpoint of the future tribulation period when the antichrist—the "man of lawlessness" (2 Thessalonians 2:3)—sets up an image of himself inside the Jewish temple (see Matthew 24:15). This amounts to the antichrist enthroning himself in the place of deity, displaying himself as God (compare with Isaiah 14:13-14; Ezekiel 28:2-9). This blasphemous act will utterly desecrate the temple, making it abominable and therefore desolate. The antichrist—the world dictator—will then demand that the world worship and pay idolatrous homage to him. Any who refuse will be persecuted, and many will be martyred.

Major Themes

1. *Strong covenant.* Daniel 9:24-27 contains an important prophecy in reference to the future seven-year tribulation period. This period begins when the antichrist signs a covenant with Israel: "He shall make a strong covenant with many for one week" (verse 27). Crucial to our present study is the fact that the seven years (the "one week") that follow the signing of this agreement will be the seven worst years of human history (see Isaiah 24:1-4,20-21; 26:20-21; Jeremiah 30:7; Joel 1:15; Amos 5:18; Zephaniah 1:15,18; Revelation 14:7). This means that in the end times, the antichrist will seem to have solved the Middle East problem—but only for a time. At the midpoint of the tribulation, he will double-cross the Jews, who will be forced to flee for their lives out of Jerusalem (Matthew 24:16-20).

2. *The abomination of desolation.* In the book of Daniel, the term "abomination of desolation" conveys the outrage and horror of a barbaric act of idolatry inside God's holy temple (Daniel 9:27; 11:31; 12:11). This abomination will apparently take place at the midpoint of the future tribulation period when the antichrist—the "man of lawlessness" (2 Thessalonians 2:3)—sets up an image of himself inside the Jewish temple (Daniel 9:27; Matthew 24:15). Such an abomination took place once before in Israel's history. Antiochus Epiphanes desecrated the Jewish temple by erecting an altar to Zeus in it and then sacrificing a pig—an unclean animal—on it.

Digging Deeper with Cross-References

Prayers answered— Genesis 17:20; 19:21; 25:21; 30:22; Exodus 8:31; 32:7-14; 33:17; Judges 3:9; 13:9; 1 Samuel 1:20,27; 1 Kings 9:3; 17:22; 1 Chronicles 4:10; Ezra 8:23; Psalms 21:2; 118:5; Luke 1:13

Names and titles of Christ—Isaiah 7:14; 9:6; Matthew 1:1,23; 16:20; Mark 14:61; Luke 9:20; 23:2; John 1:29,41; 6:48; 8:12; 10:11; 15:1; Ephesians 2:20; 5:23; Colossians 1:18; 1 Timothy 2:5; Titus 2:13; Hebrews 4:14; 6:20; 13:20; 1 Peter 2:4; 2 Peter 1:1; Revelation 1:8,17; 3:14; 5:5; 19:11,16; 22:13

Life Lessons

1. *Gabriel.* The name Gabriel literally means "mighty one of God." It speaks of Gabriel's incredible power as endowed by God. His high rank in the angelic realm is obvious from both his name and his continuous standing in the presence of God (Luke 1:19). When carrying out God's bidding, Gabriel apparently has the ability to fly swiftly—perhaps faster than the other angels (Daniel 9:21). Scripture

portrays Gabriel as the deliverer of revelation to God's people regarding God's purpose and program (Daniel 8:16-17; 9:21; Luke 1:11-17,26-38).

2. *The Anointed One—Jesus the Messiah.* The word "Messiah" comes from the Hebrew term *masiah*, which means "the anointed one." The Greek parallel to this term is "Christ" (*christos*). That the terms are equated is clear from John 1:41: "[Andrew] found his own brother Simon and said to him, 'We have found the Messiah' (which means Christ)." Hundreds of Old Testament messianic prophecies point to the coming of the Messiah, Jesus Christ (for example, Isaiah 7:14; 9:1-7; 11:2-5; 52:13–53:12). Jesus made His identity as the Christ the primary issue of faith (Matthew 16:13-20; John 11:25-27). He warned that others would come falsely claiming to be the Christ (Matthew 24:4-5,23-24).

Questions for Reflection and Discussion

1. Why is it important for us to confess our sins to God, as Daniel did (Daniel 9:20)? What insight does 1 John 1:9 give you?

2. Do you think an angel has ever intervened in your life? Why or why not?

3. What impacts you most from the cross-references on answered prayer?

Daniel Is Visited by an Angel

Daniel 10:1-9

Scripture Reading and Insights

Begin by reading Daniel 10:1-9 in your favorite Bible. As you read, keep in mind that God desires for you not only to hear His Word but also to do it (James 1:22).

In yesterday's lesson, we considered Daniel's prophecy of the 70 weeks. Now let's look at a preliminary introduction to Daniel's special visitation from an angel, which we'll continue to study in the next lesson. With your Bible still accessible, consider the following insights on the biblical text, verse by verse.

Daniel 10:1

The third year of Cyrus king of Persia (10:1): This would be 536 BC. Daniel's prayer to God had been answered. The Jewish exile in Babylon was over. By now two years had elapsed since the first decree to allow the Jews to go back to Jerusalem (see Ezra 1:1–2:1; 2:64–3:1). A remnant of Jews returned to Judea under Zerubbabel and Jeshua's leadership. These Jews were now laying the foundations of the second temple (see Ezra 3).

Meanwhile, Daniel remained in Babylon, perhaps because he was less mobile at 84 years old. While still in Babylon, he received a "word" and a "vision" about Israel's future.

Who was named Belteshazzar (10:1): Recall from chapter 1 that

Daniel and his friends all had Jewish names that honored the one true God of Israel. Daniel's name, for example, means "God has judged," or perhaps "God is my Judge." (The ending of Daniel's name, *el*, is a Hebrew term for God.) The Babylonians believed their gods were superior to Israel's God, so Daniel and his friends were given Babylonian names to honor Babylonian deities. Daniel was renamed Belteshazzar, meaning "Bel, protect his life," or "Bel, protect the king's life." (Bel was a Babylonian deity.)

The word was true (10:1): "The word" Daniel received was quite obviously true because it was a revelation from God. In syllogism form: God is true; revelation is from God; therefore revelation is true.

It was a great conflict (10:1): Daniel had earlier been prophetically made aware of the end-times conflicts that awaited his people (Daniel 7:21,25; 8:24-25; 9:27). He knew of the significant persecution that would fall on them at the hands of the "little horn," who is the antichrist (8:10-14). Now the new word given to Daniel was also "a great conflict." The phrase "great conflict" can be translated "great warfare" or "great suffering." Daniel was distressed to hear that pain and suffering lie ahead for the Jews of Israel. Details of this particular suffering are found in Daniel 11:2–12:3, which we will examine in a later lesson.

He understood the word and had understanding of the vision (10:1): This is in noted contrast to Daniel's visions recorded in Daniel 7–8, which Daniel needed help to understand.

Daniel 10:2-3

Mourning for three weeks (10:2): Bible expositors offer various explanations as to why Daniel mourned. Some say he mourned as a result of the visions he had about the future of his people. Others suggest that he mourned because of the extremely poor condition of the captives returning to Judea. They had encountered great difficulty in resettling in the land. Still others suggest he may have mourned because the reconstruction of the temple had stalled due to resistance from the Samaritans (see Ezra 4:5,24). This would have been extremely disconcerting to Daniel, for his great desire was the full restoration of Jerusalem and its temple.

Ate no delicacies (10:3): Daniel said, "No meat or wine entered my mouth, nor did I anoint myself at all, for the full three weeks." He engaged in a partial fast in order to commit himself fully to prayer. He limited himself to basic nourishment. One recalls the commitment of a much younger Daniel: "Daniel resolved that he would not defile himself with the king's food, or with the wine that he drank" (Daniel 1:8).

Daniel 10:4-6

Standing on the bank of the great river (10:4): Daniel was standing on the bank of the Tigris on the twenty-fourth day of the first month. This provides positive proof that Daniel had not gone back to Judea with the other exiles, for the Tigris River is only about 20 miles from Babylon. The Tigris is a major river in Mesopotamia with a number of significant cities along its banks. Nineveh was one of the most famous.

A man clothed in linen (10:5): Some have taken this as an appearance of the preincarnate Christ, for he is described in similar terms to Christ (see Revelation 1:13-14; see also Daniel 7:9). However, it is more likely that this is one of God's glorious angels (compare with Daniel 10:16,18; 12:6-7). Some believe it may have been Gabriel, who had previously appeared to Daniel (8:16). (See Major Themes.)

As was true previously in Daniel, the angel is called a man simply because he took on the appearance of a man. This is often the case in the Bible. When three angels appeared to Abraham, he "lifted up his eyes and looked, and behold, three men were standing in front of him" (Genesis 18:2). Angels can appear as human beings so realistically that Hebrews 13:2 exhorts us, "Do not neglect to show hospitality to strangers, for thereby some have entertained angels unawares."

Body...face...eyes...arms and legs...sound of his words (10:6): This verse contains the language of analogy. Notice the repetition of the word "like." This is an attempt to use finite human language to describe the indescribable glory of one of God's angels. Even our Lord used analogical language, for He often said "the kingdom of heaven is like..." (Matthew 13:31,33,44-45,47,52).

Daniel 10:7

I, Daniel, alone saw the vision (10:7): Those who were present with Daniel sensed a terrifying presence, but they saw nothing. One is reminded of Saul's vision of the risen Christ on the road to Damascus. "The men who were traveling with him stood speechless, hearing the voice but seeing no one" (Acts 9:7). Paul described the account in Acts 22:9: "Now those who were with me saw the light but did not understand the voice of the one who was speaking to me." One also recalls that when the Father spoke audibly to His Son, "the crowd that stood there and heard it said that it had thundered" (John 12:29). This is a curious phenomenon. Somehow, when a person experiences a supernatural encounter, those nearby may sense something without seeing everything the person sees.

Daniel 10:8-9

No strength was left in me…I retained no strength…I fell on my face in deep sleep (10:8-9): We recall that when Joshua saw the Lord, "Joshua fell on his face to the earth and worshiped and said to him, 'What does my lord say to his servant?'" (Joshua 5:14). When Abraham beheld the Almighty, he "fell on his face" (Genesis 17:3). When Manoah and his wife saw the Angel of the Lord (an appearance of the preincarnate Christ), they "fell on their faces to the ground" (Judges 13:20). Ezekiel saw the glory of God and said, "I fell on my face" (Ezekiel 3:23; 43:3; 44:4). Leviticus 9:24 tells us, "Fire came out from before the LORD and consumed the burnt offering and the pieces of fat on the altar, and when all the people saw it, they shouted and fell on their faces." First Chronicles 21:16 tells us, "David lifted his eyes and saw the angel of the LORD standing between earth and heaven, and in his hand a drawn sword stretched out over Jerusalem. Then David and the elders, clothed in sackcloth, fell upon their faces." The apostle John, upon seeing Christ in His glory, "fell at his feet as though dead" (Revelation 1:17; see also Isaiah 6:5). Daniel's response to this supernatural encounter put him in good company.

Major Themes

1. *King Cyrus of Persia.* Cyrus, king of Persia, engaged in conquests with lightning-like rapidity. His empire became vast. Babylon was among the many nations he conquered. He ultimately issued a decree for the liberation of the Jews, allowing them to return to Jerusalem and rebuild their temple (Ezra 1:1-2; Isaiah 44:28; 45:1-2). Daniel's encounter with the angel took place in the third year after Cyrus's conquest of Babylon in 539 BC (see Daniel 10:1). Cyrus died less than a decade later in 530 BC.

2. *The man clothed in linen.* Daniel's description of the "man clothed in linen" has been taken by some expositors to be an appearance of the preincarnate Christ. After all, his face was like lightning, his eyes were like torches, and his voice was as the sound of a multitude (Daniel 10:6). This is similar to the description of the resurrected and glorified Christ in Revelation 1:13-14. The problem with this view, however, is that this (apparently) same "man" said, "The prince of the kingdom of Persia withstood me twenty-one days, but Michael, one of the chief princes, came to help me" (Daniel 10:13). If this were truly the preincarnate Christ, he would be all-powerful, and no one could withstand him. Jesus, of course, exercises power and authority over the devil (Matthew 16:23). In view of this one pivotal fact, it seems best to take the "man clothed in linen" as a glorious angel, and not the preincarnate Christ.

Digging Deeper with Cross-References

Appearances of the preincarnate Christ—Genesis 5:22; 16:7-13; Exodus 3:6-8,14; Judges 6:11-23; 13:1-21; 1 Kings 19:4-8; Psalm 34:7; Zechariah 1:12-13; 3:1-2; Daniel 3:15-20; 6:16-25

Mourning—Genesis 50:10; 1 Samuel 15:35; 25:1; Ezra 9:4-7;
Job 2:5-8; Psalms 30:11; 42:9; Jeremiah 31:13; Joel 1:9-10;
Matthew 5:4; Revelation 18:11

Life Lessons

1. *The Word is true.* Daniel acknowledged that the heavenly
message he had received was true (Daniel 10:1). This brings
to mind the reality that God's Word is truth. Proverbs 30:5
tells us, "Every word of God proves true." This is similar to
Psalm 18:30: "The word of the LORD proves true." Psalm
19:8 likewise affirms, "The precepts of the LORD are right."
Psalm 33:4 states, "The word of the LORD is upright." In
the New Testament, Colossians 1:5 refers to God's Word
as "the word of the truth." John 17:17 likewise affirms,
"Your word is truth." We would expect God's Word to be
true, for everything God says is true. "I the LORD speak the
truth; I declare what is right" (Isaiah 45:19).

2. *Abstinence.* Various kinds of abstinence are found in the
Bible. Manoah's wife abstained from wine, strong drink,
and unclean foods (Judges 13:3-4,7). Samson abstained
from using a razor (Judges 16:17). Hannah abstained from
wine and strong drink (1 Samuel 1:15). Daniel abstained
from the king's food and wine (Daniel 1:8). He later
abstained from delicacies, meat, wine, and anointing
himself (Daniel 10:3). John the Baptist abstained from
wine and strong drink (Luke 1:13-15). Husbands and
wives sometimes abstain from sexual relations for a
time (1 Corinthians 7:5). Generally speaking, believers
sometimes abstain from certain things for a season so they
can focus their attention on the Lord.

Questions for Reflection and Discussion

1. Have you ever engaged in any form of abstinence for spiritual reasons? Was it a positive spiritual experience?

2. Do you believe the Bible is absolutely true in all its parts? In other words, do you believe in an inspired and inerrant Bible?

3. In view of the great glory of angels (see Daniel 10:6), is it more understandable to you that some humans were initially inclined to worship them (see Revelation 19:10)?

The Angel Explains the Future to Daniel

Daniel 10:10–11:1

Scripture Reading and Insights

Begin by reading Daniel 10:10–11:1 in your favorite Bible. As you read, stop and meditate on any verses that speak to your heart (Joshua 1:8; Psalm 1:1-3).

Yesterday we focused on a preliminary introduction to Daniel's special visitation from an angel. Now let's find out how the angel strengthened Daniel so he could receive revelation about Israel's future. With your Bible still accessible, consider the following insights on the biblical text, verse by verse.

Daniel 10:10-12

A hand touched me (10:10): Our previous lesson concluded with Daniel falling asleep: "I fell on my face in deep sleep with my face to the ground" (Daniel 10:9). Today's lesson begins with an angel touching Daniel to awaken him so he could receive new revelation about Israel's future. Upon awakening, Daniel was so frightened, he trembled on his hands and knees.

Man greatly loved (10:11): The way the angel addressed Daniel may indicate that the angel was Gabriel, for just earlier, Gabriel had informed Daniel, "You are greatly loved" (9:23). This carries the idea, "You are very precious to God."

Understand the words (10:11): The angel then instructed Daniel to "understand the words that I speak to you, and stand upright" (compare with Daniel 1:17). Daniel stood trembling, apparently still frightened.

Fear not, Daniel (10:12): The angel recognized Daniel's anxiety and tried to calm him. The angel's explanation that followed would help alleviate all his fears.

From the first day (10:12): The angel informed Daniel, "From the first day that you set your heart to understand and humbled your-self before your God, your words have been heard." Daniel may have been concerned about the apparent delay in God's answer to his prayer (compare with Daniel 10:2-3). We now learn that the prayer was actu-ally answered from day one. This was no doubt a great encouragement to Daniel.

I have come because of your words (10:12): Here is a clear example of God sending an angel to earth in response to the prayers of a human being.

Daniel 10:13-14

The prince of the kingdom of Persia withstood me (10:13): This is why the answer to Daniel's prayer was delayed three weeks. There are different ranks among God's holy angels as well as the fallen angels (Ephesians 6:12; Colossians 1:16). Michael and Gabriel are preeminent among the holy angels. If the angel who was assigned by God to go to Daniel was Gabriel, then the "prince of Persia" must have been an extremely high-ranking fallen angel, working under Satan's command. This demonic spirit was called the "prince of the kingdom of Persia" apparently because he was assigned by Satan to try to influence the kings of Persia to stand against God's people Israel and thus oppose God's plan.

Michael, one of the chief princes (10:13): Michael the archangel— presumably heaven's most powerful angel came to help the angel that had been assigned to visit Daniel.

Your people in the latter days...days yet to come (10:14): The angel then revealed to Daniel that his mission was to help Daniel under-stand what was to happen to his people in the "latter days...days yet to come." The Old Testament use of the term "latter days" (and similar terms) typically points to the future tribulation period, leading up to the coming of the Messiah to set up His millennial kingdom on earth. The angel informed Daniel that his people will go through the tribulation period.

Daniel 10:15-17

Turned my face toward the ground and was mute (10:15): Daniel's reaction was likely due to several factors. He was likely still weak being in the presence of a glorious angel (see Genesis 17:3; Judges 13:20; Ezekiel 3:23; 43:3; 44:4). He may also have been stunned to discover the level of spiritual warfare that had erupted in response to his prayer. Most important, he was apparently greatly saddened to discover what awaited his people in the "latter days"—the future tribulation period.

Touched my lips (10:16): Responding to Daniel's muteness, an angel (in the appearance of a man—see Hebrews 13:2) touched his lips (compare with Isaiah 6:7; Jeremiah 1:9).

Pains have come upon me (10:16): This verse is better translated by the Holman Christian Standard Bible: "My lord, because of the vision, anguish overwhelms me and I am powerless."

No strength remains in me (10:17): Daniel was still weak. Some Bible expositors suggest that he may have felt unworthy to speak to the angelic messenger, not only because the angel was so glorious (see Revelation 19:10; 22:9) but also because Daniel was continuing to identify with his people, who had grievously sinned against the Lord (see Daniel 9). Daniel's anxiety caused the physiological response of weakness and breathlessness.

Daniel 10:18–11:1

Touched me and strengthened me (10:18): Angels often did this in biblical times (compare with Psalm 91:12; Luke 4:11; 22:43).

Fear not...be strong and of good courage (10:19): Daniel was indeed strengthened, and then he asked the angel to continue his message about the future (compare with Joshua 1:6-9; Judges 6:23; Isaiah 35:4; 43:1).

Do you know why I have come to you? (10:20): The angel apparently asked Daniel this because Daniel had been so weak and needed to refocus his attention on the vision of the future.

Fight against the prince of Persia (10:20): The angel informed Daniel that he would need to resume his battle against the demonic spirit that was influencing the human leadership of Persia. Persia must not be allowed to thwart God's purposes for Israel.

Prince of Greece (10:20): This is apparently a demonic spirit assigned by Satan to influence the government of Greece. It is noteworthy that the angel mentions both Persia and Greece, since these empires have been a heavy focus in the book of Daniel (see chapters 2, 7, 8, and 10).

The book of truth (10:21): There is some debate among Bible expositors as to what this refers to. It may be a divine book that contains God's plans for human beings and the nations in which they live (see Daniel 12:1). It may be a book that contains God's sovereign decrees. We recall from Isaiah 46:9-11, "Remember the former things of old; for I am God, and there is no other; I am God, and there is none like me, declaring the end from the beginning and from ancient times things not yet done, saying, 'My counsel shall stand, and I will accomplish all my purpose.'" In any event, we find a number of references in Scripture to God's books (see, for example, Exodus 32:32; Psalms 69:28; 139:16).

Michael, your prince (10:21): The angel then informed Daniel, "There is none who contends by my side against these except Michael, your prince." Apparently, the angel speaking with Daniel (Gabriel?) would soon engage the demonic spirits of Persia and Greece with the archangel Michael by his side. Michael is called "your prince" because he guards Israel (Daniel 12:1).

And as for me (11:1): This verse actually closes Daniel 10 instead of beginning Daniel 11. The angel said, "And as for me, in the first year of Darius the Mede, I stood up to confirm and strengthen him." We are not given the context or any interpretive clues as to what this means. Some Bible expositors suggest that the angel somehow encouraged and protected Darius at the beginning of his reign. This indicates that God is active in the political affairs of the world.

Major Themes

1. *Spiritual warfare.* Spiritual warfare is evident in our
   passage. We learn most of what we know about spiritual
   warfare in the New Testament—particularly regarding the
   Christian's defense against the powers of darkness. First
   and foremost, the Lord Jesus prays for us (Romans 8:34;
   Hebrews 7:25). As well, God has provided us with spiritual
   armor for our defense (Ephesians 6:11-18). Effective use
   of the Word of God is especially important for spiritual
   victory (see Matthew 4). Each believer must be informed
   and thereby alert to the attacks of Satan (2 Corinthians
   2:11; 1 Peter 5:8). We are instructed to take a decisive stand
   against Satan (James 4:7). We must "give no opportunity
   to the devil" by going to bed angry (Ephesians 4:26-27).
   We are instructed to rely on the indwelling Spirit of God,
   remembering that "he who is in you is greater than he who
   is in the world" (1 John 4:4).

2. *Michael the archangel.* The angel Michael is mentioned
   in Daniel 10:21. He is the only archangel mentioned
   in the Bible. The word "archangel" implies a rank first
   among angels. Apparently Michael is in authority over
   all the other angels, including the thrones, dominions,
   rulers, and authorities mentioned in Colossians 1:16. The
   term "archangel" occurs just twice in the New Testament
   (1 Thessalonians 4:16; Jude 9), and in both instances it is
   used in the singular. Some scholars conclude from this that
   the term is restricted to a single archangel—Michael, who
   is called "one of the chief princes" (Daniel 10:13) and "the
   great prince" (12:1).

Digging Deeper with Cross-References

> *Jesus's divine touch*—Matthew 8:3,15; 9:29-30; 17:7; 20:34;
>   Mark 7:33,35; 10:13,16; Luke 22:51

The humility of God's servants—Numbers 12:3; 2 Samuel
22:28; 2 Chronicles 7:14; Psalm 25:9; Proverbs 3:34; 18:12;
Isaiah 13:11; Daniel 4:37; Zephaniah 2:3; Matthew 11:29;
Ephesians 4:2; Philippians 2:3; Colossians 2:23; 3:12;
Titus 3:1-2; James 4:6,10; 1 Peter 3:8, 5:5-6

Life Lessons

1. *Reverence for God.* We are not to fear God in the sense of
   being frightened of Him, but we are called to fear Him in
   the sense of living in reverence of Him (1 Peter 1:17; 2:17;
   1 Samuel 12:14,24; 2 Chronicles 19:9; Acts 10:35). Fear of
   the Lord motivates obedience to God (Deuteronomy 5:29;
   Ecclesiastes 12:13) and service to God (Deuteronomy 6:13).
   Fear of the Lord motivates one to avoid evil (Proverbs 3:7;
   8:13; 16:6). Fear of the Lord is true wisdom (Job 28:28;
   Psalm 111:10) and the beginning of knowledge (Proverbs
   1:7). God blesses those who fear Him (Psalm 115:13). Fear
   of the Lord leads to riches, honor, and long life (Proverbs
   22:4). God shows mercy to those who fear Him (Luke
   1:50).

2. *Delays in answered prayer.* God sometimes dispatches
   angels to take care of our prayer requests (Acts 12:6-19).
   Fallen angels sometimes oppose them. This happened
   when the prophet Daniel prayed. Daniel 10:13 reveals
   that an angel that had been sent by God to take care of
   Daniel's prayer request was detained by a more powerful
   fallen angel. Only when the archangel Michael showed up
   to render aid was the lesser angel free to carry out his task.
   Here, then, is an important thing to remember: We must
   be fervent in our prayers and not think that God is not
   listening simply because His answer is delayed. You never
   know what's going on behind the scenes in the spiritual
   world.

Questions for Reflection and Discussion

1. Daniel 10:21 indicates that Michael the archangel is involved in spiritual warfare. What more do you learn about Michael's role in spiritual warfare in Jude 1:9 and Revelation 12:7-8?

2. What have you learned about spiritual warfare in this lesson that will help you in your Christian life?

3. Do a little self-examination. Does your life manifest a proper reverence for God?

Prophecies Concerning Key Nations

Daniel 11:2-19

Scripture Reading and Insights

Begin by reading Daniel 11:2-19 in your favorite Bible. As you read, keep in mind that the Word of God brings spiritual maturity (1 Corinthians 3:1-2; Hebrews 5:12-14).

In yesterday's reading, an angel gave Daniel strength to receive revelation about the prophetic future. In today's lesson, we focus on specific prophetic revelations concerning southern and northern nations. With your Bible still accessible, consider the following insights on the biblical text, verse by verse.

Daniel 11:2-4

Now I will show you the truth (11:2): This truth is apparently "what is inscribed in the book of truth" (Daniel 10:21).

Three more kings shall arise in Persia (11:2): The angel told Daniel that Persia's present leadership would be succeeded by four more rulers. The first three kings mentioned would be Cambyses (530–522 BC), Pseudo-Smerdis (522), and Darius I Hystaspes (522–486).

A fourth shall be far richer...become strong (11:2): The fourth king—far richer, far more influential, and far more powerful than the others—would be Xerxes (486–465 BC), also known as Ahasuerus in the book of Esther.

A mighty king shall arise (11:3): The angel affirmed this king "shall rule with great dominion and do as he wills." This mighty king of Greece was none other than Alexander the Great (336–323 BC), who conquered the Medo-Persian Empire, Asia Minor, Syria, and Egypt, thereby building a massive empire in a little more than a decade (compare with Daniel 8:5,8). History reveals that Alexander's army featured 35,000 soldiers.

His kingdom shall be broken and divided (11:4): In 323 BC, Alexander the Great succumbed to illness and died at the young age of 32 and the height of his power. The Greek Empire was then divided among four of Alexander's prominent generals. Cassander reigned over Macedon and Greece. Lysimachus ruled Thrace and Asia Minor. Seleucus governed Syria and Babylon. Ptolemy led Egypt. Alexander the Great was anticipated earlier in the book of Daniel in the vision of the goat with the conspicuous horn, which then broke into four conspicuous horns (see Daniel 8:5-8).

Daniel 11:5-6

King of the south (11:5): In the verses that follow we encounter a somewhat tedious account of the rise and fall of various leaders of the north and south with plenty of battles along the way. This is unquestionably the most complicated part of the book of Daniel. I encourage you not to get bogged down in the details. There are still good spiritual lessons to learn here.

The angel first revealed to Daniel that the king of the south will be strong. This was Ptolemy I Soter. Formerly a general who served under Alexander the Great, he governed Egypt from 323 to 285 BC. The Ptolemaic dynasty controlled the Holy Land from 323 to 198 BC. The term "south" is to be understood as "south of Palestine." (North, south, west, and east in the Bible are always understood in relation to Palestine.) Egypt is actually to the south-southwest of Palestine.

We are then told that one of Ptolemy I Soter's "princes shall be stronger than he and shall rule, and his authority shall be a great authority." This prince was Seleucus I Nicator (born 311 BC), also a general under Alexander. Seleucus I Nicator abandoned Ptolemy I Soter and became the ruler of a Seleucid kingdom in Syria and Babylon that was more powerful and more extensive than Ptolemy's Egypt in the south.

They shall make an alliance (11:6): Later, the king of the south, now Ptolemy II Philadelphus (285–246 BC), entered into an alliance with the king of the north, now Antiochus II Theos (261–246 BC). In sealing treaties in ancient days, it was customary for a lesser king to give his daughter in marriage to the greater king. This was considered a token of friendship and sealed the relationship between the two kings. In the present case, the daughter of Ptolemy II Philadelphus, princess Berenice, was sent as a wife to Antiochus II Theos. Antiochus divorced his present wife Laodice in order to marry Berenice. However, Princess Berenice was unable to retain her power. Laodice (the spurned former wife) murdered Antiochus, Berenice, and their child. Laodice's own son, Seleucus II Callinicus, then became king of the north.

Daniel 11:7-9

From a branch from her roots one shall arise in his place...He shall also carry off to Egypt (11:7-8): The brother of now-deceased Berenice, Ptolemy III Euergetes of Egypt (246–221 BC), stood in place of his father and became king of the south. He invaded Syria (in the north) and avenged the death of his sister by executing Laodice. He seized all the treasures of Syria, returning south to Egypt with many spoils.

The latter shall come into the realm of the king of the south (11:9): Later, the king of Syria ("the north"), now Seleucus II, attacked the king of Egypt ("the south"), now Ptolemy IV. Seleucus II was soundly beaten and retreated back north (about 240 BC).

Daniel 11:10-13

His sons shall wage war (11:10): In Daniel 11:9-13 we read of a continuous conflict between the Ptolemies in the south (Egypt) and the Seleucids in the north (Syria). During this time, the land of Israel was invaded first by one power and then by the other. They were continually vying for control of the strategically located land of Palestine, which lay in between these two military powers. It was not a good time for Israel.

In Daniel 11:10 we are informed that Seleucus's sons (successors) in the north—that is, Seleucus III Ceraunus (226–223 BC) and Antiochus III (223–187 BC)—continued to wage war against the king of the south. The conflict seemed never-ending.

The king of the south...shall come out and fight (11:11): Some time later, the king of the south, now Ptolemy IV Philopator (222–203 BC), fought against the king of the north, now Antiochus III the Great (223–187 BC). He enjoyed victory, but any sense of superiority would be short-lived.

His heart shall be exalted (11:12): Ptolemy IV Philopator (in the south), in great arrogance, slaughtered tens of thousands of the northern Seleucid troops. However, he would not be able to prevail.

The king of the north shall again raise a multitude (11:13): Meanwhile, Antiochus III the Great (king of the north) had been busy conquering other lands. Thirteen years later, he had accumulated a vast, new army with plenty of military supplies.

Daniel 11:14-19

The violent among your own people (11:14): Some Jews chose to join forces with Antiochus, king of the north. These Jews had hoped to gain independence from both Egypt (the south) *and* Syria (the north) by participating in the conflict. But it was all in vain. Their hopes were not realized.

The forces of the south shall not stand (11:15): Antiochus III's newly enlarged northern army won a resounding victory over the south, even capturing the well-fortified city of Sidon.

He shall stand in the glorious land (11:16): Antiochus III of the north took dominion over the glorious land—that is, over Israel.

Shall bring terms of an agreement (11:17): Antiochus III (of the north) forced a peace treaty on the Ptolemies (of the south). He even gave his daughter Cleopatra as a wife to Ptolemy V Epiphanes (about 192 BC), hoping to control the Ptolemies through her influence (and her spying). Antiochus's plan backfired, however, because Cleopatra ended up supporting her Ptolemaic husband.

He shall turn his face to the coastlands (11:18): Antiochus III, from the north, now sought to conquer Greece, along the Mediterranean coastlands. But Rome didn't like this and opposed him. Roman commander Lucius Cornelius Scipio defeated Antiochus III at Magnesia in Asia Minor in 190 BC. Antiochus's expansionism was stopped dead in its tracks.

He shall stumble and fall (11:19): This forced Antiochus to retreat back to his own land in the north. He was assassinated a year later while attempting to plunder a temple in the province of Elymais.

Major Themes

1. *Self-will versus God's will.* In Daniel 11:3 we read of a mighty king who will "do as he wills." Self-will lies at the very heart of how the Bible views sin. In the earliest recorded instance of such self-will, Lucifer rebelled against God: "I will set my throne on high...I will make myself like the Most High" (Isaiah 14:13-14). After he fell into sin and suffered God's judgment, he tempted Eve in the Garden of Eden, and Eve by self-will ate the forbidden fruit instead of obeying God's will (Genesis 3:6). The truth is, human beings are prone to self-importance (Galatians 6:5), self-pity (Psalm 37), self-righteousness (Luke 18:9), self-seeking (1 Corinthians 13:5), self-confidence (Matthew 26:35), self-will (Acts 7:51), and self-confident boasting (2 Corinthians 11:17). Dangerous stuff!

2. *The truth.* The angel said to Daniel, "And now I will show you the truth" (Daniel 11:2). The absolute nature of truth is assumed throughout the book of Daniel. We can observe that Christianity rests on a foundation of absolute truth (1 Kings 17:24; Psalm 25:5; John 8:44; 2 Corinthians 6:7; Ephesians 4:15; 2 Timothy 2:15; 1 John 3:19), and that foundation is as sturdy as a rock. Biblical Christians believe that moral absolutes are grounded in the absolutely moral God of Scripture (Matthew 5:48). God stands against the moral relativist whose behavior is

based on whatever is right in his own eyes (Deuteronomy 12:8; Judges 17:6; 21:25). And since the absolutely moral Creator-God (Isaiah 44:24) has communicated precisely what He expects of us in terms of moral behavior (Exodus 20:1-17), we as His creatures are responsible to render obedience (Deuteronomy 11:13,27-28).

Digging Deeper with Cross-References

Being uprooted—Deuteronomy 29:28-29; Amos 9:15; Zephaniah 2:4; Luke 17:6; Jude 12

Fortresses can be strong, but they can also fall—Judges 9:51; 2 Samuel 5:9; Isaiah 17:3; 25:12; Ezekiel 33:27; Hosea 10:14

Powerless in the face of a strong army—Deuteronomy 1:44; 28:32; Joshua 7:5,12; Judges 6:2; Isaiah 21:15

Life Lessons

1. *The cause of war.* James 4:1-2 affirms, "What causes quarrels and what causes fights among you? Is it not this, that your passions are at war within you? You desire and do not have, so you murder. You covet and cannot obtain, so you fight and quarrel." As someone once said, wars may be fought on the battlefield, but they are first waged in the human heart.

2. *Earthly riches can be lost.* Earthly riches can quickly be lost (see Daniel 11:8). It is wiser to build up heavenly riches. Jesus instructed, "Do not lay up for yourselves treasures on earth, where moth and rust destroy and where thieves break in and steal, but lay up for yourselves treasures in heaven, where neither moth nor rust destroys and where thieves do not break in and steal" (Matthew 6:19-20). The apostle Paul adds, "We brought nothing into the world, and we cannot take anything out of the world" (1 Timothy

6:7). Therefore, Paul says the rich should not "set their hopes on the uncertainty of riches, but on God" (verse 17).

3. *Human leaders come and go.* Human leaders may become great for a short time, but they all eventually pass away. Job said that "man who is born of a woman is few of days" (Job 14:1). The psalmist used bold hyperbole: "Behold, you have made my days a few handbreadths, and my lifetime is as nothing before you" (Psalm 39:5). We ought to place our faith not in finite, temporal human leaders but rather in the infinite and eternal Ruler of the universe, God Himself.

Questions for Reflection and Discussion

1. Do you sometimes find it difficult to replace self-will with obedience to God's will?

2. What is your attitude toward money and material things? Are you focused on building up heavenly treasures?

3. Think about all the wars and conflicts in the world today. What do you see that confirms the truth of James 4:1-2?

Prophecies Concerning Antiochus Epiphanes

· Daniel 11:20-35

Scripture Reading and Insights

Begin by reading Daniel 11:20-35 in your favorite Bible. As you read, remember that the Word of God can help you be spiritually fruitful (Psalm 1:1-3).

In the previous lesson, we studied prophecies concerning the southern and northern nations, Egypt and Syria. In today's lesson, we zero in on prophecies concerning Antiochus Epiphanes. With your Bible still accessible, consider the following insights on the biblical text, verse by verse.

Daniel 11:20-21

Then shall arise in his place (11:20): Seleucus IV Philopator (187–176 BC) was the son of Antiochus III of the north. His tax collector, Heliodorus, collected massive amounts of money from the populace with which to pay tribute to Rome. After reigning for a short seven years, Seleucus was poisoned to death by Heliodorus.

A contemptible person (11:21): Seleucus IV Philopator was succeeded by his brother, Antiochus IV Epiphanes (175–164 BC). The throne was not rightfully his. Antiochus seized power when Seleucus's very young son—Demetrius I Soter, the rightful heir—was being held hostage in Rome. Antiochus turned out to be a contemptible, cruel, and idolatrous king. In his arrogance, he christened himself Epiphanes, meaning "the Illustrious One." Some who knew of his character assigned him the nickname "Epimanes"—a name meaning "madman."

Antiochus hated the Jewish people. During his reign he declared the Jewish Mosaic ceremonies illegal and attempted to destroy Judaism.

Daniel 11:22-23

Armies shall be utterly swept away (11:22): Antiochus's northern forces "swept away" the Ptolemaic (Egyptian) armies of the south like a raging flood. Antiochus was militarily ruthless.

The "prince of the covenant" may have been the Jewish high priest Onias III, who was assassinated by his defecting brother Menelaus in 170 BC at the request of Antiochus.

An alliance...he shall act deceitfully (11:23): During a volatile time when several Egyptian leaders were vying for supremacy on Egypt's throne, Antiochus took sides and entered into an alliance with Ptolemy VI Philometor over his rival Ptolemy VII Euergetes II. He thereby deceitfully sought to secure greater power and influence throughout Egypt. With a small force, Antiochus was also able to conquer a territory in Egypt.

Daniel 11:24-25

He shall come into the richest parts of the province (11:24): Some Bible expositors believe this means that Antiochus, under the guise of friendship, entered Egypt with some of his soldiers, seized wealth from some of the richest sections of Egypt, and then distributed his battle spoils among his followers to gain favor with them. His ultimate goal was to take over Egypt.

Other Bible expositors say that Antiochus without warning came into Jerusalem and seized the riches of the Jewish temple, exacted large tributes from the Jews living in Jerusalem, killed many Jews, and stationed his troops there. In this view, Antiochus may have spread the spoils of victory among his soldiers to motivate loyalty to him.

He shall do what neither his fathers nor his fathers' fathers have done, scattering among them plunder, spoil, and goods (11:24): Antiochus's strategy was unlike that of his father, who acquired spoils to increase his own personal wealth. Antiochus, by contrast, acquired wealth to buy favor from others.

Against the king of the south (11:25): The king of the south (in Egypt) was now Ptolemy VI Philometor (181–146 BC). Antiochus IV Epiphanes launched two attacks against Egypt between 170 BC and 168 BC. Though Egypt's army was strong, it was not strong enough.

"Plots" were "devised against" Ptolemy VI Philometor as trusted supporters double-crossed him and soon became captive to Antiochus.

Daniel 11:26-28

His army shall be swept away (11:26): Egyptian counselors who sat at the table with Ptolemy VI Philometor conspired against him, thereby ensuring his defeat. The Egyptian army was eventually "swept away" by the flood-like army of Antiochus.

As for the two kings (11:27): With Egypt's army devastated, Antiochus IV Epiphanes and Ptolemy VI Philometor—the victor and the vanquished—sat at the same table together. Both feigned the goal of a peaceful coexistence with each other, but both were deceptive. Ptolemy VI Philometor no doubt sought reinstatement to his throne. Antiochus IV Epiphanes sought control of all of Egypt, not just select territories he had previously moved against. With their perpetual lies to each other, neither had a satisfactory outcome.

Ptolemy VI Philometor was in a much weaker position than he previously enjoyed, now having to share rulership with another Egyptian ruler. Antiochus IV Epiphanes was likewise frustrated because he had desired total sovereign control of Egypt but did not obtain it.

Neither of them realized that Antiochus was actually fulfilling prophecy according to God's divine timetable.

His heart shall be set against the holy covenant (11:28): Returning from Egypt with great riches and spoils, Antiochus's hatred of the Jews intensified as never before. History reveals that on the way back to his homeland, he attacked Israel with a vengeance, executing some 80,000 Jewish men, women, and children and taking 40,000 prisoners as slaves. He also plundered the riches from the Jewish temple (about 169 BC). This is what is meant when our text says, "He shall work his will and return to his own land." His angry devastation of the Jews was likely caused in part by the frustrated outcome of the round-table meeting in Egypt.

Daniel 11:29-30

He shall return and come into the south (11:29): Antiochus moved against the Egyptians in the south two years later (168 BC). This was his third attack on the south, this time against the joint rulership of Egypt. However, this campaign would be much less successful.

Ships of Kittim shall come against him (11:30): The reason for Antiochus's lesser success was that the "ships of Kittim"—that is, a Roman fleet led by Gaius Popilius Laenas—forced his withdrawal in humiliation. This Roman general drew a circle in the sand, made Antiochus stand inside it, and forced him to concede defeat before stepping outside of the circle. Antiochus had to submit or prepare for war with Rome.

Take action against the holy covenant (11:30): Antiochus again attacked and plundered Jerusalem. He killed many and took many as slaves. He also instructed that all copies of the Mosaic Law be burned.

Daniel 11:31-32

Profane the temple and fortress (11:31): Antiochus grossly desecrated the Jewish temple by erecting an altar to Zeus in it and sacrificing a pig—an unclean animal—on it. This was an "abomination that makes desolate." He also prohibited Jewish sacrifices from that point forward.

This typologically points forward to another "abomination that makes desolate" during the future tribulation period. The antichrist—the "man of lawlessness" (2 Thessalonians 2:3-4)—will set up an image of himself inside the Jewish temple. This amounts to the antichrist enthroning himself in the place of deity, displaying himself as God (compare with Isaiah 14:13-14; Ezekiel 28:2-9). This blasphemous act will utterly desecrate the temple, making it abominable and therefore desolate. And like Antiochus, the antichrist will cause the Jewish sacrifices during the tribulation period to cease.

He shall seduce with flattery (11:32): In the interest of self-preservation, some Jews became compromisers. Convinced by Antiochus's flattery, they sided with him and thereby became corrupted. They became violators of the covenant. Other Jews, however, remained loyal to God and refused to compromise. These were the Hasidean Jews, who chose death rather than submitting to such compromise (compare with 1 Maccabees 1:62-63). There were many Jewish martyrs during this time (compare with Micah 5:7-9; Zechariah 9:13-16; 10:3-6).

Daniel 11:33-35

The wise among the people shall make many understand (11:33): Those godly Jews who understood and believed the truth as contained in the Scriptures would teach others while continuing to suffer persecution and die under Antiochus. Some Bible expositors relate Hebrews 11:36-38 in the Hebrews Hall of Fame to what happened under Antiochus:

> Others suffered mocking and flogging, and even chains and imprisonment. They were stoned, they were sawn in two, they were killed with the sword. They went about in skins of sheep and goats, destitute, afflicted, mistreated—of whom the world was not worthy—wandering about in deserts and mountains, and in dens and caves of the earth.

They shall receive a little help (11:34): This "little help" refers to the Maccabees, who instigated a national revolt—a Jewish "guerrilla uprising"—which Antiochus, who was presently occupied elsewhere, was unable to squash. Three years after Antiochus had desecrated the Jewish temple, the Maccabeans recaptured Jerusalem, removed the desecrating objects from the temple, cleansed the altar, and restored the Jewish sacrifices.

Refined, purified, and made white (11:35): Many of the faithful died as martyrs. The persecution under Antiochus had a purifying effect on the remnant who survived. Such trials refine the faith of the godly.

Bible expositors interpret "the time of the end" in various ways. Some say this refers to the end of Antiochus's oppression of the Jewish people, and not to the end of days. Others say it refers to the final tribulation period when the antichrist—foreshadowed by Antiochus Epiphanes—will be in power, and will continue persecution against the Jews.

Whichever is the case, we will focus on the antichrist in the next lesson.

Major Themes

1. *The people of the holy covenant.* In Daniel 11:28 we read that Antiochus Epiphanes "shall return to his land with great wealth, but his heart shall be set against the holy covenant." This holy covenant relates to God's institution of the Law and sacrificial worship for His people's temple—that is, the Jewish temple. Our passage points to how Antiochus profaned the Jewish sacrificial system, plundered the temple in Jerusalem, and massacred some 80,000 men, women, and children in the city (see 1 Maccabees 1:20-28). This was a first-century holocaust.

2. *Plunder.* In Daniel 11 we read of a "contemptible person"— Antiochus Epiphanes—who came into power and scattered to his followers the plunder obtained from the peoples he conquered. In ancient days, when a powerful nation overthrew a weaker nation, the more powerful nation would take possession of cattle, sheep, camels, donkeys, clothing, armor, jewelry, and money. As well, if any items of value were in a temple—such as silver, gold, or brass items—they, too, would be taken (see Exodus 3:22; Numbers 31:32; Mark 3:27; 1 Samuel 17:53).

Digging Deeper with Cross-References

Covenant breakers—Genesis 17:14; Deuteronomy 31:16,20; Joshua 7:11,15; 23:16; 1 Kings 11:11; 2 Kings 17:15; Psalm 78:10; Jeremiah 11:10

The wicked ensnared—Exodus 14:23-25; Esther 7:9-10; Job

> 5:13; 18:8; Psalms 7:15; 9:15; 10:2; 35:8; 57:6; 69:22;
> 141:10; Proverbs 26:27; 28:10

Life Lessons

1. *Flattery.* Some people try to get their way by using flattery, as we see in our passage (Daniel 11:21). Solomon, the wisest man who ever lived, points out the dangers of flattery. He affirmed, "A lying tongue hates its victims, and a flattering mouth works ruin" (Proverbs 26:28). As well, "A man who flatters his neighbor spreads a net for his feet" (Proverbs 29:5). Proverbs also warns of "smooth words" (Proverbs 7:5) and "seductive speech" (Proverbs 7:21).

2. *Treachery.* In our passage we witness leaders engaging in treachery, making "deceitful promises" (Daniel 11:23 NLT). There are many examples of treachery in the Bible. The sons of Jacob used treachery to destroy evil inhabitants of Shechem (Genesis 34:25). Treachery was used against Samson (Judges 16:9,19). Saul engaged in treacherous activities toward David (1 Samuel 19:11). David was treacherous against Uriah the Hittite (2 Samuel 11:15). Haman was treacherous against the Jews (Esther 3:8). Judas, of course, was treacherous toward Christ (Matthew 26:16,23,49).

Questions for Reflection and Discussion

1. Has anyone ever tried to take advantage of you by using flattering words? How did it make you feel? How did you respond?

2. Have you ever been tempted to engage in treacherous actions against another person?

3. What personally impacted you most in this lesson?

Day 37

Prophecies Concerning the Antichrist

Daniel 11:36-45

Scripture Reading and Insights

Begin by reading Daniel 11:36-45 in your favorite Bible. Read with the anticipation that the Holy Spirit has something important to teach you today (see Psalm 119:105).

In yesterday's lesson, we considered prophecies concerning Antiochus Epiphanes. Now let's learn about prophecies of the antichrist. With your Bible still accessible, consider the following insights on the biblical text, verse by verse.

Daniel 11:36-37

Shall do as he wills (11:36): As a preface, note that from here to the end of chapter 11, the antichrist is in view. The details of this section do not fit what we know to be historically true of Antiochus Epiphanes. Bible scholars believe Daniel 11:1-35 deals with the past, whereas Daniel 11:36-45 deals with the future.

We can make two observations about the scriptural assertion that the antichrist "shall do as he wills": (1) Instead of seeking God's will, the antichrist will be self-willed. (2) As a qualification, however, Scripture also seems to indicate that the antichrist will do as Satan wills. Second Thessalonians 2:9 tells us that "the coming of the lawless one is by the activity of Satan." Of course, Satan himself is self-willed, so it is not surprising that the antichrist will be as well.

He shall exalt himself and magnify himself (11:36): Notice that just as the antichrist will exalt himself as God and seek to be worshipped (2 Thessalonians 2:4; Revelation 13:5-8), Scripture reveals that Satan earlier sought to exalt himself to deity (Isaiah 14:12-17; Ezekiel 28:11-19).

And shall speak astonishing things against the God of gods (11:36): This is in keeping with what we read of the antichrist in Revelation 13:5-6: "The beast was given a mouth uttering haughty and blasphemous words, and it was allowed to exercise authority for forty-two months. It opened its mouth to utter blasphemies against God, blaspheming his name and his dwelling, that is, those who dwell in heaven." There is no greater blasphemy than this. The antichrist truly is *anti-*Christ, even putting himself in Christ's place (see Revelation 13:7-8). We are also told that the antichrist—the world dictator—will demand that the world worship him and pay idolatrous homage to him. Those who refuse will be persecuted and even martyred.

What is decreed shall be done (11:36): In other words, the duration of the antichrist's rule has been sovereignly predetermined by God. God elsewhere affirmed, "My counsel shall stand, and I will accomplish all my purpose" (Isaiah 46:10).

Pay no attention to the gods of his fathers (11:37): The antichrist will pay no attention to the pagan gods of his forerunners, such as Antiochus Epiphanes and other pagan leaders who worshipped false deities. The antichrist will have no respect for any such gods, especially since he will set himself up as God during the tribulation period (2 Thessalonians 2:4; Revelation 13:5-8).

The one beloved by women (11:37): This is apparently a reference to Jesus, the divine Messiah. During New Testament times, it was the desire of Jewish women everywhere to be blessed with the privilege of being the mother of the Jewish Messiah. Therefore the Messiah was "the one beloved by women." This verse thus indicates that the antichrist will give no attention to Jesus Christ.

He shall magnify himself above all (11:37): The antichrist will not only utter blasphemies against the one true God (Revelation 13:5-6) but also exalt himself to a preeminent divine status during the tribulation period (2 Thessalonians 2:4; Revelation 13:5-8).

Daniel 11:38-39

The god of fortresses (11:38): The "god of fortresses" is a metaphorical way of describing the antichrist's unquenchable thirst and quest for power. In other words, power will be the antichrist's god. He won't be satisfied until he attains world dominion. He will use the incredible material wealth at his disposal (gold, silver, precious stones) to build up his military arsenal.

A foreign god (11:39): This "foreign god" is apparently the same god mentioned in verse 38—that is, the god of power and military might, a god foreign to most religious people's thinking.

Those who acknowledge him (11:39): Just as Antiochus Epiphanes did so long ago, the antichrist will reward those who show loyalty to him. He will bestow honors on loyalists and grant them positions in his administration.

Daniel 11:40-43

At the time of the end (11:40): Our text tells us, "The king of the south shall attack him, but the king of the north shall rush upon him like a whirlwind, with chariots and horsemen, and with many ships." Recall that Jesus prophesied of the end times, "You will hear of wars and rumors of wars" (Matthew 24:6). Among the wars that will break out in the tribulation period is one involving two military powers—one from the south and one from the north—who engage in a pincer movement against the antichrist. This attack will apparently take place sometime after the midpoint of the seven-year tribulation period.

He shall come into the glorious land (11:41): The threat of these armies launching an attack will cause the antichrist to return to Palestine, making his headquarters between Jerusalem and the Mediterranean (compare with verse 45).

He shall stretch out his hand against the countries...Egypt...Libyans...

Cushites (11:42-43): As war continues to unfold, the forces of the antichrist will destroy Egypt, Libya, and Sudan.

Daniel 11:44-45

News from the east and the north (11:44): Sometime following the antichrist's relocation, he is made aware that armies from the east and the north are deploying, getting ready to attack. This infuriates him, for his plans for world dominion seem to be quickly falling apart all around him. He therefore lashes out "with great fury to destroy and devote many to destruction."

Pitch his palatial tents (11:45): The antichrist will relocate to the area between Jerusalem and the Mediterranean (compare with Zechariah 12:2-3; 14:2-3; Revelation 19:17-21). Though the antichrist will attempt to position himself in place of Christ reigning from Jerusalem, he will soon come to his end, for only the one true Christ belongs on the throne of David in Jerusalem (2 Samuel 7:12-13).

He shall come to his end (11:45): It would appear that the antichrist meets his end in connection with Israel's conversion to Christ at the end of the tribulation period (Zechariah 12:2–13:1). Scripture reveals that Israel will confess its national sin (Leviticus 26:40-42; Jeremiah 3:11-18; Hosea 5:15) and be saved, thereby fulfilling Paul's prophecy in Romans 11:25-27. In dire threat at Armageddon, as the antichrist's forces are closing in on the Jewish remnant, Israel will plead for their newly found Messiah to return and deliver them (they will "mourn for him, as one mourns for an only child"—Zechariah 12:10; Matthew 23:37-39; see also Isaiah 53:1-9), at which point their deliverance will surely come (see Romans 10:13-14). Israel's leaders will have finally realized the reason that the tribulation has fallen on them—perhaps due to the Holy Spirit's enlightenment of their understanding of Scripture, or the testimony of the 144,000 Jewish evangelists, or perhaps the testimony of the two prophetic witnesses. We are told that at the Lord's second coming, "the beast [antichrist] was captured, and with it the false prophet...These two were thrown alive into the lake of fire that burns with sulfur" (Revelation 19:20).

Major Themes

1. *Prophecy and the law of double reference.* According to the law of double reference, a prophetic passage of Scripture may seemingly blend two unique events or two persons into one picture. These events or persons may be separated by a significant time period. This means that a single prophecy might have two fulfillments, one dealing with the immediate future and one dealing with the distant future. Many scholars believe this is what we encounter in Daniel 11, where we read of both Antiochus Epiphanes and the future antichrist.

2. *The rise of the antichrist.* The apostle Paul warned of a future "man of lawlessness"—the antichrist (2 Thessalonians 2:3,8-9). This individual will perform counterfeit signs and wonders and deceive many people during the future tribulation period (2 Thessalonians 2:9-10). The apostle John describes him as "the beast" (Revelation 13:1-10), a satanically energized individual who will rise to prominence during the tribulation period. He will make a peace treaty with Israel (Daniel 9:27). But he will then seek to dominate the world, double-cross the Jews and then seek to destroy them, persecute believers, and set up his own kingdom (Revelation 13). He will glorify himself with arrogant and boastful words (2 Thessalonians 2:4). His assistant, the false prophet, will entice the world to worship him (Revelation 13:11-12). He will force people around the world to receive his mark, without which they cannot buy or sell, giving him control of the global economy (Revelation 13:16-17). The antichrist will eventually rule the whole world (Revelation 13:7) with his headquarters in a revived Roman Empire (Revelation 17:8-9). This beast will be defeated and destroyed by Jesus at His second coming (Revelation 19:11-20).

Digging Deeper with Cross-References

The God of gods—Deuteronomy 10:17; Psalm 136:2; Daniel 2:47; 11:36

Challenges to the God of gods—2 Thessalonians 2:3-4; Revelation 13:5-6

Utterly godless—2 Kings 17:34; Job 21:15; Psalms 10:4; 36:1; 52:7; 86:14; Jeremiah 44:10; Romans 1:28-30; 3:11,18

Life Lessons

1. *Prophetic signs of the times.* No one can know the day or the hour of end-time events (Matthew 24:36; Acts 1:7). Yet in the parable of the fig tree (Matthew 24:33), the Lord Jesus indicated that we can know the general season of His coming. The term "signs of the times" describes specific characteristics and/or conditions that will exist in the end times. When we witness these signs, we can deduce that we are in the season of the end times. For example, Jesus warned of the rise of false Christs, nations rising against nations, famines, earthquakes, an increase in lawlessness, and more (Matthew 24:4-14). Likewise, in 2 Timothy 3:1-5 the apostle Paul gave this warning:

   In the last days there will come times of difficulty. For people will be lovers of self, lovers of money, proud, arrogant, abusive, disobedient to their parents, ungrateful, unholy, heartless, unappeasable, slanderous, without self-control, brutal, not loving good, treacherous, reckless, swollen with conceit, lovers of pleasure rather than lovers of God, having the appearance of godliness, but denying its power (see also 1 Timothy 4:1).

2. *God is sovereign over all human history.* If there is one thing that biblical prophecy teaches us—and that is emphasized repeatedly in the book of Daniel—it is that

God is absolutely sovereign over human affairs. God rules the universe, controls all things, and is Lord over all (see Ephesians 1). All forms of existence are within the scope of His absolute dominion. God asserts, "My counsel shall stand, and I will accomplish all my purpose" (Isaiah 46:10). God assures us, "As I have planned, so shall it be, and as I have purposed, so shall it stand" (Isaiah 14:24). God is also absolutely sovereign over the affairs of individual nations in the world. In the book of Job we read, "He makes nations great, and he destroys them; he enlarges nations, and leads them away" (Job 12:23; see also Daniel 2:20-21).

Questions for Reflection and Discussion

1. What prophetic "signs of the times" indicate that we may be in the season of the Lord's return?

2. With some of the horrible things that go on in the world, do you ever struggle to believe that God is absolutely sovereign? How do you personally reconcile God's sovereignty with the bad things that sometimes happen around the world?

3. Does the teaching of the apostle Paul in Colossians 3:1-2 help you in regard to the evil things that transpire on earth?

Prophecies Concerning the Time of the End

Daniel 12:1-4

Scripture Reading and Insights

Begin by reading Daniel 12:1-4 in your favorite Bible. As you read, remember that the Word of God is alive and working in you (Hebrews 4:12).

Yesterday we focused attention on prophecies about the future antichrist during the tribulation period. Now let's zero in on more prophecies of the time of the end. With your Bible still accessible, consider the following insights on the biblical text, verse by verse.

Daniel 12:1

At that time (12:1): This phrase refers to the same time frame as the latter part of Daniel 11—the future seven-year tribulation period.

Michael, the great prince who has charge of your people (12:1): The phrase "your people" refers to Daniel's people, the Jews. Clearly God has assigned Michael the role of "guardian of Israel" during the future tribulation period (compare with Psalm 91:11-12).

Recall from Daniel 10:13 that Michael was one of the angels doing battle with the "prince of the kingdom of Persia," a demonic spirit no doubt seeking to influence Persia's leadership to move against Israel. Even then, Michael was watching out for Israel's interests (see also Revelation 12:7). (See Major Themes.)

There shall be a time of trouble (12:1): This is the tribulation period. The word "tribulation" literally means "to press" (as grapes), "to press together," "to press hard upon," and it refers to times of oppression, affliction, and distress. We learn more about the tribulation period in the New Testament. As a backdrop, the New Testament Greek word (*thlipsis*) is translated variously as "tribulation," "affliction," "anguish," "persecution," "trouble," and "burden." The word has been used in relation to...

- those "hard pressed" by the calamities of war (Matthew 24:21)

- a woman giving birth to a child (John 16:21)

- the afflictions of Christ (Colossians 1:24)

- those pressed by poverty and lack (Philippians 4:14)

- great anxiety and burden of heart (2 Corinthians 2:4)

- a period in the end times that will bring unparalleled tribulation (Revelation 7:14)

It is critical that general tribulation be distinguished from the tribulation period in the end times. All Christians may expect a certain amount of general tribulation in their lives. Jesus Himself said to the disciples, "In the world you will have tribulation" (John 16:33). Paul and Barnabas also warned that "through many tribulations we must enter the kingdom of God" (Acts 14:22).

The following facts demonstrate that such general tribulation is to be distinguished from the tribulation period:

- Scripture refers to a definite period of time at the end of the age (Matthew 24:29-35).

- It will be so severe that no period in history past or future will equal it (Matthew 24:21).

- It will be shortened for the elect's sake (Matthew 24:22). Otherwise, no flesh could survive it.

- It is called the time of Jacob's trouble, for it is a judgment on Messiah-rejecting Israel (Jeremiah 30:7; Daniel 12:1-4).

- The nations will also be judged for their sin and rejection of Christ (Isaiah 26:21; Revelation 6:15-17).

- This tribulation period will last seven years (Daniel 9:24,27).

- It will be so bad that people will want to hide and even die (Revelation 6:16).

The horror of this period cannot be overstated. This period will be characterized by wrath (Zephaniah 1:15,18), judgment (Revelation 14:7), indignation (Isaiah 26:20-21), trial (Revelation 3:10), trouble (Jeremiah 30:7), destruction (Joel 1:15), darkness (Amos 5:18), desolation (Daniel 9:27), overturning (Isaiah 24:1-4), and punishment (Isaiah 24:20-21). Simply put, no passage of Scripture alleviates to any degree whatsoever the severity of this time.

Scripture reveals that this tribulation will come upon the whole world. Revelation 3:10 describes it as "the hour of trial that is coming on the whole world." Isaiah 24:1 likewise speaks of this tribulation: "Behold, the LORD will empty the earth and make it desolate, and he will twist its surface and scatter its inhabitants." He continues along the same lines in verse 17: "Terror and the pit and the snare are upon you, O inhabitant of the earth!"

At that time your people shall be delivered (12:1): Even in the midst of such dark circumstances, there is yet hope. Indeed, due in no small part to Michael's protective ministry, the Jewish people are told, "Your people shall be delivered, everyone whose name shall be found written in the book." This means a remnant of Jews will survive the tribulation period. "The book" apparently records the names of all the saved (see Revelation 13:8; 17:8; 20:12,15; 21:27; see also Philippians 4:3).

It is critically important that this remnant survive, for this remnant will convert to Christ at the end of the tribulation period. The forces of the antichrist will be in the process of moving against this remnant when Israel suddenly experiences a national spiritual awakening (see Joel 2:28-29). In dire threat at Armageddon, Israel will plead for their newly found Messiah to return and deliver them (Zechariah 12:10; Matthew 23:37-39; see also Isaiah 53:1-9), at which point their deliverance will surely come (see Romans 10:13-14). The apostle Paul's prophecy about Israel will then have come to pass (Romans 11:25-27).

Daniel 12:2

Many of those who sleep...shall awake (12:2): Our text adds, "Some to everlasting life, and some to shame and everlasting contempt." This is speaking of the resurrection of believers as well as the resurrection of unbelievers. Many people will die during the tribulation period, but the good news for God's people is that death is not final. Conversely, the bad news for unbelievers is that death is not final. Both groups will be resurrected, but they have different eternal destinies—heaven or hell. (See Life Lessons.)

Note that the reference to "sleep" in this context does not mean that people are unconscious after they die. The believer's soul in the afterlife is fully awake and consciously active in the presence of God (Revelation 6:9-11; see also Philippians 1:21-23; 2 Corinthians 5:8). The unbeliever's soul is fully conscious in a place of great suffering (Luke 16:19-31). The word "sleep" is used only of the body, which takes on the appearance of sleep at death.

Daniel 12:3-4

Those who are wise (12:3): The wise are those who know the true God, see through the antichrist's deception, and turn in faith to Jesus, the divine Messiah. They lead others to the truth. Such individuals metaphorically shine in their witness and their example before others.

Shut up the words and seal the book (12:4): The "time of the end" is the tribulation period. The words of the prophecy were to be kept safe and preserved for future generations—especially for those living during the future tribulation days.

Many shall run to and fro, and knowledge shall increase (12:4): This apparently means that during the tribulation, as people are trying to understand what has come upon the world, Daniel's preserved revelation from God will provide the information they need.

Major Themes

1. *Michael, the guardian of Israel.* In Daniel 12:1 we read, "At that time shall arise Michael, the great prince who has charge of your people." The phrase "your people" means Daniel's people, the Jews. Apparently, Michael has a special role as the guardian of Israel. Theologian Louis Berkhof, in his *Systematic Theology*, says that in Michael we see a "valiant warrior fighting the battles of Jehovah against the enemies of Israel and against the evil powers in the spirit-world."[5] The question is, does this protective ministry take place throughout human history or just in the tribulation period? Our passage refers only to the tribulation period, for "that time" points back to Daniel 11:36-45, which focuses specifically on the tribulation period. This ministry of Michael will be especially important for Israel during the tribulation period because the antichrist will attempt to destroy the Jews (Revelation 12:17).

2. *The resurrection of Christ—the basis of our resurrection.* There is massive evidence for the resurrection of Jesus Christ, so we can rest assured that we, too, will be resurrected, as promised in Daniel 12:2.

   • The circumstances at the tomb reveal a missing body. And the Roman guards had fled their guard duty—an act carrying the death penalty.

   • The biblical account has Jesus appearing first to a woman, Mary Magdalene (John 20:1,11-17), an indicator of the authenticity of the resurrection account. In ancient Jewish culture, no one would make up a resurrection account in this way, for a woman's testimony was considered weightless.

- After the crucifixion, the disciples were fearful and full of doubt. Suddenly they became witness-warriors, willing to die for their claims. Only the resurrection explains the change.

- Only the resurrection could explain the conversion of hardcore skeptics—including the apostle Paul (Acts 9); James, the half-brother of Jesus (John 7:1-5; Acts 1:14; 1 Corinthians 15:7); and doubting Thomas (John 20:25-28).

- Only the resurrection of Jesus could explain the exponential growth survival of the Christian church, especially considering the Roman persecution of Christians.

- There were too many appearances over too many days to too many people for the resurrection to be easily dismissed (Acts 1:3).

- Jesus on one occasion appeared to 500 people at one time. Many of these were still living and could have disputed resurrection claims if Paul had uttered any falsehood (1 Corinthians 15:6). They did not do this, however, because the resurrection appearance of Christ was well attested.

Digging Deeper with Cross-References

God's book of life—Exodus 32:32-33; Psalm 69:28; Luke 10:20; Philippians 4:3; Revelation 3:5; 20:15

Eternal life—Psalm 23:6; John 3:14-16,36; 4:14; 5:24; 6:51,54,58; 10:28; 17:3; Romans 6:23; 2 Corinthians 4:17–5:1; 1 Timothy 6:12; 1 John 5:11-13,20

Everlasting disgrace and punishment—Matthew 25:41,46; Hebrews 6:2; Revelation 14:11, 20:10

Life Lessons

1. *The first and second resurrections.* The Scriptures indicate that there are two types of resurrection (Daniel 12:2). The first is appropriately called the "first resurrection" (Revelation 20:5), also called the "resurrection of life" (John 5:29), the "resurrection of the just" (Luke 14:14), and the "better resurrection" (Hebrews 11:35). This is the resurrection of believers. The second resurrection is the last resurrection (Revelation 20:5; see also verses 6,11-15), appropriately called the resurrection of condemnation (John 5:29; see also Daniel 12:2; Acts 24:15). This is the resurrection of the wicked. As noted previously, our resurrection is based on Christ's resurrection from the dead.

2. *Everlasting life versus everlasting contempt.* Daniel 12:2 tells us that "many of those who sleep in the dust of the earth shall awake, some to everlasting life, and some to shame and everlasting contempt." Believers will rise to eternal life in heaven (1 Corinthians 15; 2 Corinthians 5:1-10). Unbelievers will rise to eternal punishment in hell (see Matthew 25:46; 2 Thessalonians 1:5-10; Jude 7,13; Revelation 14:9-11). Notice that the punishment of the wicked in hell is just as enduring as the eternal blessedness of believers in heaven. Both are called "everlasting." In the New Testament, Romans 16:26 refers to the *eternal* God, Hebrews 9:14 refers to the *eternal* Spirit, and Matthew 25:46 uses the same adjective when referring to the *eternal* punishment of the wicked.

Questions for Reflection and Discussion

1. Do you think our present world is nearing the "time of trouble, such as never has been since there was a nation till that time" (Daniel 12:1)?

2. Do you fear death? How does your belief in the resurrection affect your daily mindset on death and dying?

3. Has today's lesson motivated you in any way to pursue righteousness before God?

The Words of the Prophecy Are Sealed

Daniel 12:5-13

Scripture Reading and Insights

Begin by reading Daniel 12:5-13 in your favorite Bible. As you read, notice how the Word of God is purifying your life (John 17:17-18).

In the previous lesson, we studied prophecies of Israel in the future tribulation period. In today's lesson, we learn more about how Daniel's words of prophecy are sealed until the end times. With your Bible still accessible, consider the following insights on the biblical text, verse by verse.

Daniel 12:5-6

Two others stood (12:5): Daniel beheld two angels on the banks of the Tigris River. The number two is significant, for Scripture reveals that two is the minimum number of witnesses (Deuteronomy 17:6; 19:15) required to confirm the oath that the linen-dressed angel (Daniel 10:5) is about to utter.

How long shall it be till the end of these wonders? (12:6): This question is apparently from one of the witnessing angels. The word "wonders" refers to the prophetic events described in Daniel 11:36-45.

Daniel 12:7

The man clothed in linen...swore by him who lives forever (12:7): The linen-dressed angel then uttered an oath. He "raised his right hand and his left hand toward heaven and swore by him who lives forever that it would be for a time, times, and half a time."

The raising of the hands indicates that truth was about to be uttered. "Him who lives forever" is a reference to our eternal God (see Deuteronomy 33:27; Psalm 90:2; Isaiah 44:6; 48:12; Revelation 1:8).

The word "time" refers to a year, "times" is two years, and "half a time" is half a year, totaling three and a half years—the second half of the tribulation period. So when the angel asks how long it would be until the prophetic events of Daniel 11:36-45 would be completed, the answer is, after the last three and a half years of the tribulation period.

The angel then clarified, "When the shattering of the power of the holy people comes to an end all these things would be finished." At the very end of the tribulation period, the holy people (Israel) will be shattered as the forces of the antichrist move toward them in the wilderness during Armageddon. They have no chance of surviving the coming onslaught. This causes them to turn in faith to their long-rejected Messiah Jesus. In dire threat at Armageddon, Israel will plead for their newly found Messiah to return and deliver them (Zechariah 12:10; Matthew 23:37-39; see also Isaiah 53:1-9). The second coming then occurs, and the divine Messiah delivers them (see Romans 10:13-14). This brings "to an end all these things"—that is, the prophecies for Israel are fulfilled.

Daniel 12:8-10

What shall be the outcome of these things? (12:8): Daniel heard what the angel said but didn't feel he had a firm grasp on things. The word "lord" here does not mean the angel is God. In biblical times, "lord" was often used as a term of respect, much like the modern word "sir."

We might paraphrase Daniel's words to this angel this way: "Sir, I heard what you said. But please clarify for me what God's program for Israel will be following this future tribulation period."

The words are shut up and sealed until the time of the end (12:9): As noted previously in the book, the fact that the words were to be "shut up and sealed until the time of the end" means they were to be kept safe and preserved for future generations—especially for those who may be alive during the future tribulation days.

Many shall purify themselves (12:10): In verses 10 through 13, the angel provided a few final clarifying comments to Daniel. In verse 10, he indicated that many Jews who come to salvation during the tribulation period would have their faith refined by the trials they endure. The apostle Paul, himself a Jew who came to faith in Christ, summarized how trials benefit believers: "We rejoice in our sufferings, knowing that suffering produces endurance, and endurance produces character, and character produces hope, and hope does not put us to shame, because God's love has been poured into our hearts through the Holy Spirit who has been given to us" (Romans 5:3-5).

The wicked shall act wickedly (12:10): Meanwhile, the wicked would continue in their wicked ways. These would continue to ignore God and succumb to following the antichrist's leadership.

Those who are wise shall understand (12:10): These people are wise in the sense that they have insights into God's ways, based on God's Word, and live their lives accordingly, despite their persecution in the tribulation period.

Daniel 12:11-13

From the time...there shall be 1,290 days (12:11): The abomination of desolation will take place at the midpoint of the tribulation period when the antichrist—the "man of lawlessness" (2 Thessalonians 2:3)—sets up an image of himself inside the Jewish temple (Daniel 9:27; Matthew 24:15). This amounts to the antichrist enthroning himself in the place of deity, displaying himself as God (compare with Isaiah 14:13-14; Ezekiel 28:2-9). This blasphemous act will utterly desecrate the temple, making it abominable and therefore desolate.

From the time this happens at the midpoint of the tribulation, there would be 1290 days. The three and a half years of the second half of the tribulation period is actually only 1260 days. The extra 30 days allow for Christ's judgment of the nations (Matthew 25:31-46) prior to the beginning of the millennial kingdom.

Blessed is he who waits and arrives at the 1,335 days (12:12): The

1,335-day period from the midpoint of the tribulation includes not only the 30 additional days for the judgment of the nations (Matthew 25:31-46) but also an additional 45 days. Many Bible expositors believe that Christ will establish His millennial government during this month and a half. People are "blessed" in reaching this time because they are about to enter into Christ's 1000-year kingdom on earth.

You shall rest and shall stand in your allotted place (12:13): We might paraphrase the angel's words this way: "Go your way and live in faith for the rest of your earthly life. Following death, your soul will enter heavenly rest. At the appointed time, you will be physically resurrected, with your soul rejoining an eternal resurrection body. You will stand, and you will receive your eternal inheritance."

Major Themes

1. *The divine timetable*. A witnessing angel asked, "How long shall it be till the end of these wonders?" (Daniel 12:6). It appears that God has a divine timetable for the fulfillment of prophesied events in human history. A number of phrases found in Daniel testify to this: "Behold, I will make known to you what shall be at the latter end of the indignation, for it refers to the appointed time of the end" (8:19). "The end is yet to be at the time appointed" (11:27). "At the time appointed he shall return and come into the south" (11:29). "Some of the wise shall stumble, so that they may be refined, purified, and made white, until the time of the end, for it still awaits the appointed time" (11:35). God truly is sovereign over all things (see Isaiah 46:10; 1 Corinthians 15:23-28; Ephesians 1:11).

2. *The swearing of oaths*. In our passage, the man clothed in linen "raised his right hand and his left hand toward heaven and swore by him who lives forever" (Daniel 12:7). Some well-meaning Christians have taken a stand against oaths altogether by appealing to the words of Jesus in Matthew 5:33-37. The problem Jesus was addressing in

that passage, however, was that oaths became so common in biblical times that people started to assume that when you did not take an oath, perhaps you were not being truthful. To counter such an idea, Jesus instructed His followers that they should have no duplicity in their words, that their "yes should be yes" and their "no should be no." In certain contexts, however, oaths are just fine. A number of legitimate oaths are mentioned in the Old Testament (Exodus 20:7; Leviticus 5:1; 19:12; Numbers 30:2-15; Deuteronomy 23:21-23). There are some mentioned in the New Testament as well (Acts 2:30; Hebrews 6:16-18; 7:20-22). Even the apostle Paul said, "I call God to witness..." (2 Corinthians 1:23).

3. *Blessing in biblical prophecy.* Our text tells us, "Blessed is he who waits and arrives at the 1,335 days" (Daniel 12:12), referring to the days just prior to the beginning of Christ's glorious millennial kingdom. Blessing is attached to another prophetic book closely connected to Daniel— the book of Revelation. There we read, "Blessed is the one who reads aloud the words of this prophecy, and blessed are those who hear, and who keep what is written in it, for the time is near" (Revelation 1:3). At the end of Revelation, we are reminded, "Blessed is the one who keeps the words of the prophecy of this book" (Revelation 22:7). Here we see an obvious connection between obedience to God and blessing. We recall James's instruction that we should not just be hearers of God's Word, but doers of it (James 1:22–25).

Digging Deeper with Cross-References

God's eternality (Daniel 12:7)—Psalms 9:7; 41:13; 45:6; 55:19; 90:2; 92:8; 93:2; 102:12,24; 111:3; 135:13; 145:13; 146:10

Human ignorance in the book of Daniel (Daniel 12:8)—Daniel 2:10,27; 4:7,18; 5:8,15; 12:8

The last days—Genesis 49:1; Isaiah 2:2; Daniel 2:28; 10:14;
    12:9; Hosea 3:5; Micah 4:1; John 11:24; Acts 2:17; 1 Timo-
    thy 4:1; 2 Timothy 3:1; James 5:3; 2 Peter 3:3; 1 John 2:18

Life Lessons

1. *Resting in heaven.* The angel informs Daniel, "You shall
   rest" (Daniel 12:13). This refers to resting in death—that is,
   in the afterlife. Christians in the intermediate state enjoy
   a sense of serene rest in the presence of Christ. They have
   no tedious labors to attend to. All is tranquil. The apostle
   John said, "I heard a voice from heaven saying, 'Write
   this: Blessed are the dead who die in the Lord from now
   on.' 'Blessed indeed,' says the Spirit, 'that they may rest
   from their labors'" (Revelation 14:13). This rest will be
   comprehensive, including rest from all toil of the body,
   from all laborious work, from all the diseases and frailties
   of the body, from all outward sorrows, from all inward
   troubles, from the temptations and afflictions of Satan,
   and from all doubts and fears. How blessed will be that
   rest!

2. *God's holy people.* Daniel 12:7 refers to "the holy people."
   This verse refers to Israel during the tribulation period,
   but the truth is that holiness is an important doctrine for
   all of us. Hebrews 12:14 tells us that without holiness, no
   one can see God. On our own, we are unfit for God's
   presence, for we have no intrinsic righteousness. But
   2 Corinthians 5:21 tells us, "For our sake he made him to
   be sin who knew no sin, so that in him we might become
   the righteousness of God." Because of Jesus, we are made
   fit for God's presence, for Christ's righteousness and
   holiness are imputed to us, just as our sin was imputed
   to Him at the cross. There has been a great exchange. As
   the great Reformer Martin Luther said, "Lord Jesus, You
   are my righteousness; I am Your sin. You have taken upon

Yourself what is mine and given me what is Yours. You
have become what You were not so that I might become
what I was not."

Questions for Reflection and Discussion

1. Are you inquisitive, like Daniel, about when certain
   end-time events will occur?

2. What reasons can you suggest for avoiding the tendency to
   predict the dates of end-time events? (See Matthew 24:36;
   Acts 1:7.)

3. What impacted you most about today's Scripture reading?

Day 40

Imitating Daniel

Here we are on day 40—and what an eye-opening study this has been! As we bring our time to a close, let's review some of the more important spiritual lessons sprinkled throughout the book of Daniel. I've listed these lessons in the form of resolutions. I hope you'll join me in making these resolutions. Let's resolve to imitate Daniel!

Like Daniel, let's resolve to maintain a holy fear, or reverence, for the one true God.

After witnessing God's great power in delivering Daniel from the lions' den, King Darius decreed that "people are to tremble and fear before the God of Daniel" (Daniel 6:26). Of course, no one had to tell Daniel and his Hebrew friends that, for they consistently lived their lives in the fear of God and in reverence for Him. This led to their consistent obedience to God even in the face of death.

The theme of fearing God or revering God is found not only in Daniel but throughout the whole of Scripture. Take a few moments to meditate on 1 Samuel 12:14,24; 2 Chronicles 19:9; Acts 10:35; and 1 Peter 1:17; 2:17.

Fear of the Lord motivates one to be obedient to God (Deuteronomy 5:29; Ecclesiastes 12:13) and serve Him (Deuteronomy 6:13). Fear of the Lord motivates one to avoid evil (Proverbs 3:7; 8:13; 16:6). Fear of the Lord is true wisdom (Job 28:28; Psalm 111:10) and the beginning of knowledge (Proverbs 1:7). God blesses those who fear Him (Psalm 115:13). Fear of the Lord leads to riches, honor, and long life (Proverbs 22:4). God shows mercy to those who fear Him (Luke

1:50). Clearly, it is in our best interest to follow Daniel's example in reverencing God.

Like Daniel, let's resolve to be consistently obedient to God.

Daniel and his Hebrew friends obeyed God regardless of what they faced. When King Darius banned prayer to any god but himself for 30 days, Daniel responded by going home and praying to the one true God, just as he had always done. Daniel simply would not disobey God. For that he was thrown into the lions' den. God, of course, honored Daniel's obedience by rescuing him from the lions (Daniel 6).

Nebuchadnezzar commanded Daniel's three Hebrew friends to bow down and worship his golden image. But they would not disobey the one true God in this matter. They told the king, "Our God whom we serve is able to deliver us from the burning fiery furnace, and he will deliver us out of your hand, O king. But if not, be it known to you, O king, that we will not serve your gods or worship the golden image that you have set up." God honored their obedience by rescuing them in the fiery furnace (Daniel 3). Daniel and his friends obeyed God no matter what!

As we examine the rest of Scripture, we discover that it is always in our best interest to be obedient to God. After all, such obedience brings...

- blessing (Luke 11:28)
- long life (1 Kings 3:14; John 8:51)
- happiness (Psalm 112:1; 119:56)
- peace (Proverbs 1:33)
- well-being (Jeremiah 7:23; see also Exodus 19:5; Leviticus 26:3-4; Deuteronomy 4:40; 12:28; 28:1; Joshua 1:8; 1 Chronicles 22:13; Isaiah 1:19)

Daniel and his friends enjoyed these realities. So can you and I!

Like Daniel, let's resolve to show our love for God by our obedience to Him.

Closely related to the previous resolution, Daniel makes the critically important point that our love for God is displayed in our obedience to Him. In his prayer to God, Daniel acknowledged that God "keeps covenant and steadfast love with those who love him and keep his commandments" (9:4). This reminds us of Exodus 20:5-6: "I the LORD your God am a jealous God...showing steadfast love to thousands of those who love me and keep my commandments." Deuteronomy 7:9 likewise refers to "the faithful God who keeps covenant and steadfast love with those who love him and keep his commandments." Nehemiah the prophet referred to God as "the great and awesome God who keeps covenant and steadfast love with those who love him and keep his commandments" (Nehemiah 1:5). This Old Testament backdrop sheds light on Jesus's instruction to His followers: "If you love me, you will keep my commandments...Whoever has my commandments and keeps them, he it is who loves me" (John 14:15,21).

Like Daniel, let's resolve to recognize and respond to God's work of discipline in our lives.

Daniel 1:1-2 tells us, "In the third year of the reign of Jehoiakim king of Judah, Nebuchadnezzar king of Babylon came to Jerusalem and besieged it. And the Lord gave Jehoiakim king of Judah into his hand." God was disciplining Israel for its disobedience.

As this Scripture demonstrates, when we who believe don't repent of our sin, God responds by disciplining us. We recall that following David's sin with Bathsheba, the Lord disciplined him for an extended time (Psalm 32:3-5; 51). God also disciplines us when we go astray: "My son, do not regard lightly the discipline of the Lord, nor be weary when reproved by him. For the Lord disciplines the one he loves, and chastises every son whom he receives" (Hebrews 12:5-6). Scripture also reminds us, "If we would examine ourselves, we would not be judged by God in this way" (1 Corinthians 11:31 NLT).

Like Daniel, let's resolve to always walk by faith and not by sight.

Even when things seem at their most hopeless, the God of miracles can come through in ways we would never have fathomed. We've seen this repeatedly in the book of Daniel. Daniel was tossed into a lions' den, which from a human perspective is about as bad as things can get. From a "walking by sight" perspective, death was certain. But Daniel walked by faith and not by sight. God rewarded that faith by rescuing him from the lions (Daniel 6).

The same is true of Daniel's three Hebrew friends. From a human perspective, being thrown into a fiery furnace is unimaginable. From a "walking by sight" perspective, they too had received a death sentence. But they were walking by faith and not by sight. They knew that the unseen God could deliver them from the fire (Daniel 3).

This same truth is illustrated numerous times throughout both the Old and New Testaments. From a human perspective, David stood no chance against the giant Goliath. But the invisible God empowered David to slay the giant (1 Samuel 17). David walked by faith and not by sight. In the New Testament, walking by sight tells us that dead people stay dead, but walking by faith recognizes that God can resurrect people from the dead (see Matthew 9:25; Luke 7:13-15; John 11:43-44; Acts 9:36-42).

Regardless of what we encounter, let's resolve to walk by faith and not by sight (2 Corinthians 5:7). Let's keep our faith strong (Psalms 40:4; 118:8; Proverbs 3:5; Jeremiah 17:7; Matthew 15:28; 21:21-22; Luke 17:5-6; Romans 10:17; 2 Corinthians 5:7; 1 Timothy 1:19; Hebrews 10:35; 11:1; 1 Peter 1:7).

Like Daniel, let's resolve to pray consistently, thankfully, specifically, and urgently.

Daniel 6:10 tells us that Daniel "got down on his knees three times a day and prayed and gave thanks before his God, as he had done previously." Notice that Daniel began his prayers with thanksgiving. We are reminded of Psalm 95:2: "Let us come into his presence with thanksgiving." Psalm 100:4 also comes to mind: "Enter his gates with thanksgiving."

After giving thanks, Daniel brought "petition and plea" before God, making specific requests of God. One is reminded of the apostle Paul's teaching on prayer in Philippians 4:6-7: "Do not be anxious about anything, but in everything by prayer and supplication with thanksgiving let your requests be made known to God. And the peace of God, which surpasses all understanding, will guard your hearts and your minds in Christ Jesus."

Daniel was certainly a believer in intercessory prayer—that is, praying for other people and not only for himself (Daniel 2:17-18). He also believed in confessing sin during prayer when appropriate (Daniel 9:8-15; see also Proverbs 28:13; 1 John 1:9). Still further, we notice that Daniel prayed with a great sense of great urgency (Daniel 9:16-19). We are reminded of James 5:16: "The urgent request of a righteous person is very powerful in its effect" (HCSB). The word "urgent" in this verse carries the idea of "earnest" or "heartfelt." Let's resolve to imitate Daniel in his prayer life.

Like Daniel, let's resolve to always be mindful of God's sovereign control over all things.

In the book of Daniel, we repeatedly see that God sovereignly reigns from heaven. God was sovereign over the captivity of Israel, the fiery furnace, the lions' den, the rise and fall of kings and nations, and much more.

God's sovereignty is a theological thread running through the entire Bible, from Genesis to Revelation. God Himself affirmed, "My counsel shall stand, and I will accomplish all my purpose" (Isaiah 46:10). He assures us, "As I have planned, so shall it be, and as I have purposed, so shall it stand" (Isaiah 14:24). The psalmist tells us that "his kingdom rules over all" (Psalm 103:19). Our God is "a great king over all the earth" (Psalm 47:2). First Chronicles 29:12-13 affirms of God, "You rule over all. In your hand are power and might, and in your hand it is to make great and to give strength to all. And now we thank you, our God, and praise your glorious name." You and I, too, should be thankful to God and praise Him for His sovereign oversight of our lives.

Like Daniel, let's resolve to trust that God can restore our lives.

In Daniel 9, Daniel earnestly prayed that his people Israel would be restored to God and to the Promised Land. Daniel sought this with all his heart. In the chapters that follow, God revealed to Daniel that He yet has a future for Israel. God would one day restore Israel.

God restores our individual lives as well. God can restore people spiritually: "The LORD is my shepherd; I shall not want. He makes me lie down in green pastures. He leads me beside still waters. He restores my soul" (Psalm 23:1-3). God can restore the joy of salvation: "Restore to me the joy of your salvation" (Psalm 51:12). God can restore us after we've experienced trials: "After you have suffered a little while, the God of all grace, who has called you to his eternal glory in Christ, will himself restore, confirm, strengthen, and establish you" (1 Peter 5:10; see also Psalm 71:20). Let us always remember, as Daniel did, that our God is a God of restoration.

Like Daniel, let's resolve to maintain a good reputation.

Daniel's stellar reputation began in the first year of his captivity and lasted all the way to his death. His good reputation not only brought him before kings but also brought him great honor and exaltation throughout life. Scripture provides examples of people with good reputations (1 Samuel 2:1-5; 29:3; Psalms 86:2; 87:3; 109:4; Proverbs 22:1; Acts 17:11) and bad reputations (2 Samuel 20:1; Proverbs 24:8; Acts 15:37-38). As Christians, we always ought to pursue a good reputation (see Proverbs 22:1; Ecclesiastes 7:1).

Like Daniel, let's resolve to always be people of integrity.

Daniel was consistently a man of integrity, and this integrity was evident to all who encountered him. Daniel would have agreed with Paul's words in 2 Corinthians 8:21: "For we aim at what is honorable not only in the Lord's sight but also in the sight of man."

The Bible speaks a great deal about being a person of integrity: "Better is a poor man who walks in his integrity than a rich man who is crooked in his ways" (Proverbs 28:6). "Better is a poor person who walks in his integrity than one who is crooked in speech and is a fool"

(Proverbs 19:1). "The integrity of the upright guides them" (Proverbs 11:3). "The righteous who walks in his integrity—blessed are his children after him!" (Proverbs 20:7). Good verses on which to meditate include Psalms 25:21; 26:1; Micah 6:8; Acts 24:16; Titus 2:1-14; Hebrews 13:18; and James 1:22-25.

Like Daniel, let's resolve to walk in humility.

Daniel was a humble man who consistently pointed away from his own abilities and pointed rather to God (Daniel 2:27-28). He had the same humble attitude as John the Baptist, who said of Jesus, "He must increase, but I must decrease" (John 3:30).

The Scriptures tell us that those who want to please God must walk in humility. Not only that, but God exalts the humble: "Humble yourselves before the Lord, and he will exalt you" (James 4:10; see also Proverbs 15:33; 22:4; 29:23; Luke 1:52; 1 Peter 5:5-6). Daniel humbled himself throughout his life, and God consistently exalted him.

Like Daniel, let's resolve to be people of prudence.

Daniel 2:14 tells us that Daniel spoke with prudence and discretion. We should do likewise. The prudent person always looks ahead to see what is coming (Proverbs 14:8) and foresees danger (Proverbs 22:3; 27:12). The prudent person always carefully considers his steps (Proverbs 14:15) and is consistently cautious (Proverbs 14:16). He consistently saves for the future (Proverbs 6:6-11) and consistently guards his mouth and his tongue (Psalm 39:1; Proverbs 21:23). Moreover, he is aware that consulting many counselors is one key to success (Proverbs 15:22). It is always in our best interest to maintain prudence, just as Daniel did.

Like Daniel, let's resolve to live for God now.

Daniel never delayed to live for God. For him, living as a believer was a present-tense proposition. Let's imitate Daniel and resolve not to wait one more minute in totally committing ourselves to God and living for Him. Let's begin now, with no further delay.

Join me. Let's do it.

Notes

1. John F. Walvoord, *Daniel* (Chicago: Moody, 2012), Kindle edition, location 1512.
2. Earnest C. Lucas, "Daniel," in John H. Walton, ed., *Zondervan Illustrated Bible Backgrounds Commentary*, vol. 4 (Grand Rapids: Zondervan, 2009), at Daniel 4:11.
3. Michael Green, ed., *1500 Illustrations for Biblical Preaching* (Grand Rapids: Baker Books, 1991), p. 350.
4. R.T. France, *The Living God* (Downers Grove: InterVarsity Press, 1972), p. 25.
5. Louis Berkhof, *Systematic Theology* (Grand Rapids: Eerdmans, 1982), p. 147.

Bibliography

Brown, Colin, ed. *The New International Dictionary of New Testament Theology*. Grand Rapids: Zondervan, 1979.

Brown, Francis, S.R. Driver, and Charles A. Briggs. *The Brown-Driver-Briggs Hebrew and English Lexicon*. Peabody: Hendrickson, 1994.

Bruce, F.F., ed. *The International Bible Commentary*. Grand Rapids: Zondervan, 1979.

Dyer, Charles. *The Rise of Babylon: Sign of the End Times*. Chicago: Moody, 2003.

Fruchtenbaum, Arnold. *The Footsteps of the Messiah*. San Antonio: Ariel, 2004.

Gaebelein, Frank E., ed. *The Expositor's Bible Commentary*. Grand Rapids: Zondervan, 1978.

Geisler, Norman. *A Popular Survey of the Old Testament*. Grand Rapids: Baker, 1978.

———. *Systematic Theology*, vol. 4: *Church/Last Things*. Saint Paul: Bethany House, 2005.

Hays, J. Daniel, J. Scott Duvall, and C. Marvin Pate. *Dictionary of Biblical Prophecy and End Times*. Grand Rapids: Zondervan, 2007.

Hengstenberg, E. W., and Theodore Meyer. *Christology of the Old Testament*. Grand Rapids: Kregel, 1970.

Hitchcock, Mark. *Bible Prophecy*. Wheaton: Tyndale House, 1999.

———. *The Second Coming of Babylon*. Sisters: Multnomah, 2003.

Hoyt, Herman. *The End Times*. Chicago: Moody, 1969.

Ice, Thomas, and Timothy Demy. *Prophecy Watch*. Eugene: Harvest House, 1998.

———. *When the Trumpet Sounds*. Eugene: Harvest House, 1995.

Ice, Thomas, and Randall Price. *Ready to Rebuild: The Imminent Plan to Rebuild the Last Days Temple*. Eugene: Harvest House, 1992.

Ironside, H.A. *Revelation*. Grand Rapids: Kregel, 1978.

Keil, C.F., and Franz Delitzsch. *Biblical Commentary on the Old Testament*. Grand Rapids: Eerdmans, 1954.

LaHaye, Tim. *The Beginning of the End*. Wheaton: Tyndale, 1991.

———. *The Coming Peace in the Middle East*. Grand Rapids: Zondervan, 1984.

LaHaye, Tim, ed. *Prophecy Study Bible*. Chattanooga: AMG, 2001.

LaHaye, Tim, and Ed Hindson, eds. *The Popular Bible Prophecy Commentary*. Eugene: Harvest House, 2006.

LaHaye, Tim, and Ed Hindson, eds. *The Popular Encyclopedia of Bible Prophecy*. Eugene: Harvest House, 2004.

LaHaye, Tim, and Thomas Ice. *Charting the End Times*. Eugene: Harvest House, 2001.

LaHaye, Tim, and Jerry Jenkins. *Are We Living in the End Times?* Wheaton: Tyndale, 1999.

MacArthur, John. *Daniel: God's Control Over Rulers and Nations.* MacArthur Bible Studies, vol. 5. Nashville: W Publishing Group, 2000.

MacDonald, W., and A. Farstad. *Believer's Bible Commentary.* Nashville: Thomas Nelson, 1997.

Pentecost, J. Dwight. *Things to Come.* Grand Rapids: Zondervan, 1964.

Pfeiffer, Charles F., and Everett F. Harrison, eds. *The Wycliffe Bible Commentary.* Chicago: Moody, 1974.

Pink, Arthur W. *The Antichrist: A Study of Satan's Christ.* Blacksburg, VA: Wilder, 2008.

Price, Randall. *Jerusalem in Prophecy.* Eugene: Harvest House, 1998.

Price, Walter K. *The Coming Antichrist.* Neptune, NJ: Loizeaux Brothers, 1985.

Reymond, Robert L. *Jesus, Divine Messiah: The Old Testament Witness.* Scotland: Christian Focus, 1990.

Rhodes, Ron. *The Coming Oil Storm: The Imminent End of Oil…and Its Strategic Global Role in End-Times Prophecy.* Eugene: Harvest House, 2010.

———. *The Middle East Conflict: What You Need to Know.* Eugene: Harvest House, 2009.

———. *Northern Storm Rising: Russia, Iran, and the Emerging End-Times Military Coalition Against Israel.* Eugene: Harvest House, 2008.

———. *The Popular Dictionary of Bible Prophecy.* Eugene: Harvest House, 2010.

———. *The Topical Handbook of Bible Prophecy.* Eugene: Harvest House, 2010.

———. *Unmasking the Antichrist.* Eugene: Harvest House, 2012.

Rosenberg, Joel. *Epicenter: Why Current Rumblings in the Middle East Will Change Your Future.* Carol Stream: Tyndale House, 2006.

Tenney, Merrill C., ed. *The Zondervan Pictorial Encyclopedia of the Bible.* Grand Rapids: Zondervan, 1978.

Unger, Merrill F. *Beyond the Crystal Ball: What Occult Practices Cannot Tell You About Future Events.* Chicago: Moody, 1973.

———. *Unger's Guide to the Bible.* Wheaton: Tyndale House, 1974.

Walvoord, John F. *Daniel.* Revised and edited by Philip E. Rawley and Charles H. Dyer. Chicago: Moody Publishers, 2012.

———. *End Times.* Nashville: Word, 1998.

———. *The Millennial Kingdom.* Grand Rapids: Zondervan, 1975.

———. *The Prophecy Knowledge Handbook.* Wheaton: Victor, 1990.

———. *The Return of the Lord.* Grand Rapids: Zondervan, 1979.

Walvoord, John F., and John E. Walvoord. *Armageddon, Oil, and the Middle East Crisis.* Grand Rapids: Zondervan, 1975.

Whitcomb, John C. *Daniel: Everyman's Bible Commentary.* Chicago: Moody, 1985.

Wiersbe, Warren. *Be Resolute (Daniel): Determining to Go God's Direction.* The BE Series Commentary. Colorado Springs: David C. Cook, 2008.

More Great Harvest House Books by Ron Rhodes

Books About the Bible
Bite-Size Bible® Answers
Bite-Size Bible® Charts
Bite-Size Bible® Definitions
Bite-Size Bible® Handbook
Commonly Misunderstood Bible Verses
Find It Fast in the Bible
Understanding the Bible from A to Z
What Does the Bible Say About…?

Books About the End Times
The Coming Oil Storm
Cyber Meltdown
The End Times in Chronological Order
Northern Storm Rising
The Topical Handbook of Bible Prophecy
Unmasking the Antichrist

Books About Other Important Topics
5-Minute Apologetics for Today
1001 Unforgettable Quotes About God, Faith, and the Bible
Angels Among Us
Answering the Objections of Atheists, Agnostics, and Skeptics
Christianity According to the Bible
The Complete Guide to Christian Denominations
Conviction Without Compromise
Find It Quick Handbook on Cults and New Religions
The Truth Behind Ghosts, Mediums, and Psychic Phenomena
Why Do Bad Things Happen If God Is Good?
The Wonder of Heaven

The 10 Most Important Things Series
The 10 Most Important Things You Can Say to a Catholic
The 10 Most Important Things You Can Say to a Jehovah's Witness
The 10 Most Important Things You Can Say to a Mason
The 10 Most Important Things You Can Say to a Mormon
The 10 Things You Need to Know About Islam
The 10 Things You Should Know About the Creation vs. Evolution Debate

The Reasoning from the Scriptures Series
Reasoning from the Scriptures with Catholics
Reasoning from the Scriptures with the Jehovah's Witnesses
Reasoning from the Scriptures with Masons
Reasoning from the Scriptures with the Mormons
Reasoning from the Scriptures with Muslims

Quick Reference Guides
Christian Views of War: What You Need to Know
Five Views on the Rapture: What You Need to Know
Halloween: What You Need to Know
Is America in Bible Prophecy?: What You Need to Know
Islam: What You Need to Know
Jehovah's Witnesses: What You Need to Know
The Middle East Conflict: What You Need to Know

To learn more about Harvest House books and
to read sample chapters, visit our website:

www.harvesthousepublishers.com

HARVEST HOUSE PUBLISHERS
EUGENE, OREGON